WHERE IS THE JUSTICE?

WHERE IS THE JUSTICE?

Media Attacks, Prosecutorial Abuse, and My 13 Years in Japanese Court

HIROMASA EZOE

FOUNDER OF RECRUIT

KODANSHA INTERNATIONAL
Tokyo • New York • London

Originally published in Japanese in 2009 by Chuokoronshinsha, Tokyo,
under the title *Recruit jiken: Ezoe Hiromasa no shinjitsu*.

Distributed in the United States by Kodansha America, LLC, and in the United
Kingdom and continental Europe by Kodansha Europe Ltd.

Published by Kodansha International Ltd., 17–14 Otowa 1-chome, Bunkyo-ku,
Tokyo 112–8652.

First edition, 2010
19 18 17 16 15 14 13 12 11 10   10 9 8 7 6 5 4 3 2 1

Library of Congress Cataloging-in-Publication Data

Ezoe, Hiromasa, 1936-
[Rikuruto jiken English]
Where is the justice? : media attacks, prosecutorial abuse, and my 13 years in
Japanese court / Hiromasa Ezoe. -- 1st ed.
p. cm.
Includes bibliographical references and index.
ISBN 978-4-7700-3147-1 (alk. paper)
1. Ezoe, Hiromasa, 1936---Trials, litigation, etc. 2. Rikuruto, Kabushiki
KaishaCorruption--History. 3. Bribery--Japan--History. 4. Political corruption--
Japan--History. 5. Corporations--Japan--Corrupt practices--History I. Title.
KNX42.R55E9913 2010
364.1'323092--dc22
2010020686

www.kodansha-intl.com

CONTENTS

Preface to the English Edition

I n English it's known as the "Recruit scandal" or the "Recruit affair"—
or occasionally the "Recruit incident," although this last designation
would seem a bit of a misnomer considering the scope of the event.
The "scandal" first came to light in mid-1988 after the *Asahi Shimbun*,
one of Japan's major daily newspapers, got ahold of the list of individuals who had purchased shares of Recruit Cosmos, a subsidiary of Recruit
Co., Ltd., in advance of their offering on the over-the-counter market. It
is not clear how the *Asahi* obtained the list from Daiwa Securities, which
was Recruit's managing underwriter. The *Asahi* story originated from its
Yokohama bureau, and starting in June 1988, over a span of six months,
the newspaper revealed slowly, like a steady drip, the names of these individuals, insinuating with each revelation that the purchaser had engaged in
an illegal act—which was to have accepted a bribe.

The transfers of Recruit Cosmos's pre-flotation shares had been carried out by Recruit management, including myself, altogether legally, fully
in compliance with Japan's Securities and Exchange Law. Having close
friends and acquaintances hold shares in a company before it goes pubic
was a practice common in the Japanese business world at the time, and
since there is always a risk that the value of the shares might decline, there
was no guarantee of profit.

These factors notwithstanding, other media quickly followed the
Asahi's suit, and reports of scandal grew widespread. Before long, evening
tabloids and weekly magazines joined the bandwagon, relying on black propaganda, their reports rife with speculation and falsehoods. Collectively,

this increasingly frenzied media coverage swayed public opinion into taking a hostile view of Recruit.

Media-incited public opinion had played a critical role in the Watergate scandal in the United States in the early seventies, and indeed, Takako Doi, head of the Japan Socialist Party at the time, sarcastically labeled the affair "Recruit-gate." After a half year of relentless accusation by the media, the scandal eventually reached the office of Prime Minister Noboru Takeshita, leading to the resignation of his entire Cabinet.

Between my release on bail in June 1989 and the start of my court trial in December of that year, I began compiling materials in preparation for the trial. These materials included the notebooks I had filled in during the 113 days of my detention, where I detailed the circumstances of my interrogations by the prosecutors, as well as the briefs written by my defense attorney Osamu Ishihara during the investigation phase. It occurred to me that someday I would wish to publish a book about this so-called scandal—it would be my side of the story—and so the first draft of this book was largely completed almost nineteen years ago.

When I consulted close friends about publishing this book, I was invariably advised against. The shared sense was: No matter what I wrote, it would be perceived as an attempt to justify myself, to restore my reputation. They understood why I would want my side of the story told, but said I'd be better off keeping quiet and maintaining a low profile.

The Recruit scandal was so famous—or infamous—that it came to be discussed in the nation's high school textbooks. The truth behind the scandal, however, was always hidden from the public, and I continued to feel the urge to speak up before I went to my grave—if only for the sake of my children and grandchildren and the very excellent employees of Recruit. I was aware that some readers might view whatever I wrote cynically, and while this kept me from publishing the book sooner, I now feel that the time is right.

One motivating factor is that Japan, after ten years of deliberations, is at last moving to reform its judicial system. Needless to say, I have had intimate experience with this judicial system, and I have very strong feelings about it.

Progress has been seen on many fronts, including the trial system and the training of legal professionals. A new system of lay judges has recently been inaugurated, even as debate on its value remains brisk; a full review of the new system is scheduled after three years. Personally, I believe that instead of creating a judicial system unique to Japan, it would be preferable to introduce the jury system that has served justice well in the courts of the United States for over two hundred years and revised when deemed necessary.

The debate surrounding these judicial reforms focuses too much on the lay judge system, and fails to address the more important point of accountability and transparency in investigations: to that end, there is need to institute rules to have a video record of the interrogation process. In Japan, interrogations by public prosecutors are conducted behind closed doors, and this lack of transparency has been the repeated cause of problems in the dispensation of justice. As I know from personal experience, anything can happen behind those closed doors—from inhumane tactics to outright coercion.

The conviction rate in Japan is close to 99.9 percent—which is to say that out of a thousand persons indicted for an alleged crime, only one might be found innocent. While on the surface this would seem a laudatory rate, it also masks the less-than-just-and-fair way that signed statements and confessions are obtained by prosecutors during interrogations. Furthermore, because Japanese courts rely on these very statements as representations of truth—even as they may have no basis in fact—the court all too often hands down judgments that are miscarriages of justice. (In a recent case in the news, the court exonerated a man who spent seventeen years in prison for a murder that he was coerced into confessing and that prosecutors claimed to have had DNA evidence for.) This deplorable situation is unlikely to change until the day Japan introduces a law requiring that all criminal interrogations be video-recorded.

In my own interrogations, detailed in this book, I was subjected to a range of threats—unending detention, arrest of Recruit employees, including its president, collapse of the company—that drove me to sign my name to statements contrary to fact. There was, moreover, physical abuse by a prosecutor. If my interrogations had been recorded on video, such prosecutorial misconduct would have been unlikely to occur.

For the benefit of readers outside Japan, let me offer this brief introduction to the company that gave its name to this scandal. I established Recruit Co., Ltd., in 1960 as a publishing house of information magazines. The company grew steadily throughout the era of Japan's high-paced economic growth, and even after it came to be viewed with hostility by the media owing to the scandal, the company's growth remained firmly on track. Recruit's operations do not require authorization by any government agency, and even after I withdrew entirely from involvement in its management after the allegations of the scandal broke, the company's business results stayed on course. They have continued to do so to this day.

In addition to publishing information magazines, Recruit also provides information through different media, including the Internet, mobile phones, and other new-generation formats. In the fiscal year ending March 2009, Recruit Group–wide sales exceeded 1.8 trillion yen (almost US$20 billion). Today Recruit is Japan's top performer in the information industry, and operations now extend into the Chinese market as well. In contrast to Japan's typical large corporations of long standing, Recruit is also known for its capable alumni starting their own successful businesses.

The Recruit trial—*my* trial—started in 1989 and dragged out for more than thirteen years; there were 322 court sessions. According to my lawyers, the trial could probably qualify for listing in the *Guinness Book of Records*. For the purposes of this book I have pared down the content of this lengthy process to its main points, largely based on the briefs written by my defense team and the court records. I wish to point out that what is presented here equates to less than one percent of the content of those records.

Cited passages have been modified for ease of reading, but fidelity to the original texts has never been compromised. The titles of individuals and the names of government agencies are referred to as they were at the time of the events.

HIROMASA EZOE
June 2010

I

HOW IT ALL BEGAN

In January 1988, as the age of fifty-one, I resigned my position as the president of the Recruit Company and assumed the role as chairman of the company. Recruit was about to post Group sales of one trillion yen and ordinary profit of 100 billion yen, but after having served as president for some thirty years, I felt that time for a change in management had come. I wanted to distance myself from the day-to-day running of the company and instead focus on overseeing the Recruit Group and to pursue extra-company activities.

By "extra-company activities," I don't mean financial activities. I was chairman of the Japan Opera Foundation; a member of the government's Tax Commission, Ad Hoc Committee on Land Policy, and University Council; a trustee of Konan Gakuen Educational Corporation, after having attended Konan Gakuen middle school and high school; and a supporter of Asahide Gakuen, a facility for the disabled founded by a mentor from university days. Furthermore, as the exceptional diligence of Recruit employees had become well known in Japanese business circles, invitations to speak on ways to energize organizations and boost employee motivation were pouring in. Personally, I was eager to share what I had learned about organizational strength over the years.

In April, Recruit welcomed guests from a wide range of fields to a reception at the Hotel Okura commemorating the appointment of a new chairman and a new president. I announced my intention to remove myself from active involvement in Recruit's management, stating that the day might come when people noted how much the company had improved after the presidency was passed on to Naotaka Ida. When Ida took the microphone, he expressed his own aspiration in this way: "Like the second runner in a relay, I aim to do my utmost to keep my team on the path to victory."

Out of the Blue

Two months later, on June 18, 1988, lightning struck. The morning edition of the *Asahi Shimbun* broke the story of what would eventually become known as the "Recruit Scandal." The headline blared: "Deputy Mayor Accepts Shares in Exchange for Opening Recruit's Way into Kawasaki."

The article alleged that, in December 1984, Hideki Komatsu, deputy mayor of the city of Kawasaki, was allowed to purchase shares of Recruit's real estate subsidiary Recruit Cosmos before the shares were publicly listed on the over-the-counter (OTC) market. Recruit, at the time, was looking for a site to build its intelligent building "Technopia," and Komatsu was in charge of finding investors for the city's redevelopment of its Japan Railway (JR) station.

The truth of the matter was, Komatsu had eagerly invited Recruit to build Technopia as part of the redevelopment of Kawasaki Station, and Recruit agreed. Recruit had not initiated the discussion, nor had it requested favors of any kind. For reasons unclear, Kawasaki City Police were investigating.

Earlier, Masao Tatsumi, who was in charge of Recruit building operations, had informed me that someone from the Kawasaki City Police had approached him, treated him to a cup of coffee, and asked for his cooperation in the police investigation.

Our company lawyer, when he heard about this, thought it highly unusual for a police officer to treat a citizen to coffee. "They must be hard-pressed to build a case," he said. Then he explained: "The statute of limitations is five years for accepting a bribe and three years for making a bribe. Since more than three years have elapsed, the statute that would have anything to do with Recruit has expired. It isn't likely the police will make a case against only one party."

I was somewhat concerned, but didn't think the issue would develop into a problem. That was when the *Asahi* article came out.

The mayor of Kawasaki was the left-leaning Saburo Ito. Komatsu, the deputy mayor, was preparing to challenge Ito in the next mayoral race and had secured the backing of city council members in the Liberal Democratic Party (LDP). These circumstances pit the two men in battle for leadership of the city.

Two days after the *Asahi* article, Komatsu was fired. The *Asahi*'s investigative reportage on the ex-deputy mayor continued for nearly six months, but in the end Komatsu was never charged.

I thought that the matter was closed. However, on June 24, the evening edition of the *Sankei Shimbun* reported that Diet member Yoshiro Mori, whom I was a close associate of, had made a significant profit from the sale of shares of Recruit Cosmos that he had purchased through his secretary. The article marked the start of an endless flow of coverage about Recruit and its provision of Recruit Cosmos shares.

Similar reports appeared in morning editions of *Asahi* and the *Yomiuri Shimbun* the following day. On June 30, the *Asahi* and *Sankei* reported transfers of Recruit Cosmos shares to the family and the secretary of Diet member Michio Watanabe, to the secretary of lawmaker Mutsuki Kato, and directly to lawmakers Koichi Kato and Saburo Tsukamoto.

In early July, the now-defunct *Asahi Journal* published an article based upon a bedside interview with Ko Morita, president of Nihon Keizai Shimbun Company (Nikkei), and which focused on Morita's purchase of Recruit Cosmos shares. The headline bewailed Recruit's business practices as "contaminating both the government and the media."

The article quoted a string of unidentified sources: "According to remarks made by the editor of a small magazine . . ."; "From what we were told by one business commentator . . ."; "According to one individual who is closely involved. . . ." The article also claimed that I had flown in a helicopter with Morita to play a round of golf. I have never played golf with the man in my life.

The article concluded with this statement: "Feelings among members of the bar with good conscience are that police could make arrests under Article 58 of the Securities and Exchange Law if they were inclined to do so—but they are not. They also note how comparable laws in the United States are regularly brought to bear."

I was incensed. On the one hand, the writer was maligning Recruit's business practices when his only source was the interview with Morita. He had not bothered to speak with me to verify anything Morita had said. And on the other hand, the article was full of conjecture and unsubstantiated claims. Especially when an article could force the resignation of the president of a rival news firm, journalistic ethics required fair and impartial reportage based on indisputable evidence. Nor did it allow for any comment or explanation from Morita himself.

I had been a regular subscriber of the *Asahi Journal* during the heyday of the student protest movement in the late sixties, and I was aware that its articles had a leftist bent. This article, though, gave me a deep sense of foreboding.

On July 5, the rumor that Morita was about to step down reached Recruit. That evening, just after nine, I telephoned Takuhiko Tsuruta, senior managing director at Nikkei. Tsuruta was not optimistic. "Who can say what will happen?" he said. "But now that *Asahi Journal* has gone this far on record, Morita probably has no choice but to resign."

Dismayed at the state of affairs, I telephoned Jiro Enjoji, the chairman of Nikkei, at his home, and asked that we meet. Enjoji, knowing full well I was being targeted by the media, kindly suggested I come to his office at seven the next morning. He would inform the security guards.

On July 6, at Nikkei's headquarters in Otemachi, I explained to the chairman of Nikkei how the *Asahi Journal* article had no truth to it and was based on false claims.

"At this point, I think it's too late," Enjoji responded, somewhat indifferently.

"I see," I replied, and quickly took my leave.

Nikkei takes matters of compliance quite seriously, and before the evening, an ad hoc meeting of the board was called and the decision made for Morita to step down. His replacement would be vice president and former political affairs reporter Akira Arai.

Morita and I had a long history. We shared, of all things, an interest in ballroom dancing. Rarely does one find the head of a large company who also enjoys dance. But then there was also Seiya Matsumoto, president of

Pioneer, who was a former winner of the All Japan Students' Competitive Dancing Contest. Naturally then, the three of us would occasionally attend dance events together.

Morita was a visionary. He launched Japan's first online business, "QUICK," which provided users with financial information relating to stocks and share prices. He set up "Nikkei NEEDS," an in-house data-bank bureau that distributed breaking news. Nikkei NEEDS even provided information to leading national and local newspapers—a move which could aid the competitors. Nikkei NEEDS was the forerunner of today's Nikkei Telecom21, a Nikkei operation with corporate clients that generates robust earnings for the company.

Morita also foresaw how newspapers were destined to change. In the mid-1970s he'd read about Herman Kahn, the futurist; John von Neumann, the mathematician who laid the groundwork for the computer; and Norbert Wiener, who was the founder of cybernetics; their work fueled expectation that the age of man-machine interface was not far off. When that happened, the use of paper would eventually become obsolete, and the day would come, Morita believed, when news and data would be sent directly via networks to end-users' computers and mobile terminals.

At the time, Recruit's sole medium of information was paper. The probability, according to Morita, that an era of widespread computer ownership would begin soon was threatening. At Recruit, the managing directors would discuss ways to deal with this new era at board meetings that sometimes entailed overnight trips.

Ei Shikiba, head of sales operations at the Nippon Telegraph and Telephone Public Corporation (NTT), approached me around this time. "We've recently succeeded in developing a map database using the computers at our research lab in Yokosuka," he said enthusiastically. "Could I interest you in using this technology to start a new business?" He added that Tokyo Gas had already expressed interest in mapping its gas-line network to create a crisis management system offering quick response in times of disaster.

This clearly merited serious consideration. Recruit officers took a tour of the lab developing the map database, and we were astonished at the scale of the facility. One thing we learned was that if all the data in the system were integrated with available aeronautical maps by the Zenrin

Company, it would be possible to make a car navigation system—a completely fresh concept at the time. Following this presentation, the Recruit board made the unanimous decision to study the feasibility of business opportunities from this new technology.

I began meeting regularly with Naotaka Ida, then Recruit's senior managing director, Naomichi Sugino, senior managing director at Nikkei, and Morita. Our discussions resulted in the creation of a business planning company that we named Data Map Corporation. The company launched with Recruit and Nikkei holding equal equity. We agreed that once business feasibility became clear, NTT and Tokyo Gas would also make capital investments. Nikkei's Shuji Oishi became founding president and Recruit director Hiroyuki Maishi was appointed managing director.

Due to our shared professional pursuits, Morita and I met for dinner discussions two to three times a year.

I truly admired his business philosophy. "Nikkei's mission is to provide accurate news to the reader," he used to say. "We make every effort to refrain from publishing articles seeking to persuade the reader through the power of the pen." It was this rapport that spurred me in late 1984 to ask Morita to purchase Recruit Cosmos shares three years before its public offering. He accepted my offer.

Because of the tremendous influence of *Nikkei*—articles appearing in its pages can at times spark fluctuation in share prices—the newspaper has a company rule that bans all its employees from owning shares of listed stocks. Morita was forced to step down from his post due to his purchase of Recruit Cosmos shares in violation of this rule and the profit he reaped from their sale. The *Nikkei*'s own article reporting its president's resignation quoted Tetsuo Ohta, managing director in charge of public relations, as attributing the move to "illness and various circumstances."

Morita's secretary rang me to say that, in keeping with the internal rule at Nikkei prohibiting ownership of publicly offered shares, Morita had sold off his shareholdings when the stock went public. "Mr. Morita sees nothing wrong with what he did," the secretary explained, "and he agreed to be interviewed by that reporter from the *Asahi Journal* in his hospital room. Then the reporter went and wrote that unconscionable article. . . ."

Soon after, *Asahi* approached Recruit for an interview on the rumored sale of Recruit Cosmos shares to the former secretary of Prime Minister Noboru Takeshita. This secretary was not alone; in fact, secretaries of other politicians had also bought shares. I knew news coverage would only get worse in the coming days, and I determined that the best thing to do was to quit Recruit immediately.

I called an emergency board meeting for six P.M., July 6. I informed the board of my intention to step down as Recruit chairman.

"I'm against your resigning," one board member said. "If you quit now, it will appear to the public there was something unscrupulous behind the transfers of Recruit Cosmos shares."

Another board member agreed: "Mr. Ezoe, I don't think there's any reason for you to quit just because Mr. Morita resigned, or because it was reported in the press that shares of Recruit Cosmos had been sold to some politicians."

But their sentiments aside, the list of yet-unknown purchasers of shares was long, and it was just a matter of time before the names of the purchasers were revealed. Although I knew I had done nothing wrong, I worried the media wouldn't think so. I feared they would pounce on Recruit from every angle.

"I want to cut my ties with Recruit," I said. "I will resign as chairman and representative director and take up a post as advising director."

Hearing these words, some board members seemed to hold back tears, while others seemed to think that once news reports quieted down, I would again become involved in Recruit Group management in some capacity. No one—not me certainly—ever imagined in the slightest that this would develop into a criminal case. I, too, thought that once the negative news began to ebb, I could be active in Group management as advising director; that would be involvement enough.

Next, I called an emergency board meeting for Recruit Cosmos and tendered my resignation as chairman. Since the company had already completed its initial public offering, it was possible the widening news coverage would have an adverse impact on share price or on company operations. The board accepted my resignation as unavoidable.

In the span of a few hours, I had resigned as chairman of both Recruit and Recruit Cosmos.

At eleven P.M., Recruit held an emergency meeting of managers. In my opening remarks, I spoke of my intent to distance myself from Recruit's management for a while. "In light of the events reported so widely in the newspapers," I said, "I have resigned as chairman and taken up a post as advising director." My words were met with unabashed astonishment.

News of the meeting had apparently leaked out, and a crowd of people from the media were gathered at the entrance to the building. "If you're asked anything by the press, just remain silent and hold your head high as you leave the building." With these parting words from Seishiro Ikushima, managing director of public relations, the meeting was brought to a close.

I stayed behind, inside the building.

In response to my sudden resignation, Nanae Fukunishi, the editor of our in-house magazine *Kamome*, suggested that we publish a special edition. Starting at one A.M., we sat down to work out a series of questions that I would answer. Fukunishi felt it would be unnatural for me to say I was resigning just because Recruit had been tied to several politicians in the news or because Morita had stepped down. "Employees won't be convinced," she said.

I considered the matter from various angles, but since I couldn't claim to be resigning for health reasons and there was no other plausible explanation, we eventually settled on this statement: "It has been widely reported in the press that I sold shares of Recruit Cosmos stock to the secretaries of some politicians. This turn of events will cause inconvenience to Recruit. Moreover, I bear ultimate responsibility for Mr. Morita's resignation from Nikkei. I ask you, from here on, to rally around Mr. Ida and to devote your collective strength toward the further development of Recruit."

Fukunishi wrote up the article, I added a few touches, and the text went to the printer at six-thirty A.M. By that time the morning editions of the dailies had been delivered. I was amazed to discover that my resignation was given top billing on the front page of all five of the nation's major dailies: "Ezoe Resigns Recruit Chairmanship: Takes Responsibility for Sale of Related Shares" (*Asahi, Yomiuri, Nikkei*); "Ezoe, Recruit Chairman, Resigns: Takes 'Social Responsibility' for Sale of Pre-flotation Shares" (*Mainichi*); "Ezoe Resigns as Chairman: Takes Responsibility for Broad Impact" (*Sankei*).

Usually, a front-page article on the resignation of a company chairman was followed up with related articles in the business section, but only in the *Asahi* was there a single article in the business section. The general news section of the papers, however, had my resignation as a top story there as well: "Niche Industry Leader Gone Astray: String of Political Maneuverings Brought to Light" (*Asahi*); "Overrules Board of Directors: "I Caused Social Stir" (*Sankei*); "Ezoe, One-time Hero, Makes Agonizing Exit: Voices Regret for 'Shallow Thinking'" (*Yomiuri*); "Reigning Information Company Shaken to the Core: Success Story Comes to Abrupt Ending" (*Mainichi*).

Why was my resignation getting such attention? I felt deep tension start to well within me.

I sat down and wrote a letter to all concerned parties, informing them of my resignation as Recruit chairman. I asked my secretary, who kindly stayed by my side until morning, to mail them out. Then, just after midday, I walked to the Ginza Nikko Hotel via Recruit's underground parking lot, checked in, drank a beer, and laid down. But the comfort of sleep escaped me.

Thoughts of Going Abroad

The following day, I moved to a room at the Imperial Hotel that one of my secretaries, Hiroaki Tsuru, had reserved in his name. I holed up in the room all day, eating only a sandwich, vegetables, and other things I asked him to buy from the hotel delicatessen. I had no appetite, but I tried to eat. I've had a weak digestive tract throughout my life and I have a history of stomach ulcers. Perhaps due to the extreme stress of the situation, my digestive system seemed literally to stop functioning, and the dinner from the previous evening was like a stone in my gut.

A close friend called and suggested that I go abroad for a while. I agreed that that would beat hiding away in a hotel room, and immediately phoned Atsushi Toyama, a freelance tour guide who had formerly worked for Recruit Young Tour. Toyama said he'd be pleased to accompany me wherever I wanted to travel.

For nearly twenty years I had worked regularly late into the night, even on weekends and holidays. Here was an opportunity for me to take an extended vacation, maybe for a year or two, to recharge my batteries. I thought of Zurich, which had caught my fancy the first time I traveled to Europe. I thought of Baur au Lac, a stone hotel on the shore of Lake Zurich, in the German-speaking part of Switzerland, which had beautiful views and exquisite French food. I could stay there for a while and then, once things settled down, tour the world.

I thought of visiting Beirut, "The Paris of the Middle East"; I thought of Istanbul, Nairobi, the Indian holy city of Benares; of Kathmandu, Buenos Aires, home of the tango; of Montevideo, the Andes, . . . People who lived in these places experience life that was little different from that of their parents' and grandparents' generation. It would largely be the same for their children. Such a life afforded them stability and rare peace of mind.

For me, change was energy, and I enjoyed it thoroughly. In my life and career, I always tried to stay one step ahead of everyone. But economic riches and richness of heart are completely different things. Travel to places like these would offer me new perspective, I thought, and as I considered taking such a break, the weight of recent events seemed to lighten. I felt new hope, I felt excitement and anticipation.

The following day, I discussed my travel plans with Hitoshi Kashiwaki, who was a key member of Recruit's business planning office. Kashiwaki, at thirty-one, was already considered by many of us on the board as someone capable of taking the Recruit helm one day. We placed great trust in him.

Kashiwaki's response was straightforward: my going abroad wasn't a good idea. "If your whereabouts remained unknown for any length of time, the press will say that you 'ran away overseas.' This obsession with Recruit in the news isn't going to last. Once the current session of the Diet ends, they'll have something else to write about, and all this coverage of Recruit will end."

Kashiwaki was right, I decided. At the time, the Diet was the scene of fierce battles between the ruling and the opposition parties over the introduction of a sales tax; the press would be having to deal with the fallout of that. And supposing I did take some time off to travel, if the press were to insinuate I "ran away overseas," I would be humiliated. I abandoned the idea of going abroad.

Two days after I stepped down, quotes from the *Kamome* article appeared in all the dailies. Senior managing director Takeshi Osawa had warned that sending our in-house magazine to reporters was risky, but I ignored him. I insisted on disclosing company information because I believed doing so would, on balance, be to Recruit's advantage. It would help outsiders know more about the company and how it worked.

In numerous *Kamome* issues, I had written articles to bolster employee motivation. I told them one day Recruit would surpass the Asahi Shimbun Company and Dentsu and become the largest information provider in Japan. Actually, *Nikkei Business*'s rankings of unlisted companies showed that Recruit's profits exceeded both Asahi's and Dentsu's at the time.

But I may have miscalculated. Recruit's core business was publishing information magazines that contained only advertising. The nature of the company's business operations coupled with my comments and actions may have fanned the antagonism journalists felt toward Recruit.

Asahi Fires the First Shot

During the time I was staying at the Imperial Hotel, Recruit public relations managing director Ikushima fielded several requests for interviews from the *Asahi* as well as its news magazine *AERA*. He turned them down.

On July 7, Hiroshi Matsubara, head of the secretariat at Recruit Cosmos who oversaw Cosmos public relations, reported that the editor-in-chief of *AERA*, Takao Tomioka, had called with an offer to "call a ceasefire" if I granted the magazine an exclusive interview.

AERA had just started publication, its inaugural issue having come out two months before. Four months before the magazine's launch, Tomioka and Toshitada Nakae, senior managing director at *Asahi*, had visited Recruit and asked my advice about production. *AERA* was Asahi's first new product in twenty years, and Recruit had been enjoying success with its *Travaille* magazine. I told them about our reliance on desktop publishing, which afforded use of a wide variety of fonts and the ability to make changes at will, and our decision to print on lightweight coated paper, which was good because the reader's hands stayed clean. "All this makes for a very attractive magazine," I said. Tomioka, who seemed pleased for this information, asked that I write a short piece for the magazine's pre-launch issue—which I did, joining some twenty others.

But before the evening was over, Nakae, Matsubara—who was an old acquaintance of Nakae's—and I went down to the piano bar that was on the lower level of the Recruit building. After a few drinks and some hors d'oeuvres, we got up to sing to the accompaniment of a live piano. Nakae was quite good at it, and he knew the lyrics to quite a few songs by heart.

This was the background of Tomioka's approaching Matsubara directly to request an interview with me. I was hesitant to agree to an interview, but I found Tomioka's offer of a ceasefire hard to resist. I thought that an interview with *AERA* alone would not be a problem. I felt it would be smart to guarantee exclusivity.

Later that evening I telephoned Nakae, reaching him while he was at a dinner engagement. "The interview will be limited to *AERA*, right?" I asked.

"I give you my word," Nakae replied.

At Recruit, Ikushima and Yasuhisa Fukaya, a member of the public relations team, voiced misgivings over my agreement to the interview, Nakae's promise notwithstanding, but I went ahead and granted the interview.

The interview was set for three P.M. on July 23 at the Nippon Kokan Building in Otemachi, which Recruit was renting half of. As the time approached, I was surprised to see the number of people arriving for this promised exclusive interview. There were Tomioka, *AERA*'s editor-in-chief; Shunji Taoka, his deputy editor-*cum*-reporter; Keiichi Suzuki, from the *Asahi*'s Yokohama Bureau, who was involved extensively in the probe surrounding Kawasaki deputy mayor Komatsu; Hiromitsu Ochiai, deputy manager of the *Asahi*'s general news department, who was a former colleague of Ikushima's; as well as several roving reporters and four photographers. On the Recruit side was myself, Ikushima, and Fukaya.

Obviously this was not an interview limited, as promised, to *AERA*, and Ikushima protested strongly, but Tomioka would not budge. Finally, completely outnumbered, I reluctantly agreed to continue on the condition the interview be capped at thirty minutes.

Thirty minutes passed, and still there was no end in sight. Ikushima and Fukaya tried repeatedly to end the interview, but the *Asahi* team pressed on. The interview did not end until just before five P.M., cameras flashing relentlessly from start to finish.

The following day, July 24, the morning editions of the major newspapers were full of news about an accident at sea caused by the *Nadashio*, a Maritime Self-Defense Forces submarine, with front-page coverage continuing through the next day. The exception was the *Asahi*, whose July 25 morning edition's top story, of considerable length, had the headline: "Ezoe Admits Selling Shares of Recruit Affiliate to Politicians."

My stock transfer had more news value than a maritime accident with thirty casualties? What was going on! A wave of anxiety washed over me. The headlines on the front page screamed, "Recruit Scandal!," "No Relationship with Secretaries," "Ezoe Says Ready for Diet Questioning," and on and on. On the general news page were the headlines "Public Opinion Sees Ezoe as Defendant" and "Exclusive Interview with Ezoe," where the article made note of my "furrowed brows and a tear-choked voice."

All newspapers have copy writers who create attention-grabbing headlines without being involved with the actual information gathering, and the copy writers at the *Asahi* were particularly adept at this.

At nine o'clock, Nobuyuki Nakahara, president of Toa Nenryo Kogyo, the oil-refinery firm, rang. "Why on earth did you agree to the interview with the *Asahi*?" he exclaimed. "That was not a wise move." Nakahara was right, of course, but by then I knew that for myself. I regretted the interview. It was careless, but I also knew that it was, by now, too late.

The interview itself appeared in *AERA*'s issue the following day, July 26. The article, with the headline "The Recruit Scandal: Former Chairman Ezoe Breaks His Silence," commandeered five pages and ended with a remark by editor-in-chief Tomioka: "It was an array of reporters following this case—powerful reporters I certainly wouldn't want to meet if I were in Mr. Ezoe's position. . . ."

A year later, when I was released on bail, I read the *Documentary of Our Reports on the Recruit Scandal* that the *Asahi* had published. It contained the following passage: "Through Recruit management, Ochiai tried bargaining for an interview repeatedly. After taking the full brunt of our probe, the last thing we expected was for Ezoe to agree to a request from the very news agency that forced his resignation. But something totally unexpected happened: *AERA* pulled a quick one in having Ezoe agree to an interview. We were very lucky that *AERA*'s editor-in-chief, Takao Tomioka, suggested that we work together."

It was naïve of me to believe in the integrity of journalists. The supposed "ceasefire" was the "call to arms."

A Reporter's Indiscretion, A President's Valor

For its ongoing news coverage of Recruit, the *Asahi Shimbun* had been nominated to win an award from the Japan Newspaper Publishers & Editors Association (NSK). Meanwhile, *Asahi*'s president, Toichiro Ichiyanagi, had been unofficially tapped to become the next NSK chairman. But then *Asahi* became embroiled in what came to be known as the "Coral Reef Incident."

On April 20, 1989, the front page of the *Asahi*'s evening edition contained a color photograph of an enormous coral reef in a special protection zone off Iriomote Island in Okinawa. Onto the coral had been scraped the initials "KY." The article blamed the deed on unprincipled divers and sounded an alarm against an increasingly pervasive trend of disrespect for nature. Subsequently, however, the entire story was proved to be a fabrication.

The *Asahi*'s explanation of the circumstances of the fabrication and the excuses it offered changed again and again. In the end, Ichiyanagi stepped down as company president and senior managing director Toshitada Nakae was picked to succeed him.

As reported in the *Asahi*'s morning edition of May 27, 1989, Ichiyanagi, when he announced his resignation, recalled another case of false reporting by the newspaper: a purported interview with Ritsu Ito in 1950. Ichiyanagi said he found it loathsome even to think back on that incident—then added that the current case was even more serious.

Few people today would know the name Ritsu Ito, but at the time Ito was well known as the no. 2 figure in the Japanese Communist Party who was kicked out of the party under allegations that he was the informer in the Sorge Incident, which centered on the Soviet spy who was later executed.

After the war, Ito's whereabouts were unknown, and anyone who succeeded in interviewing him was guaranteed a major news scoop. On September 27, 1950, the *Asahi* featured a lengthy article based on a three-minute interview an *Asahi* reporter claimed to have secured with Ito in the mountains near Takarazuka, during which the reporter had been blindfolded. For the brevity of the interview, the article was long and remarkably detailed. It was all a fake.

Three days later, on September 30, the *Asahi* published a retraction. An internal investigation had found that a reporter named Nagaoka from the Kobe bureau had made up the story, and the paper offered its apologies to the readers.

With regard to the embarrassment of the Coral Reef Incident, upon Ichiyanagi's resignation, the *Asahi* was remorseful. Reporting that resorts to any means, scrupulous or otherwise, was inexcusable, the paper wrote, and it pledged to exercise even greater diligence in reporting with moderation, never chasing after undeserved fame.

During my years at Recruit I had occasion to meet with Ichiyanagi. My impression of him was that he was a fine individual of outstanding character and insightful vision. I later learned from an *Asahi* reporter that, according to Ichiyanagi's secretary, one factor behind his taking responsibility for the Coral Reef Incident was his shame over the article in the *Asahi Journal* that had driven Morita, with whom he had long been on close terms, to resign.

Hospitalization

As the days passed, the stress began to take a toll on me. I needed sanctuary, a place for solace, but being at the center of the maelstrom, I had nowhere to go. It occurred to me that the only place left to me—where I wouldn't be thought to have "run away" and where I yet could be afforded some peace—was a hospital.

On June 26, I checked myself into Hanzomon Hospital, which was the venue for my annual physical. The head of the hospital was Tsuyoshi Miura, an authority on digestive surgery—he was also the personal physician of lawmaker Shintaro Abe and his wife Yoko—and it was he who oversaw my care there. Mrs. Miura thoughtfully made arrangements so that incoming telephone calls were blocked while I still had the freedom to place calls.

I was physically and emotionally drained. When I was awakened by a nurse in the morning, I was told that I had been asleep the entire previous day and night. I had been fed intravenously because I had been in such a deep sleep and could not be roused.

As I sought respite in the security of my hospital room, I could see from my window more than a dozen press photographers lingering at the entrance to the hospital, their cameras perched on tripods. I was sorry that my staying at the hospital was such a nuisance to the staff and the other patients.

From my bed, I turned on the television. News concerning my selling of Recruit Cosmos shares was the main fare of the news. In every instance, the tone was one of insinuation: Recruit was suspected to have committed a crime.

Watching the news—and witnessing the formidable power of television—was even more stressful than reading the news. One moment the camera would zoom in on Recruit Cosmos share certificates; the next moment, it would flash on Recruit's head office. Every time the word "Recruit" appeared on the screen, I felt a pang in my chest.

No footage was too old or shown too often. My earlier appearances on television were dug out of the archives and shown as if new; shots of Hanzomon Hospital appeared time and time again—even though the images had nothing whatsoever to do with the questions surrounding the sale of Recruit Cosmos shares.

In print, the *Asahi* stood out in its dogged pursuit of me. It would not let up, even when the *Nadashio* incident would seem to have been more newsworthy—casualties numbered over thirty and responsibility of the submarine captain was being called into question. The gravity of the incident, compared to the sale of Recruit Cosmos shares—if it did turn out to be a violation of the Securities and Exchange Law, the maximum penalty was a fine of one million yen and a one-year prison sentence—might take some of the media heat off me. I was wrong. Coverage of the *Nadashio* incident faded after about two weeks, and by then, events surrounding the sale of Recruit

Cosmos shares were being questioned in the Diet and the proceedings heavily reported each day in the news.

If Recruit were under contract to perform public works or if it were a company required to receive government approval or authorization to operate, raising doubts about a sale of a subsidiary's shares would be completely warranted. Recruit, however, was in the business of publishing information magazines, and the only governmental authorization it received was as a dispatcher of third-class mail. It received no special treatment of any kind from the government. In this regard, it seemed very strange that the opposition parties—even if their primary aim might have been to block the introduction of the sales tax—kept asking the same questions each day over and over again.

Before long, the media expanded their investigation from individual purchasers of Recruit Cosmos stock to the fundraiser tickets the Recruit Group had purchased from politicians over the years. Reports alleged these politicians thereby received donations from Recruit. Buying tickets to political fundraisers is a common occurrence: there is nothing illegal about it. Nonetheless, it was not long before some of the politicians named were forced to step down from their post.

Psychologically, I was suffering. My blood pressure, which the nurses took every morning, fluctuated wildly between 120 and 180.

Amid the relentless speculations in the news about my motivations for selling Recruit Cosmos shares, Yusaku Kamekura, the highly respected graphic designer who was an outside director of Recruit, contacted me. He got to the point quickly: "I'm moving my office to the second floor of Recruit."

"That could sully your reputation," I said. "I greatly appreciate your sentiments, but I'd prefer you not do this."

Kamekura said his mind was made up. He had talked it over with Shiseido president Yoshiharu Fukuhara, whom he knew well from Shiseido's advertising, and Fukuhara agreed that it was a strong symbolic move to make. "I just canceled my office lease," Kamekura said.

I knew Fukuhara quite well myself. We both had lived in Zushi, and our children had attended the same kindergarten. In addition, we were students of the same teacher of *kouta*, traditional ballads sung to samisen accompaniment.

I later learned from Nobumitsu Oseko, who had worked for Kamekura, that Kamekura had once angrily rebuked a reporter from the *Asahi*. "Having people close to you hold shares in your company before it goes public is something that's been done everywhere for years!" he was reported to have said, fuming.

I understood both Kamekura and Fukuhara were trying to protect Recruit, and I was grateful to them both.

Questioning in the Diet

When the press lays hold of an issue, the government roars into action. On July 29, three days after my interview appeared in *AERA*, the Ministry of Finance's Securities Bureau conducted an on-the-spot investigation of Recruit, Recruit Cosmos, and the managing underwriter for the stock transfers. Everyone involved in the transfers was questioned by the bureau as to possible violations of the Securities and Exchange Law; my understanding was that purchase agreements and the means of payments were also investigated.

After the bureau's investigations, my secretary Hiroaki Tsuru informed me that the official in charge indicated he did not expect any problems. Indeed, this was not a surprise since the sales of shares in February 1984 were officially authorized after submission of the necessary financial reports to the Kanto Local Finance Bureau, and the actual sale was carried out following submission of a request to the Japan Securities Dealers Association (JSDA) through the managing underwriter.

Moreover, in response to questioning at a Lower House Budget Committee meeting on August 5, Securities Bureau Director General Masahiko Kadotani stated that the share price was calculated using an accepted method and, to his thinking, Recruit's word on how shares were sold should be accepted for the most part. Kadotani added the bureau was presently conducting various investigations related to Article 4 of the Securities and Exchange Law, which deals with violations of the stipulation on mandatory reporting in conjunction with sales of securities.

Kadotani was called to testify before the Diet on repeated occasions, and at the fifth session of the Upper House Budget Committee on August

31 he was asked about possible violation of the law as described in Article 4. He was also asked how such a violation should to be treated. "Under the current Securities and Exchange Law," he replied, "there is currently no legal basis requiring submission of a report. We've asked Recruit Cosmos to submit a report in line with administrative guidance, but so far the company has not acquiesced. We will continue to exercise administrative guidance hereafter, and in the event that Recruit Cosmos continues to demur, we plan to take such necessary actions as working through the securities firm to curb any equity increases by Recruit Cosmos through public offerings in the near term. As for penalties to be imposed on Recruit Cosmos, the statute of limitations—three years—has already passed. If we fail to get the company to submit a report voluntarily, there's no legal basis that would enable us to force such a submission."

Concerning movements of shares prior to over-the-counter registration, Kadotani indicated that, under a self-imposed JSDA rule, movements of shares by special related parties are prohibited during a set period of time immediately before a public offering. "When this rule is violated, we reject the application for OTC registration. Insofar as this point is concerned, we conducted an investigation through the JSDA, and they reported finding no evidence of share movements by any special related parties."

Despite his testimony, the opposition parties weren't convinced. They wanted to pin responsibility on the Ministry of Finance (MOF). But while shares listed on First and Second Sections of Tokyo's Stock Exchange fall under the purview of the ministry's Securities Bureau, shares registered on the OTC market (created by the securities houses under the JSDA) operate under rules decided autonomously by the JSDA. The Securities Bureau has no direct involvement. Recruit Cosmos's shares were offered publicly on the OTC market. The various Diet opposition parties took their shots questioning Kadotani about violations of the Securities and Exchange Law, asking him repeatedly about the same matter. In a pained demeanor, Kadotani consistently replied, "We will continue our investigations."

Three lawyers—Wataru Sueyoshi of Mori Sogo Law Offices, who was the Recruit Cosmos's corporate counsel, and Koichi Tamura and Takeshi Ohara, who were experts in the Securities and Exchange Law—submitted reports on two occasions to the Public Prosecutors Office and the MOF

Securities Bureau, stating that no violation of the Securities and Exchange Law was committed. The first report was submitted on February 28, 1989; it was 569 pages in length—forty pages stating their views, with the remainder filed as supplementary material. The second report, submitted March 2, was 222 pages in length—twenty pages making their case, with the remainder supplementary material. I read both reports after being released on bail and found them to be straightforward and easy to understand.

Kadotani was asked to respond to questions concerning allegations of Recruit's violations of the Securities and Exchange Law a total of thirty times over a period of four-and-a-half months—from August 4, 1988, at a Lower House Budget Committee meeting, to December 16, at the meeting of the special Lower House committee investigating the Recruit issue.

In retrospect, the tenacious questioning of Kadotani by the opposition parties appears to have been part of their strategy to buy time to block the vote on the introduction of the sales tax. Their aim was to force the scrapping of the bill altogether. As a result, the 113th extraordinary session of the Diet was extended repeatedly, becoming the longest extension in the history of the governing body. The record shows that 70 percent of the session was taken up by questions regarding responsibility in the *Nadashio* incident collision and 30 percent taken up by questions regarding Recruit's alleged violation of the Securities and Exchange Law.

According to my secretary, however, investigators from the Securities Bureau would show up at our offices each day and kill time in one of the conference rooms until it was time to go home at five P.M.

Assault with Bullets, Assaults with Words

On August 10, 1988, gunshots were fired at my home in Minami-Azabu, a quiet residential area in the center of Tokyo. A group calling itself "Sekiho-tai" (Blood Revenge Division) claimed responsibility for the deed in written statements sent to the major news wire services. Its reason: "Recruit Cosmos's engagement in anti-Japanese activity by giving money to the anti-Japanese *Asahi*."

This made no sense to me. Why would I be targeted, when I was the one targeted by the *Asahi*?

The National Police Agency added the incident to Case File No. 116, which included a series of assaults against the *Asahi*, most notably the May 3, 1987, shooting death of Tomohiro Kojiri, an *Asahi* reporter with the Hanshin Bureau. Following this incident, Metropolitan Police Department officers were assigned guard duty at Hanzomon Hospital and at my home in Minami-Azabu. Fortunately, because of my wife's religious faith, my family lived in a condominium not far away in Minami-Aoyama, and she and my two daughters were safe.

My emotional state remained unstable, and I thought it wise to seek treatment. Hanzomon Hospital did not have a mental health department, however, so I arranged for visits from Hiroshi Inoue, a psychiatrist and internist who had attended the same university as I did. Dr. Inoue provided counseling and prescribed a tranquilizer and the antidepressant Dogmatil as well as a digestive aid.

I was advised repeatedly—by all the doctors overseeing my care—to avoid watching television and reading the newspapers, because the inevitable result would be my blood pressure skyrocketing. But I could not help myself.

Any detail relating to Recruit, no matter how trivial, was considered "newsworthy." As if it were big news, the inordinately large headline of one newspaper article read: "Recruit Cosmos Condos See Cancellations." There is nothing unusual about real estate cancellations; after the contract fee is paid but before a building is completed, prospective buyers will cancel their contracts for any of a variety of reasons—a common reason was their transfer for work to a different region in the country. Anyone in the real estate business will attest to cancellations being part and parcel of the condominium business.

There were other bits of "news": such-and-such company stopping orders with Recruit, or such-and-such company forgoing doing business with Recruit. Any business having anything to do with Recruit was itself presented as a questionable enterprise. And starting with the *Asahi*, all newspapers asked that Recruit cease advertising in their publications. Television stations did the same thing as regards Recruit's commercials.

Although the mainstay of Recruit's advertising was ads on trains, I worried that the loss of our TV spots and advertising space in the press might erode sales. This, at least, proved not to be the case. My secretary reported that sales volumes were level and earnings were solidly on point with the targets set. The other bit of good news was that, the controversy notwithstanding, talks were held with a group of Recruit's core banks, led by Sanwa Bank, and the banks agreed to support the Recruit Group and continue to provide it loans.

This gave me some strength at a time when I was feeling battered by ill winds. I was reassured: society remained accepting of the services provided by Recruit.

The weekly magazines chose to focus on my personal life. I was cast as a "profiteer" and a "business mogul with political clout," and I was supposed to have done "business steeped in lavish entertainment." I was alleged to have an untold number of sexual affairs: "The Wives and Women Who Cried in the Shadows of the Recruit Scandal"; "Confessions of Hiromasa Ezoe's Former Mistress"; "Hiromasa Ezoe's Days of Gluttony and Greed"; et cetera, et cetera.

While these articles were conjured up to entertain and attract readership, I worried what Recruit's own employees might not be impervious to the gossip. Kamekura, the graphic designer and outside director of Recruit, laughed as he related his speech to the managers: "I told them you aren't the sex-crazed rabbit the weeklies are talking about. Superman maybe, when it comes to your work, no Superman when it comes to romance!"

My wife, meanwhile, was keeping a low profile, which prompted the weeklies to speculate that she had fled the country. Then, a photographer from one weekly caught her hanging laundry on the balcony. The scoop of the photo included the caption: "Could the Mrs. have put on a little weight?" Other articles with attributions to neighbors or "parties concerned," were equally imaginative: "The Opulent Underground Life of Recruit's 'Empress,'" "The Puzzling Separate Lives of Hiromasa and Midori Ezoe," . . .

My wife, not easily flustered, later took two publishers to court and sued them for defamation of character. She won.

The Matsubara Case

On August 9, the questioning within the Lower House Budget Committee concerning alleged violations of the Securities and Exchange Law involving Recruit Cosmos shares finally concluded with questions posed by two lawmakers belonging to minor political parties: Yanosuke Narazaki of the Socialist Democratic Federation (SDF) and Tomoichi Noma of the Japanese Communist Party (JCP). With the end of Diet questioning, related reporting also settled down, and most of the news photographers abandoned their vigil outside the hospital entrance.

Although my well-being was impaired by all the pressure, I wasn't physically ill, so staying cooped up in a hospital room was making me antsy. I again thought of traveling abroad, and I passed the time reading guidebooks and making plans.

Then, on September 5, a totally new issue struck. The Nippon Television Network (NTV) broadcasted footage it had gotten of Hiroshi Matsubara, director of public relations and head of the secretariat at Recruit Cosmos, visiting the SDF's Narazaki, bowing deeply, and offering him a gift of cash. The footage was broadcast over and over again.

I was in shock. Why had Matsubara attempted to pass on a hefty sum of money to Narazaki just when questioning in the Diet had come to a close and reports of the so-called scandal were beginning to quiet down?

As Matsubara himself later explained, Narazaki had visited Recruit and Recruit Cosmos on many occasions since July under his authority as a Diet member, demanding the complete list of everyone who had purchased Recruit Cosmos shares.

Company management was at a loss as to how to respond because such a list, if turned over, would mean trouble for those individuals who had not previously been brought to light. At this point Tatsumi Tanaka, who after a career at an automotive parts manufacturer had joined Recruit, pitching himself to Matsubara as an expert in risk management (he eventually left Recruit and set up a corporate risk management firm called Risk Hedge), was adamant in his belief that Narazaki's request was in fact a demand for money. Acting on this counsel, Shunjiro Mamiya, a Recruit managing director, instructed Matsubara to take a large sum of cash and visit Narazaki at his residence in Akasaka.

On the evening of August 4, Matsubara went to see Narazaki. "Please forgive us for not divulging the list of share buyers," he said, bowing. When he attempted to proffer the cash, Narazaki refused.

Nearly four weeks later, however, on August 30, Narazaki phoned Matsubara, summoning him to his residence with the "item" in hand. Around three that afternoon, Matsubara paid a second visit to Narazaki, carrying a paper bag filled with cash. Once again, Narazaki refused the cash. Matsubara was perplexed. He recalled thinking that something strange was going on.

NTV's broadcast of the footage taken by hidden camera occurred six days later, on September 5. Why didn't NTV show the footage immediately after it came into its possession? I have to think the company was involved in internal debate on the ethics of the footage.

The next day, September 6, NTV broadcast a special program hosted by a popular newscaster during which the scene in question was shown repeatedly.

Speaking in the Diet press conference room on September 5, Narazaki revealed his intent to press charges "to protect the authority of the nation's lawmakers." With this, news coverage of the case, which had finally abated over the previous days, flared up again.

On October 11, an *Asahi* headline announced that the JCP investigation of the Recruit transfer of shares had uncovered names of nine recipients— "including Minister of Finance Kiichi Miyazawa." The other eight were former Labor Vice Minister Takashi Kato; Fumio Shimizu, secretary to LDP secretary-general Shintaro Abe; Ihei Aoki, former secretary to Prime Minister Noboru Takeshita; NTT director Ei Shikiba; University of Tokyo professor Shunpei Kumon; Yasuo Tsuihiji, secretary to former Prime Minister Yasuhiro Nakasone; former NTT director Hisahiko Hasegawa; and Tsunehachi Tagaya, tax consultant for Recruit.

Among the nine individuals newly named, six—Miyazawa, Kato, Shimizu, Shikiba, Kumon, and Hasegawa—subsequently resigned their posts. Kumon, who had provided guidance to Recruit in setting up in-house communications networks, gave up his position at the University of Tokyo immediately after the news broke, then assumed a position as a professor at an American university.

On October 15, the *Asahi* reported that the Tokyo District Public Prosecutors Office was stepping up its investigation to unravel the details of the share transfers. Four days later, on October 19, teams of special investigators from the Public Prosecutors Office conducted in-house searches at Recruit and its affiliate companies on suspicion of Recruit's attempting to bribe Narazaki.

The volume of material confiscated on that occasion amounted to 1,700 cardboard boxes of documents: 1,000 from Recruit's offices in Ginza and 700 from Recruit Cosmos. Materials included employees' notebooks, address books, accounting slips, and floppy disks, among other items. This impeded performance of regular work duties at the company, but there was nothing that could be done under the circumstances. A search was simultaneously carried out at Hiroshi Matsubara's home.

On October 20, a month and a half after the video footage was aired on NTV, Matsubara was arrested for attempted bribery.

Why, I wondered, when there seemed to be the rock-solid evidence of the video footage, was Matsubara not arrested immediately? Why had it taken the prosecutors so long to act? It seemed very strange. I suspect one reason is that prosecutors could not find clear evidence during their in-house searches. But after pursuing such a grand investigation, they could not simply back down. They needed to buy time. They knew that without solid evidence, the bribery case could not stand.

In 2007, *Seigi no wana* (The Justice Trap), by the journalist Soichiro Tahara, looked back on the Recruit scandal. This is what he had to say about the Matsubara case:

> It was this incident that spurred the prosecutors' office to pursue the Recruit matter in earnest. At the very least, they could mount a case against Matsubara, head of the secretariat, on a charge of bribery.
>
> Narazaki filed charges against Matsubara and Ezoe with the Tokyo District Public Prosecutors Office on September 8. The office's Special Investigation Department carried out raids at several locations, including Recruit's head office and affiliate companies, on

October 19. Roughly thirty people, including prosecutors from the department, were mobilized for the raid on Recruit's head office, and some twenty others were mobilized at Recruit Cosmos's head office.

Starting September 5, the Diet was supposed to be debating the sales tax, but its focus shifted entirely to the Recruit scandal. The opposition parties, seeking to delay the tax debate and force the proposal to be scrapped, contended that fully unraveling the Recruit scandal was the Diet's topic of highest priority.

Ultimately, the Matsubara case became a major turning point in the Recruit affair.

Bedside Interrogations

On October 12, I underwent questioning at Hanzomon Hospital by a special committee of the Lower House studying problems relating to the tax system and "other matters." My room was small so it was like a Tokyo commuter train with committee members representing each political party packed in.

The questioning began with committee chairman Shin Kanemaru. Why, he asked, had I resigned as chairman of Recruit and Recruit Cosmos? What was my current relationship with the companies? Then, other committee members took turns asking me questions. I responded to each as best I could.

"Do you have anything you'd like to say about the charges against you as pressed by Mr. Narazaki?" Kanemaru began.

"I have nothing I wish to say."

Takashi Yonezawa, of the Democratic Socialist Party, was next. "When did you start making donations to politicians? Did you have any specific objectives in doing so?"

"The Recruit Group has made political donations for the past ten years," I replied. "I didn't have any special aims in mind; I just hoped our contributions would be of help in enabling the performance of good government."

Toshiki Kaifu, of the LDP, asked if I was aware what I did amounted to unreported sales of shares in violation of the Securities and Exchange Law.

"I don't consider what I did to be a violation of that law," I said.

"Did you ever request anyone's cooperation so you would be appointed a member of a government council?" Kaifu asked.

"Never. I accepted my membership on government councils at the behest of the government."

Kaifu went on: "A variety of issues have been raised concerning your selling of pre-flotation shares. Do you have any opinion on this matter, or about ways to remedy these issues in the future?"

"I just want to say how deeply sorry I am for the trouble caused to so many people. I'm in no position to offer any thoughts on how to remedy the issues at hand."

The questioning continued for nearly two hours. Meanwhile, outside the building, an unseasonable thunderstorm raged.

On the following day, October 13, the *Asahi* devoted more than half its front page to my bedside questioning. "Ezoe Refuses to Reveal Share Recipients," the headline blared. Equivalent space was accorded related stories on two inside pages, one titled "Even Criminal Punishment Won't Get Me to Speak," and the other "Ezoe's Responses Avoid Heart of the Matter." Another page featured a full account of the questions and my responses, with subheadings proclaiming "Limited Results from Bedside Questioning" and "Even Outline of Stock Transactions Proves Elusive."

On average, the other major dailies devoted about half as much space as had the *Asahi*.

The opposition parties' relentless grilling of Prime Minister Noboru Takeshita and the LDP concerning Recruit Cosmos shares continued unabated. Instead of launching the debate over the sales tax bill, the Diet remained stalled.

On August 1, at the 4th plenary session of the Diet, Takako Doi, chair of the Japan Socialist Party (JSP), questioned the role of the LDP as regards Recruit and made thirteen references to what she termed "Recruit-gate"—her attempt to connect the events to the Watergate scandal under U.S. President Richard Nixon. Ironically, however, Doi herself was on the list of politicians Recruit supported through purchase of tickets to her fundraising events.

In the days when I was vice chairman of the Japan chapter of the Young Presidents' Organization (YPO), I once invited Doi to lecture at one of our seminars. To my surprise, Doi was an advocate of sound fiscal health and she conveyed worry that Japan's fiscal soundness would deteriorate in the future. "We must not leave fiscal debt to future generations," she stressed. She added that sooner or later it would be necessary to introduce a sales tax. She was also remarkably well versed in matters inside the LDP's various factions, and given her abundant and wide-ranging insight, she was a very interesting speaker. Those were the days when, other than Diet Affairs Committee meetings, clandestine meetings were held at *ryotei*, exclusive traditional restaurants, where opposition camps reached compromise on various issues. At the reception after her lecture, she was an excellent conversationalist and, it turned out, an outstanding singer when she took her turn at karaoke.

When Doi was inaugurated as the new JSP chair, Recruit purchased tickets to the party to celebrate the event. The Ministry of Labor had asked Recruit to contribute, saying that it had a quota of tickets to sell and few places to turn. I later learned that Ichiro Ozawa, deputy chief cabinet secretary at the time, requested that Recruit submit a list of its purchases of JSP party tickets but was refused. Nonetheless, an article appeared in the morning edition of the *Mainichi* on February 10, 1989, reporting that Recruit bought some two hundred thousand yen worth of tickets to Doi's inauguration party at the request of higher-ups in the Labor Ministry. I cannot guess how that information was obtained.

On November 7, while still at Hanzomon Hospital, I underwent questioning about the Matsubara affair. Toshiaki Hiwatari, prosecutor from the Special Investigation Department, impressed me as a gentleman with a brilliance and composure.

"Were you involved in Hiroshi Matsubara's attempt to bribe Mr. Narazaki?"

"No. The first I knew about it was on the television news."

"Where did the money come from?"

"I have no idea."

"You really weren't involved at all?"

"No. As I said, the first I knew of it was from the television news."

"OK, then just as a reference I'll move on and ask you about the shares that traded hands. Who sold the shares to the Labor vice minister?"

"I don't know."

"The sale to Yuzuru Ikeda—wasn't that really a sale to his brother, lawmaker Katsuya Ikeda?"

"I know nothing about that."

It seemed clear from these questions that the prosecution was attempting to build a case.

Hiwatari apparently refused to comment to the media about our exchange. The newspapers mentioned the bedside questioning session, but articles based solely on speculation used different words and lacked a common thread.

I had no appetite whatsoever. Because I wasn't consuming enough calories, the hospital supplemented my nourishment with glucose drips three times a day. The drips also contained tranquilizers, so I could sleep.

My mood swings were not yet under control, so once a week I went to see another psychiatrist, Kiyoshi Ogura, at Kanto Central Hospital in Setagaya. I would go by car, entering and leaving the hospital through the employees' entrance. At Hanzomon Hospital, my room was directly across from a fire station, and so as not to be visible through the window, I kept the curtains tightly closed all day. After living like this way for so long, the scenery along the route to Kanto Central was soothing.

Under Dr. Ogura's care I tried several antidepressants. Ultimately, Ludiomil worked best for me. Dr. Ogura also recommended exercise. I purchased a treadmill and tried running in my hospital room, but to no avail. Every day my head felt heavy, as if I were being forced to wear a helmet made of lead.

One night I waited until the hospital was quiet, and I stealthily left my room and made my way downstairs to the basement. Then I climbed up the stairs to the roof—six stories—then back down to the basement, then back up to the roof. I did this six or seven times. I started perspiring. By around the twentieth time I was sweating from head to toe and my head felt lighter. The lead helmet was melting away. All told, I had gone up and down a total of 120 floors. I was dripping sweat. In my room I took a shower, put on a fresh change of clothes, and still I was sweating. When the sweat finally stopped pouring out and I had changed clothes again, I felt totally refreshed. My depression had vanished, and I felt more like my normal self. After that, I was able to sleep soundly. From that day on, I repeated my stairs workout every evening.

During that time I felt most at ease when I was asleep. But then morning would come, and I'd awaken to the reality of the news and invariably fall back into the depression I'd escaped in the night.

Testimony before the Diet

Although my bedside interrogations were over, the opposition parties kept the pressure on. Debate in the Diet over the sales tax stalled. After a series of discussions between ruling and opposition parties in the Diet Affairs Committee, special new committees were created in both houses to investigate the Recruit scandal. On November 21, I was summoned to testify before the Lower House.

I was told I could testify in the hospital, but I decided to appear before the Diet, thinking this would be a prime opportunity to demonstrate my innocence.

The night before my appearance, I borrowed Dr. Miura's office and met with Recruit's legal counsel. "Whatever you do, don't commit perjury," he cautioned me. "During the Lockheed scandal, witnesses who said repeatedly that they had 'no recollection' of issues were later charged with perjury. The maximum penalty for violation of the Securities and Exchange Law is one year. Perjury carries a maximum sentence of ten years.

"One other thing," he continued, "regarding Recruit's purchase of the Cray supercomputer, NTT's lawyers ask that you exercise discretion. If you were to testify that NTT had purchased the computer and then sold it to Recruit, thereby suggesting NTT was merely a middleman, it could reignite trade friction between Japan and the United States."

But Recruit did purchase a Cray supercomputer through NTT and not directly from Cray Japan. Here is how that came about:

In the mid-1980s, Kobe Steel possessed technology that efficiently connected multiple computers. Recruit and Kobe Steel established a joint venture, called ARK Systems, whereby Kobe Steel would provide the engineering staff and technology and Recruit would provide the sales capability. The venture launched a mainframe computer time-sharing business called Remote Computing Service (RCS).

The building where RCS was located, formerly occupied by the Nippon Light Metal Company, was built by the Takenaka Corporation using a caisson construction method. The building had four underground basement levels, and investment was made in equipment to maintain constant pressure in the basement where the computer center was located. An IBM 3090 and a compatible Fujitsu FACOM M-360 were installed, and as soon as the time-sharing business launched, RCS quickly got solidly on track.

In those days, city banks were developing third-generation online systems, and large capacity computers were in high demand. Since general mainframe systems once used for development were no longer required, time sharing was an option that met these market needs. RCS's business expanded rapidly, and it soon outgrew its initial location. We took a lease on a computer-friendly building in Harumi, and from this venue the business continued to expand.

Recruit then constructed Technopia in the redevelopment zone of Kawasaki city. Around the same time, the company also rented property in New Jersey—a former grain elevator retrofitted into a high-tech "intelligent" building. The plan was to take advantage of the time difference between New York and Tokyo and provide connection services through the international telecommunications company Kokusai Denshin Denwa (KDD) lines to Japanese companies. This business was gaining solid momentum as well.

We then learned from staff in New York that Boeing had made its computer center an independent company and was leasing its Cray supercomputer to other companies for use in aeronautical and automotive wind tunnel testing. Our response was that we should add a supercomputer to our list of offerings as well.

Without delay we requested cost estimates from Fujitsu, NEC, and Cray. Although Cray's system, launched before the supercomputers of either Fujitsu or NEC, was advanced in terms of software, Fujitsu's FACOM VP series excelled in cost performance. We particularly liked the newly developed FACOM VP-400, which boasted the world's fastest processing speed. Fujitsu president Takuma Yamamoto assured me personally that the company would support us fully in all aspects of software. Also, Fujitsu was one of Recruit's biggest clients. We eventually opted for Fujitsu's VP-400, and Recruit became the maiden user of this supercomputer.

It was at this point, however, that Duncan Otis, president of Cray Research's Japanese subsidiary, decided to make his move via NTT.

More than a dozen supercomputers were already in Japan. These were purchased by national research organizations and national universities and, in every case, procured from domestic manufacturers. Cray supercomputers—most popular worldwide because of Cray's renowned software excellence—were used at a number of private Japanese companies but were not yet used at any national research institutes or universities. When U.S. Trade Representative Clayton Yeutter criticized Japan for its "protectionist trade policy," it was reported that if Japan continued preferential treatment toward domestic manufacturers, the United States would not hesitate to press the matter as a violation of the General Agreement on Tariffs and Trade (GATT).

The supercomputer issue was therefore a centerpiece of U.S.-Japanese trade friction and NTT was taking the brunt of the criticism. Despite entering into an agreement to purchase U.S. products, NTT failed to meet its procurement quota because of using telecommunications equipment produced by the "NTT family." To refute this criticism, NTT chose to demonstrate a proactive stance toward purchasing U.S.-made products and began holding seminars in the United States on material procurement.

NTT president Hisashi Shinto was slated to attend these seminars in Washington, D.C., and Santa Clara, California, beginning September 18, 1985, when I received a call from Ei Shikiba, then head of NTT's sales division, as I was driving to my office.

"Mr. Shinto's leaving for the U.S. tomorrow," he said, "and we've received word from vice president Yasusada Kitahara, who went to the States ahead of him, that arrangements were made for him to hold a press conference. We can't let him go empty-handed, and we were wondering if you'd consider buying a Cray computer through NTT."

After receiving Shikiba's call, I decided to add a Cray X-MP/16 supercomputer to our shopping list, with the purchase being made through NTT. Besides being an opportunity to do NTT this favor, there were two other reasons I chose to buy a Cray computer rather than stick exclusively to Fujitsu systems. First, the X-MP/16's price tag was relatively inexpensive at 1.3 billion yen. Second, I thought Cray's name and the excellence of its supercomputer design could be helpful in our recruitment of engineering students with backgrounds in telecommunications and control technology.

Haruo Yamaguchi, a managing director at NTT, contacted me with a message from Shinto saying he wished to meet me and thank me in person. The next day, I went to NTT's head office, just five minutes by car from Recruit, where Shinto offered me kind words of appreciation during our brief meeting.

Years later, on April 23, 1998, at the 224th session of the Recruit case, Yamaguchi appeared in court as a witness in this matter. His testimony was largely as I have described here.

These are the factual circumstances behind Recruit's purchase of the Cray supercomputer through NTT. I was well aware, however, that if it came to light in the Diet that the computer in question had merely passed through NTT's hands straight into Recruit's possession, trade tensions between the United States and Japan would flare up again. It was a situation to be avoided.

Fully reconciled to the prospect I might be arrested on a perjury charge, I therefore decided to testify that the computer system did not merely pass through NTT's hands, but that in purchasing it through NTT, Recruit was expecting to receive NTT's backup support.

Testimony before the Lower House

My testimony before the House of Representatives was slated for ten A.M. on November 21. It was scheduled for two hours. Since responses made during sworn testimony are subject to charges of perjury if proven false, the witness is allowed legal counsel. In my case, however, I was more concerned about my physical condition, so instead of legal counsel I requested the accompaniment of my doctor from Hanzomon Hospital, Katsuto Kobayakawa.

A swarm of cameras were hovering outside the hospital entrance. As I stepped out, reporters could be heard shouting into their microphones. "Recruit's former chairman, Hiromasa Ezoe, has just emerged from the entrance of Hanzomon Hospital. . . ." I was blinded by the blazing lights and the flashing strobes of countless cameras. I could almost feel my heart stop beating, the blood in my veins ceasing to flow.

Leaning on Hitoshi Kashiwaki, our young trusted colleague, for support, I made my way into the waiting car. A police car escorted us along the route to the Diet building, and the entire time photographers on motorcycles were racing along both sides of the car trying to get a photo of me. Facing straight ahead, I pretended to be calm and collected.

Arriving at the Diet, I noticed Shintaro Abe, the LDP secretary-general, just ahead of me. The media frenzy went on, as photographers ascended the steps alongside me, photographing me constantly. Once inside, I was escorted by a guard down the red-carpeted corridor to a waiting room. At the entrance, I spotted a reporter wearing an NHK armband. "Mr. Ezoe has just entered the waiting room outside the Lower House No. 1 Committee Room," he spoke into his microphone.

At precisely the appointed hour, committee chairman Ken Harada declared the proceedings open, and I was called to the witness stand. I was so nervous, I could feel the muscles in my face tighten. Slowly, I read the standard oath: "I swear, according to my conscience, that I will tell the truth, conceal nothing, and add no embellishment to the facts." I then signed my name to the document.

The last time witnesses were summoned to testify before the Lower House was nine years before, in connection with a case against McDonnell Douglas and Grumman Aerospace. On that occasion one of the witnesses was so nervous, his hand shaking so violently, he could barely sign his name; it was a scene that the media loved to show over and over. Following that debacle, to protect the rights of witnesses, new Diet testimony legislation was introduced that limited all related news coverage to still photos.

I would be testifying before a large number of Diet members and even with photography limited to still shots, my testimony would be broadcast on live TV for the full two hours. I did my best to look composed, but inside my nerves were completely frazzled.

The first question was posed by committee chairman Harada: "The lists submitted by Recruit and Recruit Cosmos supposedly contained the names of all the members of government and bureaucrats who received shares,"

At the start of prolonged questioning in the Diet. Tomio Sakagami of the Japan Socialist Party wanted me to name names. I preferred not to. This did not please him.

he began, "but media reports are saying Shigezo Hayasaka, secretary to former prime minister Kakuei Tanaka, also received shares—twenty thousand shares, they say—so regrettably this has cast doubt on the credibility of the list. Mr. Ezoe, are the lists complete or not?"

"From the reports I have received, Mr. Hayasaka was the only one inadvertently omitted," I replied.

Harada then asked me some questions, none of which mentioned a specific politician or asked what the motive was for providing him with shares. Most questions pertained to issues reported in the press, and these were easy to answer.

The next questions came from committee member Tomio Sakagami of the JSP: "Mr. Ezoe, there are other recipients whose names still haven't been revealed, aren't there?"

"With your permission, I would prefer not to name any names."

"That would qualify as a refusal to testify, I believe, so let me ask you again what your reasons are."

"There have already been a large number of people whose names have come out and who, as a result, have resigned their posts and been placed in awkward positions. With your permission, I would prefer not to name any names."

Hearing this, Sakagami switched to a very aggressive tone of voice. "As I see it," he addressed the committee members, "Mr. Ezoe has chosen to remain silent on this point, which I construe as a refusal to testify. I therefore demand that charges be pressed against him."

A hush fell over the room. What will happen now? I thought as rivulets of sweat coursed down my back.

After a few moments, Sakagami resumed his questioning, this time waving a copy of *AERA* magazine. "When you were interviewed by *AERA*, you claimed you had no personal dealings with any secretaries of politicians, correct?"

"The only occasion when I might become acquainted with a politician's secretary would be at a gathering of his supporters or something like that—occasions also attended by secretaries. Since I'm young, I would often take a seat most distant from the politician in the limelight. Often, I found myself sitting next to the secretary and I would speak with him, but I've never had any personal dealings with any secretaries."

The aim in asking me such a question was apparently to get me to say that though the shares in question had been registered in the secretaries' names, I knew full well that they were actually intended for the politicians themselves. Sakagami didn't press the matter any further.

Exchanges of this nature continued for two hours. When all the questioning was done, I was escorted by guard back to the waiting room. Here I met Katsuro Tanaka, one of Recruit's attorneys.

"I was watching the proceedings on TV," he said. "I was worried how it might turn out, but I saw no problem in particular." He was smiling.

I then left the Diet and headed back to the hospital. Again, we were surrounded by motorcycle-borne photographers intent on getting a shot of me during the ride.

The moment I reached my hospital room, every ounce of energy still remaining instantly evaporated. Even the simple task of changing out of my business suit took major effort. After I finally lay down on the bed, I was asleep in minutes.

"Suspicions Deepen," According to the Press

I awoke a little after six in the evening. My secretary, as always, brought me the evening editions of the various papers. I lost my breath as I checked the news of the day. In nearly every paper, news relating of my Diet testimony was front page news—with the suggestion that my appearance failed to clear away any suspicion: "Ezoe Cleverly Avoids Revealing Truth behind the Scandal" (*Mainichi*); "Ezoe Testimony: Answers Exactly as Expected" (*Nikkei*); "Ezoe-style Testimony Articulate and Evasive: Suspicions Build" (*Yomiuri*); "Ezoe Tightlipped, Tense: Commotion Fills Testimony Room" (*Asahi*).

Throughout my testimony, the room had been perfectly still—there was no "commotion." The TV evening news toed much the same line. Some stations even extended their news programming.

The next morning papers again purported the same details and all restated their claim of deepening suspicions: "Quest for Truth Unsatisfied: Testimony Filled with Blatant Contradictions" (*Asahi*); "LDP's Aim to Close Case Foiled: Testimony Raises Doubts Further" (*Tokyo Shimbun*).

Although the headlines composed by copy writers trumpeted suspicions surrounding the case, the articles themselves did not elaborate on the suspicions or specify where my testimony was contradictory.

I was particularly floored by the headline in *Mainichi*: "Opposition Parties Eager to Summon Ezoe Again." If they had more they wanted to ask, why didn't they ask me yesterday?

I was overcome by anxiety.

Once the media start treating you like a villain, no amount of self-vindication will convince them otherwise. Similar reporting continued for days. Yet, even so, I never imagined I would eventually be arrested.

With each passing day, the coverage ballooned. TV Asahi was especially zealous, creating a daily "Recruit Segment" on "News Station," its popular late-night news program.

Mari Matsunaga, editor-in-chief of *Travaille*, Recruit's employment information magazine for women, in 2002 wrote the following in her book *i-mode izen* (Before i-mode):

On Saturday, June 18, 1988, the Recruit scandal kicked off in a big way.

Starting that day, it became painful to look at the morning papers, and I flinched when turning on the TV news. As the affair dragged on without knowing where it might lead, with Recruit constantly the butt of the nation's scorn, I became mildly afflicted with nervous anxiety and began to feel frightened of the media. What hit me hardest was watching "News Station" at home. Its reporting just went on and on, endlessly.

"Today, the inquiry by the special investigators discovered that Recruit had been paying three hundred thousand yen a month to the wife of a lawmaker as an advisor's fee," said Hiroshi Kume, the show's charismatic anchor. And as he reported this "fact," what was he holding but a copy of *Travaille* magazine! "The advisor's fee was paid by this information magazine, on the pretext of receiving advice on how women can advance in society." Then, thumbing through its pages, he quipped flippantly, "Where on earth is there anywhere in this magazine that would need such advice?"

I began to feel dizzy and thought I might collapse on the spot.

I also was watching Kume's show that evening and was absolutely stunned by his claim. While there were instances when the Recruit Group paid advisory fees to lawmakers' secretaries, no payments were ever rendered to a lawmaker's wife. Thinking the incident rather strange, I asked people in public relations the following day whether any articles to this effect were published in any of the newspapers. The answer was no.

I began to wonder if the special investigators were leaking certain information to TV stations and different information to other media.

The Reporting Heats Up

Reporting on the Recruit affair grew more heated each day, and it began to have an impact where least expected.

On November 30, the *Asahi*, in its column devoted exclusively to the Recruit scandal, reported that the Tokyo Metropolitan Government and Minato ward, which had earlier agreed to provide 360 million yen in subsidies toward the construction of a building in the Kaigan redevelopment zone, were rescinding the offer. The reason: Recruit would be occupying the building. Mayor of Minato ward Keiji Yamada indicated that because of the deluge of criticism Recruit was facing, public sentiment would not allow tax money to go toward the project.

The building in question was in the warehouse zone of the Kaigan district. It was being built at the request of Recruit, as it sought to expand its office space. The landowner, Sanshin Warehouse, had committed no crime, and Recruit had had no administrative penalties imposed. Allegations of violations of the Securities and Exchange Law were being made against me, but I had not been arrested or charged.

Administrative authorities pay close attention to the press, but is it right for them to withdraw a subsidy merely because of something they read in the media? In this case, I would say these authorities were guilty of committing an illegal act.

The building was already under construction, and without the 360 million yen in subsidies, the landowner might be unable to complete the job. If Sanshin Warehouse were to sue Minato ward, the ward would likely lose. Fortunately, Sanshin Warehouse had the requisite funds and the building was completed on schedule. Recruit Cosmos rented the property as originally planned, but Sanshin ended up losing the 360 million yen it was promised.

During this time, the Special Investigation Department of the Public Prosecutors Office was questioning Recruit's management as well as its business partners on a daily basis. The central issue up to this point was alleged violations of the Securities and Exchange Law, but the thrust of their inquiry now shifted to suspicions surrounding the provision of Recruit Cosmos shares to Shikiba and other NTT officials. A headline in the *Tokyo Shimbun* on December 3 read: "Cozy Relationship between Recruit and NTT Comes to Light." The *Sankei Shimbun* ran a story with the headline "Special Investigators Have Shikiba Explain; Documents on Circuit Resale Business Submitted."

The relationship between Recruit and NTT was purely business, but the media kept implying that the provision of shares to individuals at NTT was done to curry favor. Claims of the "cozy relationship" were based on the newspaper's discovery of Recruit telephone exchange equipment installed at an NTT site in Yokohama. What the reporter for *Tokyo Shimbun* failed to understand was that because the Cray supercomputer Recruit purchased through NTT was water-cooled, dedicated equipment was necessary at the site in Yokohama, which NTT was no longer using. NTT also bore the installment costs.

As I've said, NTT's attorney had asked me not to talk about Recruit's purchase of a Cray supercomputer since it could lead to trade friction between Japan and the United States. For this reason, Recruit offered no explanation concerning the supercomputer, but our cooperation had the effect of raising suspicions of collusion between Recruit and NTT.

On December 9, Kiichi Miyazawa resigned his position as Minister of Finance. His parting words were: "Recruit has become a name that will not easily be forgotten."

All along, Miyazawa had maintained that it was his secretary, Tsuneo Hattori, who had purchased the Recruit Cosmos shares, Miyazawa claiming to have known nothing about the transaction. For this reason, the issue put before the Diet was whether the signature on the document of receipt was Miyazawa's or his secretary's.

On December 14, the media reported that profit from the sale of Recruit Cosmos shares had been remitted to a bank account held under the name of Kozo Murata, secretary of now NTT chairman Shinto. Later on this day, Shinto resigned.

"To a person in my position," Shinto explained, "his secretary is like a second wife. I left my bankbooks completely in Murata's hands, so I feel intensely responsible for the fact that profit from the sale of the shares was in such an account." Shinto's remarks were given wide coverage both in the papers and on TV.

Subsequently, when it came to light that shares were purchased by Jiro Ushio, chairman of Ushio Incorporated and vice chairman of Keizai Doyukai (Japan Association of Corporate Executives), and Ken Moroi, chairman of Chichibu Cement, both men immediately announced their resignations from all official positions. At his press conference, Ushio conceded that practices considered normal in the past were no longer acceptable. He said that by resigning he was taking responsibility for the social criticism he faced.

These resignations were followed by a string of other resignations by politicians who had been found to have received donations from Recruit or Recruit Cosmos.

Lawmakers who reach cabinet level often relegate sales of tickets to fundraising events entirely to their secretaries. Hidetaka Kashihara, private secretary to Ken Harada, the chairman of the Lower House special committee investigating the Recruit scandal, had been an elementary school classmate of mine. At Kashihara's request, I bought tickets to a fundraising event for Harada. When this was revealed, Harada resigned as director-general of the Economic Planning Agency—despite, I would assume, Harada's having no knowledge of my purchases.

Similarly, Yukio Hayashida, a member of the House of Councilors, resigned as Minister of Justice because Recruit had purchased tickets to his fundraising event. He was succeeded by Takashi Hasegawa, who at the press conference marking his appointment announced: "It's because I have no connection with Recruit that I can confidently show my face before you today." Two days later, however, when it was reported that Recruit had earlier purchased fifteen tickets to Hasegawa's fundraising events, Hasegawa immediately resigned.

I was in my hospital room, watching these proceedings on TV. I asked myself how Hasegawa could be made to resign for something he knew nothing about. The reason, I realized again, was the power of the media.

Once the media targeted an individual, anyone or anything having even the slightest connection to him could come under attack. Issues of trivial consequence under normal circumstances got denounced. Those who suffered this condemnation had surely never imagined this happening.

Even as the Tokyo District Public Prosecutors Office continued its questioning of Recruit management, the media reported that prosecutors were holding joint meetings with the High Public Prosecutors Office as well as the Supreme Public Prosecutors Office.

Keiji Takehara, in charge of legal affairs at Recruit, inquired about these joint meetings and was told that since no precedent existed for charging high government officials with simple acceptance of bribes, prosecutors were building their cases on charges of acceptance of bribes in return for provision of favors. "You've got nothing to worry about, Mr. Ezoe," Take-hara tried to assure me. "You made no requests of any kind."

Nonetheless, the questioning of Recruit president Ida and Recruit managers—as well as Shikiba at NTT—went on. I knew that, since the special investigators had come this far, turning back was not an option for them. But why were they investigating everyone around me, but not me directly? At this point, I simply wanted them to investigate me quickly and resolve the issue as soon as possible.

The waiting was difficult. To calm my nerves in the hospital I listened to some of my favorite singers—Hibari Misora, Masashi Sada, Nat King Cole, and Perry Como. After a while, though, the music no longer struck a soothing chord within me.

As the central figure in the corruption case involving members of the government and the bureaucracy, I continued to draw intense criticism from the media. But I was not alone: children of Recruit employees were being bullied at school because their father worked at Recruit.

Hiroshi Tsuruoka, who had been with me since Recruit began, visited me in the hospital and offered encouragement. I was hardly in a frame of mind to feel encouraged, however. My secretary, Hiroaki Tsuru, would come every week to report on Recruit's business performance, and what kept me going was his assurance that on that front all was well.

I had not had much of an appetite, but now I began to lose my sense of taste. For meals, I continued to be fed from a drip; now and then I would have an energy bar. Meanwhile the intensifying stress sent me into an even bleaker mood.

Hospital Days

While I was in the hospital, an array of items arrived for me in the mail. There were post cards with scribbled messages like "Die!" and "Hell awaits you!" But the majority was notes of encouragement from Recruit employees and their families as well as from the general public—people I'd never met. Quite a few parents of employees urged me not to do anything "rash"—a euphemism for taking my own life. These letters gave me strength, incentive to live, and I felt sincere gratitude to them.

Some people sent books. One was *Nezumi* (Rat), by Saburo Shiroyama, which told the life story of Naokichi Kaneko, head manager of Suzuki Shop Inc., a trading company that dated back to the Meiji era and was the forerunner of Sojitz Corporation, giving birth to such companies as Kobe Steel and Teijin. In his lifetime Kaneko endured his share of trials and tribulations: he was exceedingly successful but subject to relentless criticism in the press and accused of rice hoarding, which resulted in the shop being burned down by a mob in 1918. What Kaneko experienced resembled in some ways what I was going through, I thought, and I read the book with interest, deeply impressed with how Kaneko lived his life. He was a frugal man who died virtually penniless.

Another book I received was *Ippai no kakesoba* (A Bowl of Soba), by Ryohei Kuri, which had been on the bestseller list. It was the story of a destitute mother and child whose dire circumstances made it necessary for them to share a single bowl of soba noodles to welcome in the New Year. Seeing their desperate straits, the soba shop owner silently placed an extra helping of noodles into their bowl. Like most people, I found the story quite moving.

Then there was *Zen to Yomeigaku* (Zen and Neo-Confucianism), by Masahiro Yasuoka. It contains a passage that I've paraphrased as follows:

Combining the radical for "man" 人 with the symbol for "to lament" 憂 results in the Chinese character 優, which normally means "to excel" but also has overtones of "resting at ease" or "enjoying latitude." Man cannot be man unless he experiences a great many things and knows sorrow. When he lives a life altogether ordinary without care, he cannot become an "excellent" person. Only when he has experienced great sorrow and distress, endured agony and worry, contemplated his lot and learned from it, can he rest at ease and know peace of mind. From that point on, he begins to excel.

I also received an unexpected letter from a former lawmaker that was penned elegantly with a brush: "From what I read in the newspapers, I don't believe your political donations were made out of a desire to receive anything in return. I'm writing to let you know there's an 81-year-old former member of the Diet out here, a representative of the JSP, who thinks you have been made a political scapegoat and who feels sorry for you. But as the saying goes, 'Fate works in strange ways.' Please keep firmly in mind that good days will come to you again, and be strong." I was deeply moved to receive such encouragement from someone on the inside who was familiar with the workings of politics.

About two weeks after my testimony before the Diet, a close friend from university days came to visit me in the hospital. He said he had been in touch with a lawyer who had advice he wanted to impart, and wondered if I would be willing to meet the man. The following evening I left the hospital through a back entrance and went to the Diamond Hotel, which was next door. There, in a guest room, I met with my friend and the lawyer.

"If things continue this way," the lawyer began, "it's very possible, Mr. Ezoe, that you'll be arrested on charges of making bribes and others will be arrested for receiving them. So far there's no talk in the press of your being arrested. Why don't you consider going abroad? If you left the country, proceedings in the Diet would go smoothly, and the LDP would be grateful to you. The statute of limitations in bribery cases is three years. The statute's efficacy would be suspended while you're overseas, but would run out for those on the receiving end during your absence. The maximum sentence for a violation of the Securities and Exchange Law is one year. Even if a case against you were to stand, your offense would be minor. The opposition parties are making this scandal a political issue only in order to avoid bringing up the sales tax; once time passes, charges aren't likely to be pressed against you. And once debate in the Diet comes to a close, the press will stop dwelling on this topic and the entire issue will be dropped."

I'd heard these arguments before. Going abroad at this point, however, was something I just couldn't do—even if it would be appreciated by the LDP.

Mingling with Politicians

When three of my classmates—from Konan Gakuen and the University of Tokyo—first became lawmakers, they had expressed surprise at the conditions they were expected to work under. The size of the offices assigned to them were no larger than a studio apartment, the funds allotted to them could support only two official secretaries, and they were expected to get around by train, as official cars were provided only to ministers and the top three officials in the ruling party; even reporters got chauffeured.

They needed to maintain offices at the Diet as well as in their electoral districts. They needed staff in both places. They needed to attend weddings, funerals, and other functions involving their supporters. As lawmakers, it was impossible to conduct political activities unless they were constantly fundraising.

They asked me to help if I could.

When I had occasion to visit the Diet members' office building, the anteroom where a lawmaker could meet with his visitors was barely large enough to accommodate four people. Even a branch manager at a bank had more space. With only two secretaries and no car, how could lawmakers be expected to conduct political activities, campaigning included, with such limited resources?

Lawmakers from outlying regions were especially hard-put. Generally, they left Tokyo and returned to their home districts on the weekends. If there were a wedding or funeral or some other function of a supporter, they would be expected to attend. Monetary gifts were part of this attendance. In addition, lawmakers regularly sponsored trips, golf competitions, and the sort, and it was customary for them to foot at least part of the cost.

In the days when multiple-member constituencies (three to five representatives) of a district were the norm, leaders and core members of the LDP factions—which were comparable to parties within the party—would back certain candidates as a way of expanding the influence of a faction through election. Once a candidate was selected, the faction would hold events to show its support for the candidate. Faction members and their secretaries would be under intense pressure to sell quotas of tickets to these fundraisers. A candidate who was plucked from the bureaucracy often had no self-created funds in his campaign coffers. So, from early in the campaign, core faction members who supported the candidate would travel to various electoral districts to demonstrate support. This also required funds.

When I learned about this situation, I decided to help where I could. I started purchasing tickets to their fundraisers and thereby made my political contributions. That was about forty years ago. Today, lawmakers have improved salaries and allowances, although their situation remains hard-pressed.

A comparison between Japan and the United States shows that while Japan pays for three secretaries per Diet member—two regular secretaries in addition to a secretary in charge of political policy (a position introduced in 1993), the United States pays for forty-four secretaries per senator. The cost outlay per U.S. lawmaker is over ten times that of Japan's. I have also heard that aides to a senator have their own separate offices and that each senator has his or her own library.

Japan, of course, has its bigwig politicians who maintain individual offices away from the Diet and have their own chauffeured automobiles. Politicians of this rank usually have a number of secretaries who remain within the local electoral district and who attend weddings, funerals, and such on their behalf. However, only a handful of lawmakers would meet this description.

Many countries, the United States included, show greater leniency toward political contributions than does Japan. Here, the situation is not conducive to increasing semi-public political contributions from organizations like Nippon Keidanren (Japan Business Federation; until 2002, it was known as Keidanren) or the People's Political Association.

Without donations, a good politician cannot come to the fore; and without good politicians, it is difficult to forge a good country. Japan's lawmakers want to make the nation stronger and better, but the very nature of their position puts them in need of money. When I understood this, I began to increase my political contributions and my purchases of tickets to political fundraisers.

After entering my forties, with the construction of Recruit's head office in Ginza and the purchase of the Nippon Light Metal Building complete, I began to direct my attention outside the company. I joined Keidanren (Japan Federation of Economic Organizations), became an executive member of Keizai Doyukai (Japan Association of Corporate Executives), and member of the policy committee at Nikkeiren (Japan Federation of Employers' Associations). In the course of Keizai Doyukai's summer seminars in Karuizawa and training camps in Fujiyoshida organized by Nikkeiren, I got to know other corporate leaders.

These executives would occasionally approach me, saying they were core backers of a certain politician's book publication party, which was a way to fundraise, and then suggest I become one as well. Generally, I would acquiesce to such requests even when I did not personally know the lawmaker in question. In most cases, a lawmaker's book publication party would have been held by five-to-ten core backers. For a cabinet-level politician, a typical contribution would be made by purchasing fifty tickets at twenty thousand yen apiece.

I invited politicians to speak at Recruit's board meetings. At times I would invite them to speak at our companywide managers' meetings—in the same way that I would invite scholars or economic experts. They would speak on subjects not directly related to business—on, for example, national economic policy or diplomatic issues. Many politicians are outstanding speakers, and Recruit's managers often commented on how beneficial it was to have these speakers.

Politicians tend to socialize with other politicians. The same is true of politicians' secretaries. Recruit apparently acquired a reputation among them as a generous company that, when asked, would buy tickets to fundraising events. During this time, I also contributed to the Japan Opera Foundation (where I was serving as general director), various psychology associations, and the local Grand Ginza Festival, among other groups. Overall, though, Recruit's percentage of contributions to politicians was higher than at other companies.

The Recruit Group at the time was generating annual profits of 40 to 50 billion yen. Contributions of up to one percent of that amount—400 to 500 million yen—were tax-exempt, and it was within those limits that I purchased tickets to fundraising events. In addition, I made substantial political donations on my own—from the profit I personally received when Recruit Cosmos went public.

In retrospect, I see my actions were rash and not well thought through. At the time, however, I thought I was doing a good thing.

Acquaintance with Shintaro Abe

I first met Shintaro Abe in 1974 at a party to celebrate his appointment as Minister of Agriculture, Forestry, and Fisheries. I had been invited to this gathering by Motonari Niikura, president of Niikura Scales Company, an old friend who was hosting the party at a *ryotei* in Akasaka.

It was the first time I had spoken with a cabinet minister. It seems there were a number of celebrations planned for him and the one I attended was second on the schedule. It began at nine P.M. and was attended by a small group of people. Niikura was the kind of person who didn't mince words, so no sooner had we finished toasting Abe than our host turned to him and asked, "Well, Mr. Abe, how does it feel to be a cabinet minister?"

"It feels great!"Abe beamed. "It was always my aspiration, once I became a politician, to become a minister."

"At your press conference on TV, you said the appointment came as a surprise to you."

"I've long wanted to become a cabinet minister, but I never imagined I'd become Minister of Agriculture and Forestry."

"But at the press conference, you were rather specific about the issues you'd initially be dealing with."

"The speech was prepared by the chief cabinet secretary. The content would be the same no matter who became minister. About an hour before meeting the press, I was handed my speech, and I was also told how to respond to questions the press was likely to ask."

"So you mean cabinet ministers just spout what bureaucrats write for them?"

"Hey, wait a minute!" Abe laughed. "From now on I'll be learning all about my new position!"

Being somewhat argumentative by nature, I thought this was a good opportunity to broach a subject I'd had on my mind for some time.

"Mr. Abe, the broiler chicken and egg businesses are boosting their productivity levels by shifting to large-scale poultry farming. But in the case of rice and beef, I think Japan's domestic products are going to be replaced by foreign products unless the government takes action. For example, it should liberalize the selling and buying of farmlands so that the scale of farming in this country can expand. And with livestock, large-scale cattle breeding farms should be approved and the large-scale beef cattle industry developed."

"This nation's rice lands are where the LDP has its biggest base of support," the new Minister of Agriculture replied. "If I were to say what you just suggested, I'd get beaten to a pulp! People like you think prices will decline if we liberalize imports of beef and oranges; but if we did that, LDP lawmakers would lose their support base—and lose their seats in the Diet. The one who wins the most votes in an election is the one who gets elected: that's the way parliamentary democracy works. Democratic government isn't rational the way running a company is. In order for politicians to implement policies, we have to make compromises."

Abe spoke with a gentle smile on his face. I found him to be candid, even-tempered, and charismatic. At the time, he was tagged to assume leadership of the Fukuda faction of the LDP.

Increasingly Close Rapport

About a month later, I received a phone call from Abe's secretary, Fumio Shimizu. The Minister of Agriculture's dinner engagement for that evening had suddenly canceled, and he was wondering if I would be free to join him. The offer pleased me greatly, and I accepted.

We were to meet at the same *ryotei* in Akasaka where we first met. I left my office somewhat nervous at the thought of dining alone with him.

After the usual exchange of pleasantries, Abe began to talk about himself:

"After I graduated from college, I became a reporter for the *Mainichi*. Then, when I got married, my father-in-law was a politician [former prime minister Nobusuke Kishi] so I entered politics. Politicians eat with the same kind of people night after night—there were regular dinners with members of the Fukuda faction, informal dinners with the leaders of other factions, dinners with members of the Diet Affairs Committee, dinners with supporters. Since becoming minister, I've also dined with leaders of Zen-noh [National Federation of Agricultural Cooperative Associations] and Zen-chu [Japanese Central Union of Agricultural Cooperatives] and with lawmakers in my faction. I've also spoken at fundraising events for newly elected lawmakers in my faction. So I end up having most of my evening meals with familiar people I interact with during the day. Obviously, policy is very important for us. However, what I personally want is to hear what young people working on the economic front lines have to say."

As dinner proceeded, he then turned to the following topic: "From as long back as I can remember, my father told me that my mother had died. But later, I learned that my parents had in fact divorced, and my mother had gone to Tokyo, remarried, and had another son. I now know that my younger half-brother works for the Industrial Bank of Japan, and I've made up my mind to go meet him. I'm quite looking forward to it."

I was stunned. By total coincidence, I had recently found myself at a similar moment in life.

My parents had divorced when I was young, and my mother left the family. I hadn't seen her since then. But about a month ago, the woman who had looked after me as a child approached me. "I've grown old and weak," she said. "Before I die, I want to bring you and your mother together."

My mother had remarried and had had two children. I agonized over what I should do, but in the end decided not to see her. It was soon after making this decision that I was having dinner with Abe. Here he was, telling me, someone he hardly knew, how much he was looking forward to meeting his half-brother, a smile on his face the whole time. He struck me as being a very big-hearted man.

Abe's half-brother, it turned out, was Masao Nishimura, whom I had occasion to meet when he became president of the Industrial Bank of Japan.

"I've learned that Shintaro Abe is my older brother," Nishimura said. "During the general elections campaign, on weekends I've traveled to Yamaguchi to support Shinzo Abe. Since I look a lot like Shintaro, when I go campaigning with Shinzo and ask people to give their support to my nephew, it wins him a lot of votes!"

I asked him whether, given his position as a bank president, he hadn't been criticized in the weekly magazines for traveling all the way to Yamaguchi to support the election campaign of a relative.

"If anyone questions me on it, I just say 'I'm campaigning for my nephew—what's wrong with that?' I never pay any attention to what's written in the weeklies."

Nishimura spoke with the same gentle smile on his face that his half-brother did. I got the feeling that they had fully acknowledged each other and grown close.

Nishimura was a man who thought about the grand scheme of things. When I sold my equity stake in Recruit to Daiei, he took pains to ensure that Recruit and Daiei's finances would remain separate.

While we were dining, Abe asked if I would introduce him to some young people. "It doesn't have to be a large number," he added. "I just want to hear what straight-talking people like you have to say."

His reference to me as "straight-talking" pleased me.

The first person I introduced him to was Minoru Mori of the Mori Building Company. We were to meet at a restaurant at nine P.M., but when Mori arrived he was already inebriated.

"Mr. Abe," Mori began, "the LDP's public investments all go to funding projects in outlying regions. Direct some of that money into Tokyo! Tokyo's infrastructure is outdated, so connecting expressways from other areas only makes the Metropolitan Expressway more congested. Investing in Tokyo should bring good returns. It's been more than thirty years since the plans to build MacArthur Road [a 40-meter-wide boulevard running from Shimbashi to Toranomon planned and approved by the U.S. Occupation Forces, which was to give momentum to Tokyo's redevelopment] were hatched. It still is not completed. Tokyo's road network lags behind the rest of the country."

A smile broke out on Abe's face. "Public spending in Tokyo will increase when the number of Diet seats occupied by LDP members representing Tokyo increases," Abe said. "Mr. Mori, please give your support to LDP lawmakers from Tokyo, so the party can increase its representation in the Diet."

At that moment, Abe had to step away for a phone call, and Mori soon fell fast asleep. When Abe returned, I tried to wake Mori, but he just grunted and could not be roused.

"Let him sleep," Abe laughed. "He can plead his case to me all he wants, but Tokyo's roads still won't get any better!"

From this time on, I would meet with Abe twice a month, normally after nine in the evening. Sometimes it was just the two of us, but mostly we were joined by a young business owner or political commentator.

Through Abe, I met a number of promising Diet members from the Fukuda faction of the LDP, among them Hiroshi Mitsuzuka, Mutsuki Kato, and Yoshiro Mori.

I gained a great deal from Abe's impressions and insights. His assessment of his party's factions: "In the LDP, factions are like parties within the party. Each faction directs its energies into seeking out new people to run in the next election, getting them elected, and expanding its own influence. There was a time when, in the face of criticism of this situation, the LDP made what looked from the outside like moves to disband the factions. But in the end, they remained strong. The energy of the factions seeking to expand their power is the lifeblood of the LDP."

On political financing: "The party with an unshakable platform is the Japanese Communist Party. Since its members pay party membership fees, the JCP is never pinched financially. The Komeito, a party funded by the Soka Gakkai, is also flush with cash. Some people say there's something strange about a religious group being a political patron, but overseas we see similar examples like Germany's Christian Democratic Union, and in Muslim countries politics and religion are inseparable. The LDP doesn't have a similar support base. Keidanren doesn't have the clout it once did, either. We have no choice but to rely on contributions from the corporate sector."

On the bureaucracy: "When you become a cabinet minister, you're allowed to take a secretary along with you. The ministry, though, provides its own secretary who is highly experienced and much better versed in the ministry's affairs. Things are constructed so that your secretary learns from the ministry secretary. The wall of bureaucracy is very thick."

On family legacies within the Diet: "I'm a second-generation lawmaker, and people say successions of this sort are strange. But the reason a retiring lawmaker tends to have a relative take his place is because it is the lawmakers' support organizations that conduct the election campaigns."

On the fortunes of one of his faction's most famous members: "Junichiro Koizumi doesn't listen to what he's told by Fukuda or by me. He tends to absent himself from faction gatherings and refuses to be part of a pack. He has his own definite opinions. He's an interesting person, one to watch in the future."

I was charmed by the way Abe would speak so candidly to a young guy like me. Every time I heard him talk, I would feel strongly that Japan would be a better place if Abe were to become prime minister.

The last time I met Abe was when he was secretary-general of the LDP. What he said on that occasion left a lasting impression:

"The secretary-general can wield his power most during elections. The LDP has party chapters in every prefecture, and they recommend the candidates the party should support. It is the secretary-general, however, who has the power to make the final decision. In the secretary-general's office there are veteran staff members who provide him with information on which faction leaders pushed certain candidates, details of the voter base in each district, and so on. The secretary-general also holds the party's purse strings, and it's up to him to decide how much money candidates are allocated. So at election times the secretary-general is able to expand his own faction. I didn't realize it when I was a cabinet member, but now that I've become the secretary-general I've come to see how powerful the position is."

Abe should have been slated to be next in line for prime minister after Noboru Takeshita. He wasn't chosen for the post, however, because his secretary, Fumio Shimizu, had received Recruit Cosmos shares. Abe became ill not long thereafter and, regrettably, passed away in May 1991.

My Connection with Noboru Takeshita

It was through Shintaro Abe that I met Noboru Takeshita. They had been elected at the same time and were old friends. I became a member of a group of Takeshita's core supporters.

At Abe's invitation, one evening in mid-December 1984, I attended a gathering of Takeshita's supporters at a *ryotei* in Tsukiji. Snow flurried around me as I arrived around nine. Takeshita was, at the time, serving as the Minister of Finance, and from the mood of those in attendance, I gathered meetings of this sort were held often.

Some people don't take kindly to politicians with strong ambitions, but unless politicians with aspirations form groups, the policies they espouse are impossible to achieve. I, for one, believe it's when people have the ambition to realize political policies for the future of Japan that the government moves forward and the nation picks up steam.

The people in attendance this December night were people who were bent on expanding the influence of Kakuei Tanaka's faction. For appearance sake, the gathering was called a study group, but news reports speculated it was actually a gathering of politicians who intended to break from the Tanaka camp to form a new faction. I went to the gathering feeling somewhat nervous, expecting to find a room filled with people burning with ambition.

The group of lawmakers sometimes referred to as Takeshita's "seven magistrates" were all present. I had met Takeshita and Ichiro Ozawa before, but it was my first time meeting the others.

Seiroku Kajiyama was speaking when I arrived. "During the Lockheed scandal, I was the first one to greet Tanaka after he was released from detention at Kosuge Prison," he said with a self-satisfied look on his face. "It got a lot of coverage on TV."

"When Tanaka was on trial, I went as an observer every day," Ozawa piped up. "I never missed a session."

As I listened, I thought to myself, "What's the point? Sitting in on every session isn't going to change the outcome." I guessed the important thing was Ozawa's demonstration of loyalty to Tanaka. I never dreamed I myself would know what it was like to be sitting in the defendant's seat one day.

The group of people were on friendly terms and the mood was very easy, without tension. They all sang Kakuei Tanaka's praises. Throughout the evening Keizo Obuchi stuck firmly to the role of listener. Takeshita, the man at center stage, spent the entire time discussing matters openly and without reserve.

Takeshita had gotten his start as a grassroots politician. He'd worked his way up to a position in the Diet after serving in the Shimane Prefectural Assembly, and perhaps owing to this background, he had an outstanding memory for people's names and backgrounds. Even more remarkable was his ability with numbers. Citing numbers adds persuasiveness to what one is saying, and when Takeshita spoke, his speech was peppered with an amazing cache of data.

From remarks he made that evening, I got the clear impression that Takeshita was waiting for the right opportunity to form a new faction.

Less than two months later, on February 7, 1985, a ceremony was held to inaugurate the study group Soseikai, the Creative Politics Society. More than forty members of the Tanaka faction took part.

According to Shozaburo Ishida, who defended Kakuei Tanaka during his Lockheed trial and who was my chief defense counsel, the creation of Soseikai was something that Tanaka found difficult to accept. He met Tanaka the morning after the ceremony, and watched as Tanaka poured himself a glass of brandy and gulped it down like water. But despite the throngs of people gathered outside Tanaka's estate in Mejiro, Tanaka did not lose his composure. Some three weeks later, on February 27, Tanaka collapsed in his home and was rushed to Tokyo Teishin Hospital.

At the time, the Tanaka faction boasted 120 lawmakers. Even if membership decreased by forty, it would still outnumber Soseikai. Moreover, it had very close ties to the Nakasone Cabinet—in fact, it was often referred to as the "Tanakasone Cabinet." Takeshita had close ties to the Abe faction, but even combined, their numbers were significantly smaller than the Tanaka and Nakasone factions.

How a person feels about someone depends on his experiences with that individual right up to a given point in time. Among Soseikai's participants were lawmakers whom Kakuei Tanaka trusted—especially Ichiro Ozawa, whom he trusted most of all. Tanaka must have found it incredulous that Ozawa had shifted his allegiance to Soseikai.

Two years later, on July 4, 1987, a ceremony was held at the Tokyo Prince Hotel to mark the inauguration of Keiseikai, a newly expanded incarnation of Soseikai. Members of the Tanaka faction abandoned their roost and flocked to Takeshita's new group. Such was the magnetism of Takeshita that this became the largest faction of the LDP.

Politicians gravitating to groups in this manner brought to mind how, in 1600, Japan's *daimyo* feudal lords ruminated over which side to join in the decisive Battle of Sekigahara: the Western Army supporting the Toyotomi line or the Eastern Army backing the Tokugawa camp. Seeing these current events unfold like a modern-day version of a samurai movie, I became all the more enthralled by the world of politics.

Deeper and Deeper into the Political Abyss

Recruit in those days, due to its launch of its business department system and its spinning off of various operations, was undergoing both diversification and expansion. Personally, though, this resulted in my being less involved in day-to-day operations of the company.

My focus shifted all the more toward external matters after I became chairman. Three or four nights a week, I would have dinner with people with no vested interest whatsoever in Recruit. In a quest to broaden my horizons and interact with people on a deeper level, I accepted invitations to join groups supporting the prime minister and new, upcoming leaders. I was impressed by the styles of this new generation, who seemed to exude a fresh individuality. These invitations would also be occasion for dining out.

Whereas politician-support events in outlying areas tend to use gatherings to make an appeal, politician-support gatherings in Tokyo were occasions for exchanging opinions on topics such as the macro-economy, economic policies, diplomatic matters, and so on. I learned a great deal by attending them.

One complaint heard frequently at cabinet minister–support gatherings was ministers' not having the right to manage their personnel. "Even if I want to appoint a woman to a position—say, as bureau chief or, at the very least, section chief—I get thwarted," a minister griped. "Only the secretariat, the person in charge of personnel management, has authority to make personnel decisions. Even becoming a minister doesn't give us that right."

To say the least, this gave me pause. If the president of a company didn't have the right to manage his personnel, neither his management staff nor his employees would ever follow his lead. By the same token, if a cabinet minister doesn't have the right to manage his own personnel, he can say what he thinks to his ministry's bureaucrats, but he's not likely to get the results he wants.

In Japan, the amount of legislation introduced by Diet members is extremely small. Our textbooks tell us that Japan is a nation with three separate branches of government: legislative, executive, and judicial. But in reality, the general outline of bills might be presented by Diet members, but it is the administrative officials who meet and draw up the actual bills. These bills are then debated by the various party committees—on education and culture, social welfare and labor, and so on—and finally, if approved by the party's Diet Affairs Committee, submitted to the Diet. Following this, enforcement regulations are drawn up by the related ministry or bureau. In cases where a bill's content works to the disadvantage of that authority, loopholes are often devised and inserted into the regulations' finer points.

At one gathering I attended, I suggested the introduction of daylight savings time. "It would offer benefits in terms of saving energy," I said. The reaction I received was this: "You're absolutely right. I wonder which agency would be in charge of that. . . ."

Even with budget matters, of utmost importance to the nation, it's the Lower House Budget Committee that makes the relevant decisions. By the time the budget and related bills are presented to the Diet in a House plenary session, the outcome is a given. Even media reports focus on the passage of budget proposals and related bills by the Lower House. Typically, after that, barring any exceptional circumstances, proposals and bills are agreed upon automatically within the Upper House.

Concerning question-and-answer exchanges within the Diet, each party selects in advance—no later than the day before the proceedings—which legislators will stand and pose their questions. The section chief of the relevant agency then finds out what is to be asked and, by the morning of the exchange in the Diet, he will have prepared responses and given a lecture to the minister who will be responding. The minister simply reads the prepared document. In the event that the questioning veers in a direction in which the minister has difficulty responding, a bureaucrat by his side hands him a memo. The future of Japan is thus, to a large extent, determined by the bureaucracy.

As for lawmakers, since these proceedings in the Diet are televised live on NHK, they, rather than dealing with the details of a bill, take up topics that will win them popularity with the viewers. As a result, they tend to rely on theatric displays and clever ploys designed to trip up their opponents.

One lawmaker told me he had been selected to pose questions at the next Q&A session. "Mr. Ezoe," he said, "what questions do you think would be received positively by the media these days?" Meanwhile lawmakers on the responding end, when faced with a question too difficult for them to answer directly, rack their brains to come up with an evasive response. This is how the Japanese Diet works.

The more closely I came to associate with politicians and bureaucrats, the more I learned about the country's decision-making system.

At the invitation of Hajime Tsuboi, chairman of Mitsui Fudosan, I joined the group supporting Yasuhiro Nakasone, which would regularly meet at Fukuden, a *ryotei* in Chiyoda ward. At the invitation of Binsuke Sugiura, who was chairman of the Long-Term Credit Bank of Japan, I also joined the group supporting Kiichi Miyazawa, which would convene at Sazanka-so, an elegant restaurant owned by the Hotel New Otani. Breakfast meetings would have two sessions—at seven A.M. and at eight A.M.—while dinner meetings would have sessions at six P.M. and eight P.M. Politicians were to attend all four sessions. A successful politician had to have a hearty appetite, I learned.

From my contact with politicians, I got to think that they were good listeners. They would listen intently to my opinions, despite my youth, and comment on them. I thought I was speaking my mind on state affairs, contributing to the nation, a perception that was very gratifying. In turn, I was induced to become even more involved in these groups supporting different politicians.

In hindsight I was foolish, but at the time I embraced the belief that by giving economic support to politicians, I was helping, even in a small way, to improve the government of our nation. It was only after the so-called scandal broke that I realized I had deluded myself—and that, as far as the public is concerned, no political donations are ever made without expecting something in return.

II

COLLUSION BETWEEN THE INVESTIGATORS AND THE MEDIA

On December 20, 1988, about a month after questioning of Recruit employees had begun, my own interrogation got under way.

The Public Prosecutors Office contacted Recruit with an offer to meet me at a venue of my choosing in order to avoid attention by the media. My legal counsel, Yoshiyuki Maki, a former prosecutor himself, escorted the investigating prosecutor to the Shiba Grand Plaza, a hotel belonging to the Recruit Group. I had decided to undergo questioning in the privacy of one of the guest rooms here. The charge against me was violation of the Securities and Exchange Law.

The prosecutor in charge of my case was Norio Munakata, the Special Investigation Department's no. 2 official. He was of average height and weight, wore thick glasses, and was dressed in a gray suit. He had the reputation of a public servant of high integrity, having made a name for himself as the prosecutor of the governor of Fukushima Prefecture on corruption charges. It was the first time in Japanese history that an incumbent governor had been convicted.

As he entered the room, Munakata looked around intently. His first words, before he took his seat, were: "I don't suppose you've hidden any microphones here, have you?" Then: "My name's Munakata. I'm the prosecutor in charge of your case, Mr. Ezoe. How are you feeling?"

"I'm doing OK."

"You're the key person in this case. The media reports are suggesting a variety of issues are involved here, but in all frankness, Mr. Ezoe, what issues in your opinion are going to be called into question here?" He spoke very politely.

Still, if there was anyone who wanted to know where the problematic issues existed, it was me. "I don't know," I said.

"What charges does your attorney worry will be brought against you? Could you please tell me that?"

"He says he doesn't know what charges will be pressed."

I was telling the truth. Kyuzaburo Hino, my defense counsel during this investigative phase, was at a loss to know where any problems existed. In his view, I wasn't likely to be arrested on anything related to the Securities and Exchange Law.

"Mr. Ezoe," Munakata continued, "have you ever met in private with former Prime Minister Nakasone?"

"Yes, I have."

"Really?" A smile broke out on Munakata's face. "I'll ask you more about that later. Why did you provide shares of Recruit Cosmos to so many people? Your close relationship with them surely contributed to your doing so, but you must have had something to gain from it also?"

"By the time you reach your fifties, separating business relationships and friendships becomes difficult. Sometimes you form friendships with people you may have met at a gathering of CEOs."

"I understand that, and that's fine as long as no favors are involved. Suppose you and I were close friends from school days; if you offered me shares of stock there would be no problem. But there must be people who weren't close to you like that."

"There was nothing in particular I sought to gain from the people who received the shares."

"Surely that's not true of the politicians? Everyone knows that no political contributions are made without expecting something in return."

"I did what I did out of a desire to support them. I didn't expect anything from them in return."

"The Recruit Cosmos shares you provided—those were your own shares, right?"

"No. Those shares were transferred from the companies of several close friends where I'd had them held for more than three years. I might also point out that proper sales agreements were concluded with everyone concerned, and all the necessary securities transaction taxes were paid."

It was at this point that this first day of interrogation drew to a close. As he was leaving the room, the prosecutor made one final comment: "Next time I'll bring a prepared written statement. All you'll need to do is sign it."

After Munakata left, I turned on the television. TV Tokyo was reporting on my case:

"Today, it appears that the Special Investigation Department of the Tokyo District Public Prosecutors Office began questioning former Recruit Chairman Hiromasa Ezoe. . . ."

The speed at which the news was reported was astonishing, and it convinced me my suspicions about the link between the special investigators and the media were true.

On December 29, the *Yomiuri* reported on Munakata's interrogation in detail. The following is an excerpt:

> The interrogation of Ezoe was conducted personally by prosecutor Norio Munakata, second in command in the Special Investigation Department, which is in charge of the case. It is highly unusual for the no. 2 prosecutor to take on such an interrogation, offering a glimpse into the extraordinary zeal with which the department is pursuing this case.
>
> Ezoe is the central figure in the scheme to liberally distribute the shares of stock in question. Many people involved in the investigation point out that unless Ezoe is made to reveal everything, there can be no elucidation of the Recruit scandal in its entirety. However, while on the surface he appears to be a soft-spoken man, Ezoe has an unyielding nature; his refusal, once he has made up his mind, to open up and speak about something was already demonstrated in his Diet testimony, where, even when pressed to reveal the names of the private individuals who had received the shares, he remained tightlipped.
>
> Prosecutor Munakata is known for the sharp skills he displayed in the corruption case against the governor of Fukushima Prefecture

and the case involving McDonnell Douglas and Grumman Aerospace. The Special Investigation Department is therefore playing its highest trump to undertake the formal questioning of the all-important key figure in this case.

On December 22, I was interrogated for a second time. Munakata arrived with a forty-to-fifty-page statement he had written relating to my alleged violation of the Securities and Exchange Law. It indicated I had bought back shares from five companies and then sold them.

Ichiro Yamanaka, senior managing director at Daiwa Securities, which was the managing underwriter of Recruit Cosmos's initial public offering, warned me. "When an initial public offering approaches," he said, "the company founder often starts wanting to give his shares to friends and acquaintances. Don't do it—it's against the law." As the IPO drew nearer, just as Yamanaka had insinuated, I started wanting shares in Recruit Cosmos to be held by the company's officers and managers, by my friends, and by prominent people outside the company. I felt that if managers on the payroll owned shares, they would have an extra incentive to boost the company's business performance and drive its share price higher. I thought that if prominent individuals became Recruit Cosmos shareholders, it would enhance the company's prestige. But, as Yamanaka had driven home to me, I knew it was illegal to transfer shares that I myself owned.

I decided to take care of the issue in this way: In December 1984, a year and ten months before the IPO, a capital increase was carried out at Recruit Cosmos at 2,500 yen per share. Of the companies that agreed to buy shares at that time, I approached five that were owned by close friends and got them to agree to sell their shareholdings to Recruit Cosmos's management staff and to prominent people outside the company, at a rate of 3,500 yen a share. Since the transactions consisted of share selling by these five companies directly to the share buyers, my only involvement was acting as the intermediary. Sales agreements were drawn up between the five companies and their respective share buyers, and securities transaction taxes were duly paid. No money passed through my bank account. I told all this to Prosecutor Munakata and said that since the statement he wrote was contrary to the facts, I could not sign it.

At that point his attitude changed completely. "It's highly regrettable you won't sign," he said in a firm tone of voice, "after we've gone and prepared the statement for you. We also went out of our way to come here, a Recruit-owned facility, as we'd felt badly that if you were forced to come to the Public Prosecutors Office you'd be surrounded by the media. But if that's your attitude, we'll just have to have you come to our office—if that's what you prefer."

Going to the Public Prosecutors Office and being mobbed by the press was actually the last thing I wanted to do. But apparently Munakata was bluffing. "I'll come again," he said, and took his leave.

Meeting My Daughter

Late that evening, I left Hanzomon Hospital through a back entrance and went to the Keio Plaza Hotel in Shinjuku to meet my elder daughter. She was wearing a white sweater and jeans and looked so well. Seeing her after so long made me very happy.

We went to the guestroom I'd reserved, and after being cooped up in the hospital, I found the view was dazzling. I spent a long time just gazing out the window.

My daughter ordered some sandwiches, then took drinks out of the refrigerator—Coke, orange juice, tea drinks—and lined them up on the table.

"Father, which would you like?"

"The oolong tea, I guess."

As she began pouring the tea into a glass, she began, "Don't let any of this get to you, Father. I know you didn't do anything wrong."

"Everyone must be casting cold glances at you these days. Please forgive me."

"Don't worry about me. I guarantee you I'll pass my exams." She was in the midst of studying for her college entrance examinations.

"Just be sure not to overdo it," I said. "Take good care of yourself."

"I'm not overdoing it. Say, Father, why don't we both stay here for the night?"

"I'm afraid I can't."

Though neither of us said anything, we were both thinking we would probably not see each other again for a while. My daughter made no mention whatsoever of the case against me. We passed the time reminiscing about happy times from her childhood, our conversation proceeding in fits and starts.

I took heart from her thoughtfulness. I left the hotel around one A.M. and returned to the hospital.

Questioning Based on Media Reports

The following day I was questioned for a third time.

"Today I'll ask you in detail about your violation of the Securities and Exchange Law," Munakata began. "The shares you sold were shares you'd bought back, weren't they?"

"No. As I told you the last time, sales agreements were exchanged between all parties concerned."

Munakata leaned forward and switched to a lower tone of voice: "I'm sure you know that in transactions involving real estate, a sale can be registered without recording an interim owner—in order to save on taxes. That's what we have here, isn't it?"

"No. Each of the companies selling their shares concluded a sales agreement with the buyer, revenue stamps were affixed to the documents, and securities transaction taxes were paid."

"How was the selling price determined? It seems too low to me."

"If a transfer price is set at a level the tax authorities consider unfairly low, they impose a tax on the buyer. To avoid causing any such inconvenience to buyers, Seiichi Tateoka, Recruit Cosmos's managing director in charge of financial matters, calculated what would be a fair price based on tax laws, using the comparable peer company pricing formula."

Munakata stared straight at me. "The newspapers are reporting this as a backflow of shares from the five companies. That's the way they're describing it, and I also think you just bought back the shares from the five companies and then passed them on."

"I asked the five companies owned by my friends to sell their shares to the buyers. All I did was act as a go-between; I didn't buy or sell anything.

The sales agreements were all concluded between the parties concerned."

Our exchange went around and around in circles like this, turning Munakata's mood sour.

"I can't seem to get you to understand, can I? Let's call it quits early today."

"I feel fine. Please, let's continue."

"In my twenty years as a prosecutor, that's the first time anyone ever said *that* to me!" He smiled wryly and left.

As my interrogation continued, Munakata pressed me again and again about the share transfers. I imagined he had never traded in stock himself. Our conversations kept going nowhere on two topics: whether or not I bought back the shares from the five companies, and the alleged certainty that the shares would go up in price.

"In the press they're saying anyone who acquired the shares before Recruit Cosmos went public was guaranteed to see their value appreciate and make a killing."

"Stocks can go up, or they can go down. That's what the market's all about."

"So, are you trying to tell me you wanted these people to have the shares thinking their price would go down?"

"Of course not. Recruit Cosmos bought properties slated for condominium construction when land prices were down, after the second oil crisis calmed, and its business was destined to improve in the years ahead. For these reasons, I thought its share price would rise as well."

"So you did want to see these people buying the shares reap profits?"

"Yes, I did. But I wasn't looking for any favors from them in return."

"They were able to make a profit by selling immediately, weren't they?"

"I didn't have them acquire the shares with instructions to sell them right away. I myself have at times been asked by friends, owners of seven or eight companies, to hold shares in their companies. I bought them before the companies went public, and I *still* have them today."

"You're a wealthy man—you didn't have to sell them. Some of the people who bought shares by borrowing money from First Finance sold them off immediately."

Share prices fluctuate. Depending on how the market moves, the start-ing price on the first day of a stock's trading can exceed the pre-opening purchase price by a wide margin, or in some cases it can undershoot the price. To illustrate, on October 5, 2007, the *Nikkei Financial Daily* car-ried an article reporting that all IPOs in September "failed," in the sense that all newly registered issues opened below their public offering price. At the time of Recruit Cosmos's OTC registration, however, nearly all issues opened above their pre-flotation price.

Also, although the five companies releasing their shares as well as those who took possession of them did conclude sales agreements—as I said—in many of these cases, the funds for purchase were borrowed from First Finance, a Recruit Group company. First Finance charged 7 percent inter-est—one percent higher than the banks—and this created a bad impression.

"First Finance is practically your personal wallet," Munakata said. "That's what makes this case all about you—these transactions were yours."

First Finance was capitalized at 50 billion yen—more than Recruit. Ini-tially Hiroshi Kobayashi was the company's president, but in the run-up to its IPO he stepped down and became vice president. Mamoru Shirakuma, of Toyo Trust & Banking, was brought in to serve in the top position.

"First Finance isn't my personal wallet," I said firmly. "Among the doc-uments you seized, there should be a lot of material First Finance submitted to the Japan Securities Dealers Association ahead of its IPO."

"Oh? Well, we're short of hands and haven't been able to look through everything."

Munakata seemed to have had the wind taken out of his sails. His whole argument about First Finance being under my control was gone. From that point the interrogation started going around in circles again, and Munakata began to get annoyed.

"Please be a bit more straightforward in answering my questions," he snipped.

"I *am* being straightforward," I replied.

"You don't seem to feel very well today," he said with a sigh. "Let's call it a day."

"Couldn't we just continue?"

"I'll come again tomorrow."

At that, he left with a look of disgust on his face.

Recruit Cosmos's Share Price

Share prices are impacted by media reports and by popular trends. I was well aware that if coverage critical of Recruit Cosmos continued, shareholders would sell off their holdings; but if the reporting quieted down and business performance improved, the share price would also rise.

I attempted to determine when the recipients of the Recruit Cosmos shares sold, but in the years since Recruit disbanded First Finance in 1992, all documentation was discarded.

Among those who purchased stock, Ei Shikiba, who had been head of sales operations at NTT, and whom I had known for many years, said he would always hold on to the shares. But after his voluntary questioning began, he sold the shares off after notifying the prosecutors of his intent. His purchase price had been 3,500 yen per share, but he sold them for less than 2,500 yen, thereby incurring a loss of more than ten million yen.

Further, believing that what he had done did not constitute a crime, Shikiba requested a separate trial. He was found guilty, however, on the contention that had he sold the shares immediately, he would have made a profit. Most unjustly, the court imposed a fine of 11.35 million yen and handed down a sentence of one year and six months in prison, with a three-year suspension.

After his sentence, NTT demanded that Shikiba return his retirement stipend, which left him in dire straits. Shikiba went back to work to earn money to return the stipend, but he fell ill and passed away not long afterward.

I felt truly sorry for the trouble I caused not only Shikiba himself but also his bereaved family.

After my interrogation began, coverage by the media heated up even more. Nearly every day, TV viewers were treated to footage of Hanzomon Hospital. First the news reports would present comments by Dr. Miura, an authority on digestive surgery, concerning the Emperor's ailing health. Then they would turn to news on the Recruit affair.

At the time, Recruit had introduced the profit center system. To strengthen a sense of unity, Takeshi Osawa had established and trained the company's women marathon team. In December, the team participated in the National Corporate Women Marathon Relay Race, which was broadcast on TV. The team members included Yuko Arimori, who would win the bronze medal at the Atlanta Olympics in 1992 and Naoko Takahashi, the gold medalist of the Barcelona Olympics in 1996. Since they ran with their number emblazoned beneath the company name of Recruit, when they ran past other contestants, the TV camera focused on other runners to avoid showing the Recruit name. I could imagine the frustration—and even the insult—that Recruit employees watching the marathon must feel, and I felt ashamed things had come to this.

In the year-end ranking of the biggest news stories of 1988, the Emperor's ill health and the Recruit scandal were placed on equal footing.

Reserving a Burial Plot

On January 1, 1989, the headline on the front page of the morning *Asahi* read: "Compulsory Investigations to Begin This Month: Charges to Include Violation of Securities and Exchange Law." The sub-headline read: "Probe to Get to Heart of Recruit Scandal."

The gist of the article was that with the start of a new calendar year, the investigation would finally be kicking into gear. More than five hundred people had been interrogated by the Tokyo District Public Prosecutors Office, allowing authorities to paint a fairly clear picture of what had occurred. The Special Investigation Department would begin compulsory investigations—as well as making arrests—within the month. The article made no mention, however, of exactly what the charges would be.

On January 2, a holiday on which there would be no interrogation, I went to Shinshoji Temple in Narita to make customary prayers at the start of the new year. It was a brilliant day, and as we drove along, the forests stretching far off into the distance stirred me with their beauty. The area all around Shinshoji was terribly congested, so about two kilometers before the temple I asked the driver to pull off into the parking lot of a restaurant, and from here I clasped my hands and paid my respects to the deities. As it was near lunchtime, I went into the restaurant and, from the menu, ordered a Salisbury steak. It was the first time in a long while that I had something other than hospital fare, and the savory meat sizzling on the cast iron serving plate tasted very special.

On January 4, I phoned Recruit and spoke with the office of public relations. The staff said no articles had appeared in other newspapers suggesting compulsory investigations would get under way within the month. The article in the *Asahi* was, in industry terms, *maeuchi*—a disclosure, written anonymously, based on a leak from an authority.

On the night of January 6, I met Naotaka Ida and two of Recruit's senior managing directors—Kunio Okuzumi and Eiko Kono—at a condominium apartment near Hanzomon Hospital that was owned by Recruit Cosmos. Ida, as the president of Recruit, was being summoned by the Public Prosecutors Office day in and day out, even on Saturdays and Sundays, and as the interrogations continued until as late as one A.M., he was unable to return to his residence in Fujisawa and ended up taking up lodging in a hotel. Moreover, since he was going into the office at about nine every morning, he was getting only about four hours of sleep a night. The fatigue seemed to be taking a toll.

Kono had also received calls from the Public Prosecutors Office requesting she come in and submit to questioning. "I keep turning them down," she said, "because if I went every time they asked, I wouldn't get any work done." She went on to say that Recruit's sales were trending in line with the targets set at the start of the term, so there was no need to worry about the company's business performance. "Many clients offer us words of encouragement."

Okuzumi was equally reassuring. "Both Recruit and Recruit Cosmos are in position to record growth in sales and profits when accounts close in March. Talks were held with our main banks, and they've assured us they'll continue extending us loans as they have until now."

Hearing that earnings were growing in spite of the daily criticism of Recruit in the news, I was deeply moved to hear that employees were all working together and exercising their capabilities to the fullest.

"Thank you all," I said, bowing to them. "I'm sorry to be causing you so much trouble."

The meeting was short, only about thirty minutes, and I thought it was likely to be our last discussion like this for some time. I suspected I would be arrested before very long.

Those days I often slipped into a foggy mental state, feeling the urge to do away with myself. I thought that if I were to die, all the commotion would settle down, so I began saving up the sleeping pills, Benzalin, the hospital issued me each day. One day when Dr. Kobayakawa was making his rounds, I casually asked what the lethal dosage of Benzalin would be.

"It depends on the individual, but I would guess around fifty pills," he said. "But with recent improvements, sleeping pills are now designed to make the stomach reject anything more than twenty or thirty pills, after which the person will involuntarily disgorge the whole lot. A lot of people still try to kill themselves using sleeping pills, but most of them don't succeed."

So that option was foreclosed.

Still thinking of ending it all by one means or another, I considered a gravesite.

Historically, the Ezoe family was part of the Soto sect of Zen Buddhism, headquartered at Eiheiji Temple in Fukui Prefecture. There's a branch of that temple, called Chokokuji, in the Nishi-Azabu area of Tokyo. I went and spoke with the head priest about purchasing a gravesite, taking my cousin, Chikako Haraguchi, along with me.

He told me that there was a large plot owned by a family since the 1920s, but for many years the temple had had no contact with the owner. A plan was now afoot to divide the plot into twelve or perhaps sixteen smaller plots and sell them off. I immediately indicated that if the plan went through, I wanted to buy a plot. "Even the smallest of the lot will do," I said.

During those days, just being alive was agony. My state of mind was such that, in a fit of despair, I thought of hurling myself off the roof of the hospital. I went up to the roof any number of times and peered down, but at a height of only five stories, I worried the fall wouldn't kill me. If I were to survive, it would not only be humiliating, but also the mental anguish would continue. Further, if I committed suicide, it would be a stain on Recruit. And my children would have to carry the burden for the rest of their lives.

I resolved to endure whatever pain might come my way, and to live and face judgment.

I apparently wrote a will too, but Kei Sakuma, my secretary, said that after he'd discussed the matter with Hitoshi Kashiwaki, the will had been discarded. "It just didn't seem like a will you would write," Sakuma said. I have no recollection of having written such a will.

"Proof of the Devil"

"You must have thought NTT was a purely private company, didn't you? JR [Japan Railways] and JT [Japan Tobacco] may be purely private, but NTT employees are quasi-public servants. Recruit does business with NTT—you're business partners. You should know you can't go giving Recruit Cosmos shares to someone from NTT."

This was Prosecutor Munakata in the course of my interrogation one day. And he was right: I *had* thought NTT was a private company, given that in the news the company was reportedly "privatized."

"When you provided shares to Kozo Murata, what you really had in mind was a transfer to Shinto, wasn't it?"

"Yes."

"What did you and Mr. Murata talk about?"

"I asked him about buying the shares after discussing the matter with Mr. Shinto."

"That's what I thought. Let's write that up now."

Munakata proceeded to prepare a statement stipulating that by transferring the Recruit Cosmos shares to Kozo Murata, I really had had in mind they were for Shinto, and he put it in front of me to sign. When I did so, Munakata looked quite satisfied.

"OK. This should do it!" he beamed, and then continued, "I'll have the prosecutor in charge look into the details later. One more thing: among those who received shares, there's one person I'm unclear about as to who approached him about the deal. Were you the one who broached the subject to Labor Vice Minister Takashi Kato?"

"I had nothing to do with it. I only learned about it in the newspapers. It was a complete surprise to me."

"The Education Vice Minister Kunio Takaishi received 10,000 shares while Mr. Kato received only 3,000. Why the difference?"

"I have no idea. I didn't know anything about Mr. Kato's receiving shares."

"It didn't have to be you personally. Mr. Kato testified before the Diet that he was approached by former managing director Masao Tatsumi, but Mr. Tatsumi says it wasn't he. I want to know who it really was."

"I don't know. I'd like to know myself."

"You know, Mr. Ezoe, it's about time you start giving us some earnest answers in a manner befitting your position as the founder of Recruit."

By this time, Munakata had adopted a harsh tone of voice, and the more I kept saying I didn't know anything about what he was asking me, the more awkward and unpleasant the air between us became.

In the end, I signed a statement drawn up by Munakata to the following effect: "I had nothing whatsoever to do with the transfer of shares to Mr. Kato. I wasn't involved in all the share transfers: for example, not with lawmakers Katsuya Ikeda or Keishu Tanaka, or the secretary to the mayor of Urawa City, or the Yokohama City Council. Mr. Kato fits into this category."

Munakata moved on: "Katsuya Ikeda is another person we don't know where he got his shares from. You say it wasn't you?"

"No. I have no acquaintance at all with Mr. Ikeda."

"It didn't have to be you yourself who provided him with the shares. Why don't you tell us who it was?"

"I don't know who it was."

"Isn't there anyone you could place between you and the recipient? That would lighten your crime, you know, and I promise we won't indict whomever you name. If it wasn't you who provided the shares, you'll have to prove that. You're the man in charge, so ultimately you're responsible, you know."

"As I said, I don't know who it was. I know I'm not the person who did it. And naturally, since I had nothing to do with it, I can't offer you any proof that I didn't do it."

Silence prevailed for a few moments. Then Munakata continued, this time as if he were a magician revealing the secret behind a trick: "Of course, you can't prove you had nothing to do with it," he said. "*Probatio diabolica*—proof of the devil. It's impossible to prove the devil doesn't exist. You've got no evidence to prove you didn't provide those shares— even if there's no evidence to prove you did. But still, the fact remains, you're offering no proof you didn't do it."

Questions about "My Mistresses"

On January 31, Munakata announced that from this point on my interrogations would be conducted by another prosecutor. The location was also to be changed, to the Public Prosecutors Office in Toshima ward.

The new prosecutor, Seisui Kamigaki, was an imposing man with a broad chest and deep voice. He looked like a prosecutor straight out of a Hollywood movie, with a commanding presence that would intimidate anyone who stood in his path.

"My name's Kamigaki," he said by way of introduction. "Mr. Ezoe, I've always thought you to be a fine upstanding man. I hope you won't destroy the image I have of you." A pause. "The reason I became a prosecutor is because I have a strong sense of justice. Gradually, though, I've come to think it's a job that doesn't reap its due rewards. Being a prosecutor is a very busy job, but no matter how much you put in, what you receive is always the same since you're a public servant. The higher up you go, the more the jobs are limited to graduates of the University of Tokyo. Me, I graduated from a regional college. Through the years I've handled a slew of tax evasion cases, so I was thinking I should quit this job and become a lawyer handling cases of tax evasion."

"But I've read that the chief public prosecutor is, like you, a graduate of Okayama University," I responded.

"He's a special case. Besides, now that I've been appointed to take charge of interrogating the ringleader in this big criminal case, I'm glad I didn't quit my job. If I can uncover the great evil that's been done here, it'll make my day as a prosecutor. I actually asked Mr. Munakata to put me in charge of your case. Once it came out that politicians were implicated, the

Special Investigation Department started focusing on the case and began its informal investigation."

"What kind of investigation?"

"Checking the newspapers, weekly magazines, TV—things like that. When you gave your testimony before the Diet, the whole department was watching it on TV, wondering whether you could be arrested."

So that was how it worked: the media operate like investigators and the special investigators build the case. And when political corruption was involved, the department takes a special interest.

My new prosecutor began by questioning me about my relationships with women based on what the weekly magazines were reporting—which was a hodgepodge of truths and lies. He had read them meticulously, including the women's magazines.

"The bar in the basement of the Recruit Building—the woman who runs it is a former stewardess with Japan Air Lines. Quite beautiful, they say."

"Yes, she used to be a stewardess. And she is said to be a beautiful woman."

"From what I've read, you often went there after work and drank together."

"I did occasionally go there for a drink after work, to cool down before going home."

"The weeklies say she's your mistress. You must have escorted her home at times. Where does she live?"

"I have sometimes seen her home. She lives in Minato-ku, in Kamiya-cho."

"Hmm. That would be on your way home, wouldn't it? Did you ever stop off at her place?"

"No. Never."

"Never?"

"Never."

Kamigaki was beginning to irritate me.

He apparently sensed this. "OK, then. As far as she's concerned, I'll believe you. So, tell me about this woman who's living in your condo in Minami-Aoyama. She's an employee of Recruit Cosmos, isn't she? What's your relationship with her?"

"There's nothing between us."

"According to what I've been able to find out, she's 34 and still single, isn't she?"

"I don't know how old she is. But yes, she's single."

"What sort of relationship do you have with her?"

"As I said, there's nothing between us."

"Why then, out of all the company's employees, are you allowing her to stay in your condominium?"

"A company the Recruit Group did business with was on the verge of going bankrupt, so I bought a condo the company owned. She just happened to end up renting it from me."

"The weeklies say she's your mistress, too."

"They're wrong."

"*Focus* magazine had a photo of you sailing in Okinawa with your friends, including a woman. What's your relationship with her?"

"There's nothing between us."

"The women's magazines also wrote that your secretaries are your mistresses."

"Again, they're wrong. And besides, what's any of this got to do with my case? Why do you keep harping on such things?"

"When we investigate a crime, we always start by checking into background. And like they say, *Cherchez la femme*—'Behind every crime there's always a woman.'"

By this point I was feeling very annoyed. After the day's interrogation was over, I told my lawyer about this.

"They always start their investigations this way," he said matter-of-factly. "Especially in cases involving public servants or company heads. The mere mention of a sexual relationship is enough to make some men go limp."

I explained how, when I was at university, a lecturer on criminal psychology indicated that ninety-nine out of a hundred crimes committed by juveniles were attributable to the environment in which the child grew up. So if the investigators were interested in asking me about my upbringing—rather than about my alleged affairs with women—I could see their point. My lawyer chuckled, "In a bribery case involving a man in his fifties, they're not going to ask you about your childhood!"

At Recruit, no fuss was ever raised over relationships between male and female employees. For the prosecutors to start their investigation by asking about such things was, to me, a notion well behind the times.

The Prosecutor Gets His Hackles Up

"Last time, I asked you about your relationships with women. Perhaps you were a bit offended."

At the start of his next day of interrogation, Kamigaki took a completely different, more soft-spoken tack, as he asked about the motives behind my share transfers. Once again, I denied the insinuations he made, and when he started harping repeatedly on the same point, I just clammed up. When my silence grew longer, he began to look more and more annoyed. After a while, he got fed up and raised his voice. "If you aren't going to say anything, then why did you come here?"

"I came because you summoned me."

With that, Kamigaki became all the more annoyed. He appeared to be quite irritated and puffed incessantly on his cigarette. He offered me one.

"I don't smoke," I said, and resumed my silence.

After a few moments, he took a different approach, seemingly unable to bear the silence.

"Are you remaining silent under instructions from your attorney?"

"No."

"If you refuse to say anything, then why did you come?" he asked again.

I knew that if I repeated that I'd come because he'd summoned me, he would get all the more rankled. So I just kept silent. Then, without warning, he suddenly banged on the table.

"I'll show you what a special investigation is all about!" he shouted. "You're the one who's dragging this out."

Even after this outburst, I continued to deny his allegations or simply remain silent.

Next, he put a prepared statement in front of me stating that I was aware the share transfers constituted bribes. "Here's a pen. Sign it!" he barked.

When I refused, his face turned fearsome, and he bellowed: "You think you can get away with an attitude like that toward a prosecutor? You'd better stop trying to make me look like a fool, you self-centered, arrogant idiot!"

The barrage of words continued. "You're really riling me, you know. Until now I had positive feelings toward you—but that's changed now, to contempt. Face up to what you've done, admit it. Sign the statement!"

I wanted to say I'd done nothing criminal. Instead I kept silent. The more Kamigaki raised his voice, the more composed I became.

Finally, he thrust a piece of paper in front of me that listed the various questions he had asked, each accompanied by the same remark: that I had remained silent and refused to answer. I refused to sign it. The prosecutor became more agitated, his anger reaching a peak.

"You've really riled me now! Refusal to sign a statement will work strongly against you in court, you know. If that's the way you want to play. I'll just put down that I wrote the statement, read it to you, and asked you to sign, but that you refused. Then, I'll send it right off to the court. That's all for today. Get out of here!"

I bowed my head and left the room.

The Stalemate Deepens

February 3, two days after this prickly exchange, no sooner had Prosecutor Kamigaki entered the interrogation room than his anger surfaced loud and clear.

"Headquarters is not pleased. All that statement you signed the other day said was that you had Shinto in mind when you provided the shares to Murata; it didn't say what your aim was. Today we'll take a statement that says that you offered the shares to get favors in return."

"That's not true," I said, repeating myself a number of times. When Kamigaki continued to harp on the point, I became silent. This seemed to irritate him beyond control.

"As a prosecutor, I have the authority to put you under arrest, you know. You stick to this attitude of yours and I'll throw you in jail right this minute!" He raised his voice so loud, the windows in the interrogation room seemed to rattle.

"Go ahead and arrest me!" I felt like saying. At this stage, I had come to feel that if I was going to be arrested at some point, I wanted them to do it sooner rather than later. But again, I remained silent.

"What do you think you gain by keeping silent?" he finally burst out.

Not long after my interrogations began, Sohei Nakayama, special advisor to the Industrial Bank of Japan, offered me his advice: "When I was arrested in connection with the shipbuilding scandal, I remained silent from start to finish—and was acquitted. As a result, I earned a reputation from those around me as being a man who could be trusted. There are times when you can prove your manliness by keeping your mouth shut. You'd do well to keep quiet, too."

The so-called shipbuilding scandal of 1954 was one of the biggest bribery cases in postwar Japan, leading to the arrest of seventy-one people. Of the major figures indicted, seven were found innocent and fourteen were found guilty but given suspended sentences. When the special investigation into the case spread to a growing list of shipbuilders and maritime trade companies—Yamashita Kisen, Hitachi Zosen, Iino Kaiun, and Shin Nippon Kisen among them—Justice Minister Takeru Inukai wielded his authority and halted the investigation. Although the case ultimately brought down the cabinet of Shigeru Yoshida, some have said the investigators asked Inukai to intervene because they didn't believe that further probing would serve any purpose.

I told Kamigaki about the advice I received, but I made no mention of Nakayama's name. "I agree with this advice," I said, "and that's why I'm maintaining my silence."

The prosecutor's fury quickly eased. "So that's your reason? This wasn't your attorney's advice? I thought you wouldn't sign the statement because your attorney told you not to," he said, then paused for a moment. "It's a bit early, but let's break for lunch. Go out and treat yourself to something special."

With that, Kamigaki leaned back in his chair and, in his usual fashion, struck a match and puffed on his cigarette.

After lunch, the prosecutor's first words picked up on the last line of questioning.

"You said you were advised not to say anything by someone you respect, not by your attorney. When I heard your reason for refusing to say anything, it actually made me happy. Just who was this person who gave you this advice?"

"I can't tell you that."

"Close to seventy people were arrested in the shipbuilding scandal, but only six or seven are still alive. Is this person living in Fujisawa? Or perhaps this person is living in Zushi?"

Nakayama lived in Zushi, but I had absolutely no intention of revealing he was the one who gave me the advice.

"I can't say. It would not be an honorable thing to do."

"You know, Mr. Ezoe, I find you an interesting person. Hearing what you just said, I see you're a fine person and not calculating in the way I'd thought. I agree," he continued slowly in a hushed voice, as if he were about to reveal a secret, "there are times when it's honorable not to speak. That was the purported motivation behind Akira Kato of the Seibi Group. He maintained his honor the entire time he was in detention. He may have kept his honor, but he ended up staying in detention two long years."

"I'm not going to say anything—even if it means being detained for a long time."

"That's easy to say, but detention centers are terrible places, you know—they're places where it's not easy to stay healthy. Prolonged detention is a real hardship, worse than being in prison."

I said nothing. Kamigaki glanced up at the clock.

"OK, that's enough for today," he said, motioning for me to leave the room.

I bowed slightly and took my leave.

The following day, all the morning papers reported I was denying the "alleged facts" against me.

"Shouldn't they be saying 'allegations' against me?" I complained to my attorney.

"'Alleged facts' is their way of saying that what is alleged differs from proven facts," my attorney replied.

This explanation did not sit well with me, and from this point on in the interrogation, the relationship between Prosecutor Kamigaki and me grew increasingly hostile.

He again prepared a statement listing the questions he asked and my answers to them. When he angrily ordered me to sign it, I again refused.

"OK, if that's the way you want it, I'll just have to send the statement to the court with a note stating that the accused refused to sign. You know, though, sending statements to the court like this one after another isn't going to help you when you come up for trial."

Here was this prosecutor of imposing physique blustering away at the top of his lungs to me, thin and weak-stomached, sitting with no response for him. We were like a wolf with gaze fixed on his prey and a frightened lamb looking for a means of escape.

My Arrest

On February 13, 1989, after the morning interrogation was over, I went to have a bowl of ramen for lunch. When I returned, Kamigaki asked me if I had anything scheduled for later in the day. I said I didn't.

The following day I was scheduled to appear before a special investigative committee of the Kawasaki City Council. But from the way the prosecutor was acting, hurried in a way I had never seen before, I sensed that my arrest was imminent. He left the room repeatedly, and I imagined he was keeping in close contact with the home office.

The prosecutors likely decided it would be best to arrest me today, before I had a chance to answer questions before the special committee. They must have concluded if I faced questioning by the committee about allegations reported in the press and testified in denial, it might affect the drift of the media's reports. If I was not scheduled to appear before the committee, I think my arrest may have come later.

A little after three in the afternoon, Kamigaki announced that I was being arrested on this the fifty-fifth day since the start of my interrogation. Although my questioning had concerned only alleged violations of the Securities and Exchange Law and my connections with Shinto, the charges I was arrested on were bribery involving two other people at NTT: Hisahiko

Hasegawa and Ei Shikiba. I was relieved the charges were unrelated to Shinto.

Over the duration of my interrogation, the continual threats that I would be arrested made me increasingly frightened, to the point I was not able to enjoy a good night's sleep for weeks. Once I was arrested, I suddenly felt released from this fear and anxiety and, if anything, actually felt a sense of relief.

In the car on the way to the Tokyo Detention Center, Kamigaki and I were seated beside each other.

"Now that I've been arrested, I feel quite relieved," I said.

"I thought you would. I could tell you wanted to be arrested as quickly as possible. It's something everyone who submits to voluntary questioning thinks: if you're going to arrest me, let's get it over with quickly. I would have arrested you earlier if you admitted to the charges. It took this long because you kept denying them."

"After asking me only about Mr. Shinto, why am I being arrested in connection with Mr. Hasegawa and Mr. Shikiba?"

"Murata, Shinto's secretary, said he did it entirely at his own discretion. We couldn't make any connection between the two of them."

I was glad to hear that.

Traffic was very heavy. Kamigaki, looking nervously at his watch, instructed the driver to take a different route, which turned out to be no less congested. "I told the media we'd arrive at 4:30. We wouldn't want to keep them waiting, would we?"

As we approached the detention center, Kamigaki turned toward me. "I'm putting handcuffs on you now. There will be hordes of photographers lined up as we go in. I suggest you put your hands down between your legs so they can't shoot you handcuffed. You're free to assume any posture you want, but with someone in your position I'd suggest you look straight ahead and keep your head held high."

When the car came within about ten meters of the entrance, the driver slowed to walking speed. The cameras were waiting ahead.

"Look up," Kamigaki suddenly said. "There're helicopters with photographers ready to catch you being arrested."

Indeed, there were several helicopters circling. Special investigators were certainly adept at making full use of the media.

As we reached the entrance, the car came to a halt. The photographers all leaped toward the vehicle, some even jumping on the hood to get a good shot. The flashes from their cameras were blinding, but I just kept looking straight ahead, not even allowing myself to blink. After several moments, the "photo session" was finished and the car proceeded into the building.

I was furious.

"You're just trying to make an example out of me," I said. "I'm nothing more than a suspect. This is a violation of my human rights!"

After I was released on bail, I saw a copy of the *Asahi* from the morning after my arrest. "Former Recruit Chairman Ezoe Arrested" the headline blared, followed by the subheading "Share Provision Affirmed as Act of Bribery." The article, which contended that the Takeshita administration would now be in an even more difficult position, was accompanied by a photo of me entering the Tokyo Detention Center, sitting in the car next to Kamigaki. The photo was dated February 13, at 5:47 P.M., a time of day barely light enough to allow photography from a helicopter.

A similar photo had also graced the cover of that week's *AERA* magazine. Under a title proclaiming "The Crimes of Recruit's Ezoe," the lead article enumerated the multitude of allegations made against me.

Footage of my arrest, I later learned, was broadcast repeatedly by all the TV stations, and both the newspapers and TV changed their description of me from "former Recruit chairman Hiromasa Ezoe" to simply "Ezoe." The reports were calculated to give the impression I had already been found guilty.

Interrogations at the Detention Center

The Tokyo Detention Center is located on a fairly large plot of land in Kosuge in western Katsushika, between the Arakawa and Ayase rivers. Although it has since been entirely rebuilt on a rather magnificent scale, in 1989 it was a collection of rows of low, interconnected buildings of steel-reinforced concrete construction, surrounded by a high wall. Besides holding criminal suspects undergoing investigation and defendants on trial, the center functions as a facility for convicted felons.

Most people, upon hearing that someone is in Kosuge, assume the person is serving time in prison.

"Dancing the Can-can"

When I entered the building, there was a checkpoint where my personal effects—wallet, keys, wristwatch, etc.—were taken "for safekeeping."

Next I was stripped naked and made to walk under the gaze of almost a dozen guards. Then I was made to get down on all fours, and the next thing I knew a glass rod was shoved up my rear end. The perpetrator proceeded to move the rod in and out and around, causing me great pain, discomfort, and humiliation—with the phalanx of guards watching this spectacle. My humanity had been violated.

"It's called 'dancing the can-can,'" my lawyer told me later. "It's a ritual they make you go through when you enter a detention center. I've had clients go to Kosuge all fired up, determined to prove their mettle, but they're forced to dance the can-can and they're shell-shocked. When I see them after that happens, they're so depressed they're like a completely different person. The authorities claim they're simply examining inmates for hemorrhoids, but it's inhumane. The bar association is making an issue of it these days."

I had had hemorrhoid problems for years. There was no medication to cure the problem, and the only option was an operation, but my case, my physician said, was not so serious as to warrant surgery, so he suggested I learn to live with them. I want to know what course of treatment would the detention center have administered if they did find I had hemorrhoids. The whole business of the "examination" was to humiliate. It was indefensible.

They also took away any items of clothing that I could use to commit suicide—belts, shoelaces, etc. I was allowed to keep my underwear and sweaters.

Next was my interview with a doctor. Since I had been in the hospital all this time, he wanted to know about my medical condition and what kind of medications I was taking.

"They've been giving me the antidepressant Ludiomil; Dogmatil, which works as a digestive aid and also as an anti-depressant; and sleeping pills. I hope you'll continue to give them to me here."

"We can't administer anti-depressants, but we have a variety of sleeping aids. What have you been taking?"

"Benzalin."

"We have that here. I'll prescribe it for you starting tonight."

After the interview was over, the guard who was accompanying me announced, "From now on, you are number 126. You won't be called by name, you will be called by your number. Number 126."

I was left thinking about two things: First, the cows on Recruit's farm in Kagoshima. They had no name; they only had a number. Second, my great-grandfather, who was a lower-class samurai serving the Nabeshima clan: what would he think? For a samurai, he'd said, nothing is more important than his family name, and Ezoe was our name. Now I had no name, I was a number, even though I was just a suspect. The indignity made my head spin.

The guard next took me by elevator up to the third floor. There were about fifty small, narrow cells lined up along a corridor. I was taken to one near the middle. When the thick steel door slammed shut and the key turned in the lock, a pall of gloom came over me. All my life, I'd never had any vices worse than being serious and hardworking, and *this* is where it got me.

Everything in the detention center was gray. The building, a relic from prewar days, was musty, its walls dingy with years of dirt. My cell was small and cramped and had a horrid smell, but after a few minutes somehow I got used to it and it no longer bothered me.

The space toward the front of the cell had two vintage tatami mats. Toward the rear was a tiny area with a wooden floor, outfitted with a commode on one side and a sink on the other. Except when sitting on the toilet or washing at the sink, we had to sit on the floor; lying down was not permitted. Because the cell's dimensions were so small, there was virtually no choice as to where one would sit. And since many people had sat in the same place through so many years, the concrete wall in that spot was worn down, leaving a natural hollow.

The wall facing the inner courtyard rose to a height of about 1.5 meters, above which was a window covered with bars. But because the window had no glass, the cell was open to the elements and was extremely cold. The only view from inside, while seated on the floor, was the slice of sky visible through the bars.

My attorney told me I would be monitored in my cell at all times by security camera, and he advised me to stay still. I looked around carefully but wasn't able to detect where the camera might be.

Before long it was mealtime. Under constant guard-watch, I accepted the tray passed to me through the small opening of my cell door by the inmate on serving duty. The meal consisted of boiled rice with barley served in an aluminum container and soup containing pork, *daikon* radish, carrots, and other vegetables. There was plenty to eat and it was tasty enough; the problem was the brief length of time between being served and the tray being taken away.

I've always had a weak stomach, and have suffered from stomach ulcers numerous times since middle school. My doctors had advised that I eat slowly and chew my food well. They even suggested that I should leave milk in my mouth for a time and "chew" it before swallowing. I had only finished about one-third of my meal before it was taken away.

I began feeling sorry for myself. Even a dog gets angry if his food is taken away.

The Prosecutor's Attitude Hardens

After dinner, the guard came to retrieve me for questioning. It was a fair distance to the interrogation room, a walk of perhaps five or six minutes, and I was shivering from the cold.

At Kosuge, the detention center, interrogation rooms and jail cells were all located within the same building complex. Between the detention block and the interrogation rooms you passed through a gate, and each time you entered or exited, the time was recorded on a punch card.

According to my card—which I was given access to after the fact—I passed through the gate to the Public Prosecutors Office at 7:36 P.M. The interrogation room was heated, and the twenty-degree difference in temperature made me feel physically unbalanced.

In all, there were about thirty interrogation rooms lining the corridor. I was taken to a room about halfway down. It had a frosted window, and the walls were spotless white.

The prosecutor's assistant, sitting with his back to the door, motioned me toward a chair with caster wheels and a seatback that wobbled. Before me was the prosecutor's desk, large and gray, along with a small filing cabinet on which rested a stack of papers.

After a few minutes, Kamigaki entered the room. He seemed completely different from the person who conducted my voluntary questioning. His attitude was noticeably more threatening than when he had brought me here hours before. He took his seat directly facing me and began to yell at me.

"Our house search turned up nothing! And we found nothing in the hospital, either. Where'd you hide everything?"

"I haven't hidden anything anywhere."

"Damn it, don't lie to me!"

As he bellowed loud enough to make the window rattle, I thought how strange this was. I had been arrested on the fifty-fifth day of my first interrogation, and if I *had* hidden anything there was more than enough time for it to be uncovered. It made no sense for him to be angry *now* over not finding any evidence. Besides, I had nothing to hide in the first place.

When Kamigaki was done for the evening, the guard took me back to my cell. The moment I passed through the gate back into the unheated cell block, I felt the shock of cold. The time was 9:31 P.M.

The mattress in my cell was thin and flat as a pancake. The air blowing through the pane-less window had me shivering. Several minutes later the guard came with my medication—a single tablet of Benzalin—and a paper cup of water. He watched to be sure I swallowed the pill, then left.

I was worried I would be unable to fall asleep, but perhaps because my arrest had released me from all the anxiety of the past weeks, I fell asleep immediately.

The wake-up bell rang the following morning, February 14, at seven o'clock. I immediately got up, folded the bedding, and placed it in a corner. Then came roll call. I kneeled down, torso erect, resting on my heels, facing the corridor. When the guard appeared, he yelled, "Number!"

It happened so suddenly that I couldn't recall my number. "Umm . . . ," I mumbled.

"126! You're number 126! Don't forget it."

This time I engraved it indelibly in my memory. Over the course of 113 days, I never forgot it. In fact, 126 became a number I would never forget for the rest of my life.

After breakfast, the guard announced I was to be taken to the courthouse. I was let out of my cell and placed in handcuffs.

Suspects being taken from the detention house to the courthouse were all handcuffed and tied together by rope at one-meter intervals. We lined up in the corridor. Among us were tattooed gangsters and a few people from other Asian countries. Never in my life did I imagine I would one day be part of group like this.

Throughout the bus ride from Kosuge to Kasumigaseki, screens were drawn over the windows to prevent our being seen from anyone outside. These screens, however, did not prevent us from seeing out. Peering at the streets I had known for so many years, I pondered how much my world had changed. I felt a tightening in my chest.

When we reached the courthouse, the bus entered the building through the underground garage. We were let off, untied, and handed over to the courthouse guards, who proceeded to lead us to individual cells on the basement level. My cell had a toilet but no window and was small and stuffy. To pass the time, I was handed two cheap novels.

After a short while I was taken by the guard to the judge's chamber. The judge first informed me of my right to remain silent, and then announced that he made the decision to keep me in detention. The whole business took no more than five minutes.

Afterward, I met with my lawyer, who told me Hiroshi Kobayashi, vice president of First Finance, had been arrested the same day I was. Like me, he was accused of passing bribes to Hasegawa and Shikiba of NTT. I was stunned.

Kobayashi was the founder of First Finance, which was a member of the Recruit Group, but which had no connection whatsoever with Recruit. For more than a dozen years, Kobayashi had had no involvement in Recruit's operations, and he knew nothing about the transfers of shares in Recruit Cosmos. His only involvement was in conjunction with extending financing to the people buying the shares. He had done nothing criminal! It pained me deeply, thinking about the difficult situation he was in.

That evening, at the hour when all the courtroom sessions had adjourned, the guard came for me. In the same way that we were brought to court in the morning, we were tied together by rope and led to an open area to wait for the bus back to Kosuge. By the time the bus pulled out of the garage, it was already dark.

When I returned to my cell at the detention center, my meal was waiting for me in the opening of my door. The rice was ice-cold, dry and crumbly, the soup cold, everything was cold. I could only manage to eat a little.

At 7:47, it was time for my evening interrogation with Kamigaki. This time he wanted to know about my connections with Hasegawa and Shikiba. It was the same dogged accusations: that I had provided shares to the two men in order to receive favors from them. I denied having any motive of the kind.

I always assumed it was the job of a prosecutor to arrest someone and then investigate whether he is guilty or innocent. I now knew firsthand how it really worked: A prosecutor wrenches statements from the accused that will ensure a guilty verdict in court.

Kamigaki's persistence brought him no results. Few words were exchanged between us, and I could monitor his growing annoyance.

Further Arrests

On February 15, there were snow flurries. My interrogation this day was a continuation from the preceding evening, focusing on my provision of shares to Hasegawa and Shikiba.

KAMIGAKI: "You must have expected favors of some kind in return for what you did?"

EZOE: "Recruit and NTT were in a business relationship. Recruit is one of NTT's major users, and in that capacity is a paying customer of NTT. The company never received any favors from Mr. Hasegawa or Mr. Shikiba."

KAMIGAKI: "Stop lying, damn it!"

EZOE: "I'm not lying."

KAMIGAKI: "Get this straight. You've been arrested. The chances of you getting off once you've been arrested are about as good as a camel passing through the eye of a needle."

EZOE: "No matter what my chances are, I still proclaim I'm innocent."

KAMIGAKI: "This investigation isn't as simple as you think. You stick to this attitude of yours, and the number of people arrested will only increase. You heard those helicopters flying overhead again today? Two people from Recruit were arrested on charges of violating the Securities and Exchange Law. If you don't believe me, just ask your lawyer!"

Which I did the following day. My lawyer told me Seiichi Tateoka, a director at Recruit Cosmos, and Shunjiro Mamiya, a managing director at Recruit, had in fact been arrested and charged with violating the Securities and Exchange Law.

I had been interrogated by Prosecutor Munakata on suspicion of having violated the Securities and Exchange Law, yet when I was arrested, the charge was making bribes. I was overcome again by anxiety.

February 16 was yet another day of denials and silences. During the afternoon interrogation, Kamigaki again let loose his anger.

"I don't like this defiant attitude of yours. If the truth be known, there was no need to arrest Tateoka and Mamiya, but you refused, so we took them in. If you don't want to talk, we can make another round of arrests, and then another round of arrests. We'll bring in the president of Recruit, we'll bring in the president of Recruit Cosmos. We know you gave ten million yen to Ichiro Ozawa, thirty million yen to Shintaro Abe, and a hefty sum to Koichi Kato. Unless you start talking, we'll release this news to the press—which, as you know too well, would lead to the dissolution of the Diet and the holding of new general elections."

Again, this was rather strange. The ten million yen to Ichiro Ozawa was money paid for tickets to a fundraising party, organized by the LDP's Iwate chapter, held at the Morioka Grand Hotel, which was part of the Recruit Group. The donation was made at the request of the hotel, which asked its business partners to pitch in. Moreover, the money did not go to Ozawa but to the Iwate chapter—a move that caused the press to speculate that I was considering going into politics myself. The other donations Kamigaki was threatening exposure with had also already been reported by the media. Maybe the special investigators were bringing all this up because they wanted to shake up the current administration.

That night, lying on my thin mattress, shivering from the cold draft blowing through the open window, I couldn't sleep. The day's events weighed heavily on me.

Despite their arrest, Tateoka and Mamiya were never charged. After my release on bail, my lawyer said their arrests were, as Kamigaki suggested, a ploy to bring an end to my denials of wrongdoing. Even so, the defense team had been worried about what would happen if more arrests followed.

Ida Facing Arrest, Too?

Events of this kind continued during my interrogation of February 18.

"Yesterday Shigeru Kano of the Labor Ministry's Employment Security Bureau was arrested on a charge of bribe-taking," the prosecutor began. "And one of the people who entertained Kano was Naotaka Ida, president of Recruit. Over the three years, Ida spent a total of half a million yen wining and dining Kano and treating him to golf and so on. Half a million may not sound like much, but it's enough reason for us to bring Ida in. If you think I'm lying, just ask your attorney."

Ida and Kano were both graduates of Tohoku University, where Ida completed a graduate research program in psychology. Ida himself had told me that occasionally Kano would invite him out for drinks, usually in the company of Seigo Abe, head of sales, who also shared the same alma mater.

I knew that if I kept up my denials, it was conceivable that Ida would be arrested. This prospect worried me greatly.

The media were all reporting that Recruit was suspected of providing shares to Labor Vice Minister Takashi Kato in exchange for favors from the Labor Ministry. The focus was on the ministry's oversight of advertising.

Roughly 80 percent of all workers who changed jobs had found their new positions through sources such as private job-placement agencies, newspaper help-wanted ads, and job-information magazines; only 20 percent went through public employment offices. The Ministry of Labor, concerned that its role as employment administrator was declining, did not welcome its diminishing role.

While this was going on, the 2nd Ad Hoc Commission on Administrative Reform was also considering—in addition to privatizing the Japanese National Railways (JNR), Nippon Telegraph and Telephone Public Corporation (NTT), and the Japan Tobacco and Salt Public Corporation—the down-scaling of the nation's employment agency services.

Kano, in his role at the Labor Ministry's Employment Security Bureau, drew up an outline of a proposal for amending the Employment Security Act and distributed it to members of the press. The proposal implied the ministry's intent to impose regulations on help-wanted advertising. A copy of Kano's proposal also found its way, through a company called Diamond-Big, to Recruit.

Kano's intention in drafting such a proposal was unclear, but one thing seemed certain: if restrictions were actually imposed on job advertising, the move would deal a powerful blow to Recruit's business. To better understand the details, Ida, then senior managing director in charge of job advertising, paid a visit to Takashi Kato, head of the Employment Security Bureau. At this meeting, Ida learned that the ministry had no intention of imposing such regulations and there was no such resolution under consideration.

I myself reviewed the proposal written by Kano. It was one-page long, and what it contained would hardly qualify as the draft of a bill, which would have had to be at least twenty pages in length. Moreover, the bureau section that Kano belonged to was not in charge of drafting these bills in the first place.

All the same, to be on the safe side, I phoned Kenichiro Otsubo, a former Labor Ministry bureaucrat who was now a member of the Lower House and serving as head of the LDP's labor division, to inquire about the matter. I knew Otsubo quite well. He was elected to the Diet from Saga Prefecture, where my family was from, and my aunt led the local women's group supporting his campaign. I had also bought tickets to fundraising events when he was running for office.

Otsubo said he'd be in Ginza for a dinner meeting in the next few days and would stop by Recruit on his way there to speak with me. During his visit, he explained that if any amendments were to be made to the Employment Security Act, he, in his role as head of the LDP's labor division, would be the first to know. If indeed there were any amendments, the issue would then be debated by the House of Representatives' Committee on Health, Labor, and Welfare, and then it would be presented to the full House for consideration.

"So far," he said, "I've heard nothing about it."

Otsubo went on to recount a story about when he was still at the Labor Ministry and had been assigned as an attaché to the Japanese Embassy in Germany. At the time, in response to a spate of problems involving false advertising, Germany had done away with all help-wanted ads. All solicitation for workers thereafter was handled exclusively through the nation's public employment agencies. The outcome, however, was a jump in the unemployment rate, and in the end, job advertising was reinstated.

In Japan, exaggerated wording in job ads posted in newspapers had once been a social issue. On that occasion the Ministry of Labor sought to revise the Employment Security Act and assume a monitoring role over employment advertising, but the move was vehemently opposed by the Japan Newspaper Publishers & Editors Association. The issue was finally settled with the 1971 establishment of the Newspaper Advertising Review Council (NARC) and the introduction of self-regulation.

According to Otsubo, it was impossible to regulate newspaper advertising and job-information magazines. In fact, the 2nd Ad Hoc Commission on Administrative Reform once proposed deregulating these areas, and the Labor Ministry's regulations on job advertising were seen as an impediment to securing the labor force required by industry, and were thus seen as going against present requirements for society.

As for scaling back the nation's employment agency services, Otsubo said it would be impossible to reduce the number of public servants because such a move would be opposed by the Japan Socialist Party and by the Council of the Public Corporations and Government Workers Unions, both of which were backed by the General Council of Trade Unions of Japan (Sohyo). This made perfect sense to me.

Nonetheless, it appeared that at every opportunity, Kano was surreptitiously telling Recruit employees there was a move afoot within the Labor Ministry to regulate job advertising, and every time he intimated this, he added he would make sure to block such a move. A number of employees—including Seigo Abe, Ryogo Akabane, and Yoshiki Katsuno, managers in the department handling advertising for educational institutions—took him at his word and frequently entertained Kano—at *his* request—with meals, rounds of golf, mahjong, and the sort. Kano also had Recruit accept the tab for his own evenings out with people with no relation to Recruit. In all, he did this on forty-one occasions.

One other matter I was questioned on in conjunction with the Ministry of Labor was the establishment of the Employment Information Center.

Kano approached Recruit senior managing director Takeshi Osawa, indicating that the ministry was planning to create an employment information center and asking for Osawa's cooperation.

At the time, the Labor Ministry already had a Labor Market Center located in Tokyo's Nerima ward. The center was equipped with a UNIVAC computer featuring the world's largest processing capability, and a system was already in place that matched data on job offers and job seekers using terminals installed at all public employment agency offices. Kano had contacted Osawa immediately after the Labor Market Center's opening, and he set up a meeting at a restaurant in Shimbashi that included Osawa, Kano himself, Labor Vice Minister Hideo Seki, and myself.

I was opposed to backing the creation of a new employment information center, but Osawa suggested it would be improper to turn down a request from the vice minister. I decided that Recruit would assign one employee to the center on the condition that Recruit wasn't the only company to offer such assistance. From what we were told, companies in the industry would shoulder costs until the center became incorporated, and operating costs after it opened would thereafter be covered by the state.

Because Recruit publishes employment-information magazines, the media, in its reportage of Recruit Cosmos shares that were provided to Labor Vice Minister Kato, were making it seem as though the Ministry of Labor had direct authority over Recruit. The fact of the matter, however, is that Recruit was not under the jurisdiction of the Labor Ministry but rather under NARC—an organization over which the ministry had no authority.

The media also reported later that Recruit was suspected of having wielded its influence with the Labor Ministry so the gentlemen's agreement between universities and the corporate sector with regard to the commencement of recruiting activities would work in favor with Recruit's interests. That allegation had no factual basis, and it arose from the misconception that the Labor Ministry was in a position to exercise control over the agreement.

The prosecution contended I approached the ministry to receive favors in the form of the ministry setting the timetable for recruitment book distributions so that it would have a positive impact on our sales of the "Recruit Book." However, Recruit would have benefited more from the dismantling of the gentlemen's agreement altogether, or at least for it to be ignored. *That* would have a positive impact on the sales activities of a company that publishes information magazines, freeing it to send out its publications any time during the year.

The fact is, the Ministry of Labor had no legal authority to regulate the activities of a publisher of information magazines. But Recruit, as well as all companies publishing information magazines in those days, cooperated "voluntarily" with the gentlemen's agreement not because of its effect on their bottom line, but because they believed it to be in society's best interest.

The gentlemen's agreement was concluded between a council comprised of representative members of the industrial sector and an informal body encompassing members from the nation's universities. The former—officially known as the Central Employment Measures Council and headed by Yoshinobu Matsuzaki, senior managing director at Nikkeiren—monitored compliance with the agreement, and punishment against any violations of the agreement was carried out in the form of identifying the perpetrators in the press. No legal sanctions could be imposed.

Despite the fact that the Labor Ministry was not in a position to provide favors of any kind to Recruit, the prosecution tenaciously accused me of designating that shares of Recruit Cosmos be provided to Kato in exchange for something in return from his ministry.

As regards the Employment Information Center, the prosecution was scathing: "You put out the money so it would work to Recruit's benefit, didn't you?"

Here was another case of being only one of a number of companies that provided financial support to the center. And as for treating Kano to golf, that outing was arranged by Kano himself as both a token of appreciation and a social occasion. I did not even participate.

This was the outline of my connections with the Labor Ministry. I explained this to Kamigaki over and over, but it seemed to make no difference.

"You stick to this pigheaded attitude of yours, and just watch what happens to Recruit if Ida gets arrested? The company you started will collapse and all its employees will be tossed out with nowhere to go."

This threat was repeated endlessly.

After my arrest, one of my defense attorneys, Kyuzaburo Hino, met with Prosecutor Munakata two or three times a week at the Public Prosecutors Office. When he came to see me on the day the above exchange took place, he told me Munakata had shown him what looked like an arrest warrant for Ida.

"Mr. Ezoe, if you continue to deny all the allegations against you, Mr. Ida could very well get arrested."

At the time, Recruit as a group was carrying loans totaling 1.8 trillion yen. While the bulk was borrowed from four banks—the Industrial Bank of Japan (IBJ), Mitsui, Sanwa, and Dai-Ichi Kangyo—altogether there were twenty-one lenders, including virtually all the city and trust banks plus regional institutions like the Chiba Bank, Saitama Bank, and Bank of Yokohama.

If Ida were arrested, the lower-tier banks could conceivably pull out their money, in which case the core lending institutions would not likely make up for the shortfall due to the financial risk and public scrutiny. Ultimately, the Group would not be able to meet its financial needs and would go under.

Besides 1.8 trillion yen in loans, the Group had some ten thousand people on its payroll. If it were to go under—because the president of Recruit entertained someone to the tune of just a half million yen—the failure would be on a scale rarely seen and the negative consequences would be immeasurable. I had to assume the prosecutors had considered this. If all that were to happen, if anyone were to be lambasted by the media, it should be the Public Prosecutors Office.

Hino, though, kept repeating the possibility that Ida might be arrested. I thought the prosecutors were just bluffing and wouldn't likely go that far; but if the situation really did turn out that way, the Recruit Group would go under. The very idea prevented me from sleeping that night, and as I lay awake I composed the following haiku:

> *Alone in my cell—*
> *Gazing at the moon,*
> *Troubled by depressing thoughts.*

In the end, Kano was arrested and indicted on a charge of bribe-taking. The Recruit employees who proffered the "bribes" were not indicted because for the most part, the entertainment and payment of Kano's bills were done in response to his request.

After being released on bail, I read the *Asahi* of February 18. The main headline read: "Recruit President Ida Unable to Avoid Responsibility in Scandal." The article talked of a "major impact expected on Group operations," but it made no mention whatsoever about Ida's role in the issue or what the impact was expected to be. Even so, if Ida had gotten arrested, the impact on Group operations *would* have been major—that was certain.

I was told later that when my defense team read the article they assembled to discuss the course of action they should take in response. The whole affair seems to have been a stratagem on the part of the special investigators to leak information to the *Asahi* as a way of shaking up my attorneys.

That Cray Computer

Hino was visibly disturbed by the report in the *Asahi* that Ida could face arrest. While on the one hand I still thought it was a bluff, on the chance the article might have an element of truth to it, I told Kamigaki the next day I would cooperate in the preparation of a statement.

"So, you've finally come to see my point," he replied, his expression changing to friendly.

In matters relating to my dealings with NTT and Shikiba, Prosecutor Kamigaki appeared to be quite sure how to frame the statement, but as regards Hasegawa, he seemed to be racking his brain.

At the time of his arrest, Hasegawa was head of a department at Recruit, and Recruit's legal counsel was placed in charge of his defense. Since his alleged partner in crime was another Recruit employee, building the case against him must have been difficult.

About twenty years before, I had served in an executive capacity at The Forum (now Japan New Business Conferences), an organization founded by Kazuo Noda, an expert in business economics (later, president emeritus of Tama University and president of Miyagi University). Members of The Forum—including CSK's Isao Okawa and SoftBank's Masayoshi Son— were proactive in hosting many study seminars on business economics. Hisahiko Hasegawa was also a core member, so our connection had a long history.

When Hasegawa was working at NTT as head of the Data Communications Bureau, he was implicated in a scandal where the Metropolitan Police Department pressed charges. When news was reported in the weeklies, Hasegawa opted to leave NTT. If not for this smear, he may well have become the first president of NTT Data Corporation. I suggested he come and work for Recruit. When I approached him about buying shares in Recruit Cosmos, his joining the company had already been decided in confidence.

Concerning Hasegawa, the prosecutors were interested in the matter surrounding the supercomputer. As described earlier, however, the person at NTT who phoned me requesting that Recruit purchase a Cray supercomputer was Shikiba, second in command of the company's corporate communication system operations.

The real reason that Recruit bought the Cray supercomputer via NTT was, I repeat, as an act of cooperation to avert trade friction between Japan and the United States: NTT merely functioned as a sort of funnel. But when I testified before the Diet, to prevent the matter from becoming a new political issue I stated our intent was to receive backup support

from NTT. If I were to make a statement now that contradicted what I said under oath, it would constitute a violation of the Diet Testimony Law. I told Kamigaki the truth anyway. As I spoke, emotions suddenly welled up inside me and tears began streaming down my cheeks.

Kamigaki must already have known from the evidence seized that Recruit was mulling the purchase of a supercomputer from Cray Japan and had received a cost estimate. He must also have known, from the contract we entered into, that following our purchase of hardware through NTT, Recruit concluded an agreement on software and other backup services with Cray Japan, not with NTT. All the same, he seemed disappointed on hearing my confession.

"Here we thought, after hearing you testify before the Diet, that we could go with the argument that you provided shares as a way of thanking NTT for its help in getting the supercomputer."

Had the Public Prosecutors Office added a violation of the Diet Testimony Law to the charges pressed against me, no doubt I would have been tried for a felony of serious weight. Perhaps the prosecutors already met and completed their case blueprint after taking statements from many people based on that blueprint. I received no indication they intended to indict me on a charge of violating the Diet Testimony Law.

Snooping by the Prosecutors Office

It was around this time that one of my attorneys, Osamu Ishihara, who visited regularly, was barred from entering the premises.

Whenever we met, Ishihara had always advised that if the prosecutor said something that was not true, I should always make a clear denial of it. I thought perhaps that was why he was barred from visiting me, although conversations in the visitation rooms were not supposed to be monitored. I suspect a hidden microphone was placed there anyway—in the same way that there was a hidden camera in my cell.

The day I was taken to the Public Prosecutors Office for processing extension of my period of detention, Kamigaki was summoned as well. That night, in the course of my interrogation he allowed that headquarters had reprimanded him for being too lenient with me. This deepened my suspicion that illicit cameras had been placed in the interrogation room and that they were connected to headquarters.

While I was writing this book, I thought to ask an expert about this. During World War II, he told me, research was carried out for the use of microscopic, high-performance electronic cameras as a means to raise the hit rate when firing rifles. Night-vision cameras were developed so that the enemy could be located even in moonlight—technology that became the basis for development of gastro scopes and other high-tech cameras. Japan came to possess the world's most sophisticated technology in this area. It was the conjecture of this expert that a small electronic camera had been installed in the ceiling panel of the interrogation room, recording the goings-on through a tiny hole. By this camera and hair-thin high-speed digital circuitry or micro-waves, images were likely sent to prosecution headquarters. As for the microphone, he indicated that something as small as one-centimeter-square with a thickness of only two-to-three millimeters could be installed under the table or a chair in the visitation room. This sound could be relayed via a wireless network, amplified, and transmitted to the prosecutors' office or to headquarters.

Hearing this made me recall how, on the very first day that I underwent voluntary interrogation, Munakata asked sardonically whether I had a hidden microphone. The picture was getting clearer.

Connections with the Outside

At the detention center, inmates were allowed to receive certain requested items. Delivery of these items could only be done by two designated companies, Sagamiya and Ikedaya, which checked that anything delivered to inmates did not contain things like drugs or needles.

Through my attorneys, who then passed them to my secretary, I made several requests: chocolates, sponge cake, as well as a few books—*Norwegian Wood*, by Haruki Murakami, the Japanese translation of Erich Fromm's *To Have or To Be*, and two titles on improving one's skiing. Magazines were not allowed.

What I yearned for most, though, was music and newspapers. Music was an indispensable part of my life. For many years I was in the habit of waking up in the morning and reading the newspaper with music playing in the background. I also listened to music before going to sleep. Throughout my interrogation period, however, both were disallowed.

In my cell there was a radio, but it wasn't possible to select a channel. Suspects undergoing interrogation were prevented from listening to news, and the only programs available were baseball games, sumo matches, variety shows, and popular music. The detention center seemed to cater to the tastes of the majority of the inmates. I didn't hear the singers I like—Masashi Sada and Hibari Misora—even once. Today, when I hear songs that were popular in those days and that were played frequently over that radio, memories of my time in detention come flooding back.

Four or five days after my arrest, I learned there was a list of items I could buy through my guards. Among them were candy, chocolates, tissues, notebooks, ballpoint pens, and so on. I purchased candy to supplement my calorie intake as well as notebooks and pens, which I used to take notes of what transpired during my daily interrogations, including the statements taken from me. I did this so I could tell my lawyers exactly what happened when they visited me.

On the first page of my notebook, I wrote the following:

> Don't think about getting out quickly.
> Think of this as an ideal time for studying.
> There's no point in becoming pessimistic or angry; think of your time here as a god-given holiday.
> It's up to you to overcome your difficult environment; have the courage to think of your current environment as good.

I also dug deep into my memory in order to record all the exchanges that took place between me and the prosecutors up until the point of my arrest.

And before visits from my attorney, I would write in very fine print, on the palms of my hands, what transpired in the latest interrogations, as well as the main points of any statements taken. When I walked to the visitation room, I clasped my hands so the guard wouldn't notice. I would discuss what happened with my attorney while making reference to the notes on my palms. After the guard took me back to my cell, I would immediately rub off all traces of my notes with soap.

I thought the guards would discover this at some point, but they never did.

My Detention Gets Extended

On February 22, the tenth day after I was brought to Kosuge, Prosecutor Kamigaki announced they were extending my period of detention.

When a suspect is taken under arrest, a request for detention is issued within forty-eight hours. The detention period is ten days beginning from the day the request was made. At the end of that period an extension by up to another ten days is permitted. This means that on a single arrest warrant the maximum permissible length of custody is forty-eight hours plus twenty days. In a case like mine involving multiple charges, what the prosecution typically does is to make an arrest and indict on one charge. They will subsequently issue a second arrest warrant and bring another indictment against the suspect, and on and on.

One of my defense attorneys, Takeshi Tada, cautioned me not to provoke the prosecutor. He suggested that prosecutors, in preparing their written statements for me to sign, were known to include things I had said as well as things that were untrue. My intention was to cooperate but not to admit to things that differed from the facts. But I had no legal expertise, and admitting to certain things while denying others could be tricky.

I had two options: to admit or to deny. Since I had committed no crime, I chose the path of denial. My notes from this time confirm that day after day I either denied allegations made against me or simply remained silent. The prosecutors, likely losing patience with my stubborn refusals, on more than one occasion tried a conciliatory approach: "Denying things will only work against you. Let us help you out of this. Admit what you've done, and we'll help you where we can."

At other times they would try pleading: "Headquarters was on our backs today, accusing us of dawdling. 'Get a statement from him *fast!*' they yelled at us. Mr. Ezoe, please, won't you help us out?"

Then at other times they would come back from lunch break and immediately start berating me. This swinging back and forth from threats to appeasement and back again became the daily standard.

I built Recruit from scratch, and throughout its long development I weathered the full range of difficulties and battles. Had I been merely one cog within a large organization, I am certain I would not have been able to confront the prosecutors to the extent I did.

My attorneys warned me from the outset my detention might be lengthy. At this point I believed I no longer had anything to lose, and remaining silent was the honorable thing for me to do.

When I was informed my detention would be extended, I resolved to hold on no matter how lengthy it might get.

Modern-day Torture

Before my arrest, around the time my voluntary interrogation began under Prosecutor Munakata, my attorneys gave me a book by the title of *Keiji saiban no hikari to kage (Shadow and Light in Criminal Trials)*. The authors wrote that when bribery offenses are in question, even if one party wines and dines another party with whom he has a business relationship, he is innocent unless he admits the entertainment was intended as a form of bribe. For the prosecution to win a guilty verdict against a defendant, it must therefore secure a written confession from the defendant admitting he acted with the intent of bribery.

In order to indict me and find me guilty, it was thus imperative for the prosecutors to secure a written confession from me admitting my actions were intended as bribes. To wrest such a confession from me, they interrogated me in a way I could only describe as "modern-day torture."

Up against a Wall

On the day I was arrested, during their search of my hospital room, the special investigators apparently found the copy of this book.

During my interrogation, the prosecutor criticized me as though I did something wrong by reading it. Later, in court he made the same point, as if to make a case against me by demonstrating to the court that I knew in advance what interrogations were all about. But after being put through fifty-five days of voluntary interrogation, how could there be anything suspect about reading a book or two on criminal court proceedings?

The blurb on the back cover of *Shadow and Light in Criminal Trials* says the rate of conviction in criminal court cases in Japan is 99.9 percent, a feat it claims is unequaled anywhere else. This is touted as the "light side" of Japan's criminal justice system. It points out there also exists a "shadow side" as well—illustrated by the number of cases in which a defendant initially sentenced to death is subsequently found innocent at retrial. When this occurs, media reporting is found not to have done its job in a majority of these cases. The blurb concludes: "In this book, a former court judge and a lawyer shed 'light' on the 'dark' side lurking within the country's criminal court proceedings."

The book itself introduces four cases. The one that left the greatest impression was what became known as the "Geidai violin scandal." The case had to do with the purchase of a violin by the music department of the prestigious Tokyo National University of Fine Arts and Music (known as Geidai, currently Tokyo University of the Arts). The violin in question was a vintage Guadagnini offered through a dealer of musical instruments. A professor, Yoshio Unno, was called on to give his appraisal of the instrument. Unno, who was a renowned violinist as well, played the instrument on offer, gave it his seal of approval, and the sale went through. It was later revealed that after the sale Unno received a violin bow valued at 800,000 yen from the dealer. It also came to light that, on another occasion, Unno received one million yen from the same source for performing a similar service in conjunction with the sale of a violin to a Geidai student. Unno's actions, construed as bribe-taking, were widely reported in the *Asahi* at the time, and a case was brought against him.

A fine Guadagnini can cost upwards of 100 million yen. Guadagninis were crafted by hand roughly 250 years ago, and their value varies depending on their state of preservation and the performers who previously played them. Their true value becomes known, however, only when they are played.

As an exception to its rules, the Ministry of Education allows Geidai, which is a state institution, to invite top-class performers to serve on its faculty. If Unno were found to have played the instruments in question and merely to have given his appraisal of them, he would be innocent by law; but if he were found to have used his position as a Geidai professor to accept a "fee" for his appraisal, he would be guilty of a crime.

In cases such as this, a guilty or not-guilty verdict depends on whether or not the accused admits to the notion that he knew bribery was involved. As such, the prosecution in the case needed a statement from Unno clearly espousing that he was aware he was accepting a "reward" for his services. And to do so, they resorted to coercive interrogation. *Shadow and Light in Criminal Trials* describes how Unno was questioned. Here is a sample of what Unno had to say:

> In the interrogation room, I was on repeated occasions yelled at and subjected to remarks insulting to my character.

> In the course of the interrogation, if I made a statement contrary to what the prosecutor wanted, he would suddenly throw down his documents on the table or bang the table with a ruler. Thinking my fingers might be hurt, I kept my hands out of sight.

> The prosecutor would take a ballpoint pen, bring it close to my eyes and flip it around. When I attempted to avoid getting hit, he held the back of my head so the pen would practically touch my eyeballs.

> He suddenly kicked the flimsy steel-pipe chair I was sitting on out from under me, causing me to land hard on my backside on the floor.

> I was ordered to stand, for a long time, perfectly straight, with my face practically touching the wall.

> As a result of my fear during the interrogations and the fatigue caused by the long interrogations lasting until late at night, even after I returned to my cell I was unable to fall asleep, causing me to suffer from perpetual lack of sleep.

Even after there was a change of prosecutors, my interrogations continued late into the night; the resulting accumulation of anxiety, agitation, and exhaustion put me in a state in which I was unable to fully scrutinize the content of the statements I signed.

After my release, I asked a dealer of musical instruments, whom I had occasion to meet, about the Unno case.

"Guadagnini lived in the 18th century," he said. "The violin in question could have been made by one of his apprentices, or it may even have been a fake. Since an amateur can't judge what's good or bad, or what's authentic or not, it's standard practice when selling a stringed instrument like that to have it evaluated by a well-known performer who can actually play it. Any violinist knows this is how things are done. The case against Unno—who was enjoying a very prominent career at the time—apparently resulted from a leak by another Geidai professor. It's really a shame what happened to him."

Like Unno, during my interrogations I was frequently made to stand for long periods facing the wall.

"You must have expected something in return," Kamigaki repeated.

"Nothing of the kind. When Hasegawa left NTT for personal reasons, I invited him to come to Recruit, and the transfer of shares was carried out. I wasn't looking for any favors from NTT."

"You're so goddamn arrogant! I've never seen anyone so arrogant as you in all my years. You should be apologizing to the public for what you did! Listen, you, don't think you can pull one over on us. You don't realize just how scary we can be when we want to be!" In his rage, the prosecutor then lifted up the table and dropped it, causing all the papers to come crashing down on my side.

"Stand up! Face left and walk! Left!! LEFT!!!"

I walked slowly to the corner of the room. Kamigaki positioned himself just inches away from me.

"Closer to the wall! Closer! NOW!"

I cringed and inched closer to the wall, until my nose was practically touching it. When I closed my eyes, the prosecutor leaned even closer and bellowed in my ear.

"Who said you could close your eyes, damn it! Are you trying to make a fool of me? Make a fool of me, and you're making a fool of this country, damn you!"

I thought my eardrum would burst. With my nose pressed so close to the wall, keeping my eyes open was extremely uncomfortable. My eyes became bleary and my ears were burning.

"Open those eyes, I said! And stand still!"

Before long the wall began to take on a yellow tinge. It seemed to have a yellowish ring, perhaps from the contracting of my pupils. My eyes hurt. Tears welled up, though it was not from sadness.

Being forced to face a wall at a close distance and keep my eyes open was very stressful. So too was having someone shout at the top of his lungs in my ear. My left leg, which I had once broken in a ski accident, began to ache. Gradually, I could feel the blood descending into the soles of my feet.

I asked to use the toilet, and was allowed to go to the lavatory, escorted by a guard. With a guard monitoring my every move, I sat on the toilet for four or five minutes. I raised my feet, placed the soles against the wall, and rotated my ankles to let the blood flow more freely. The guard said nothing.

When I returned to the interrogation room, Kamigaki made me stand again. He meanwhile pored over documents. At lunchtime, a guard escorted me back to my cell. When I was brought for the afternoon interrogation, Kamigaki again ordered me to stand where I had stood all morning, facing the wall. From time to time he would come close by my side to be sure my eyes were open, and if they were not, he would again yell into my ear: "Damn it! I told you to keep those damned eyes of yours open!"

Since this treatment continued day after day, my legs gradually stiffened to the point I could no longer walk normally. As a guard in the interrogation area took me to the checkpoint, a guard in the detention block would then take over and escort me back to my cell. The guards in the detention block seemed to understand my situation, and they always slowed their pace to match mine. Every night, in my futon before falling asleep, I would rotate my ankles and stretch my feet to improve the blood circulation.

The pain in my eyes persisted, and even after I returned to my cell at night the image of the yellow ring on the wall would linger whenever I closed my eyelids. Even after my release, my eyes felt pain, so I had them checked. I was told I had become increasingly nearsighted, but before too long, the condition improved, so it appears to have been a case of pseudo myopia.

My interrogations were even harsher than what I had read in *Shadow and Light in Criminal Trials*, and during a visit from Hino I complained about being made to stand facing the wall. It seems he took up the issue immediately with Prosecutor Munakata, yet I continued to receive the same treatment. According to my notes, I was forced to stand morning, afternoon, and night four days straight: March 7 through 10.

During my trial, on June 27, 1996, Prosecutor Kamigaki took the witness stand on this matter. He denied having ever made me stand. However, prior to that, on May 7, 1993, Prosecutor Munakata appeared in court as a witness and testified that Hino spoke to him concerning Kamigaki's interrogation methods. Munakata told the court that in light of what I had said about the matter, plus the protest lodged by my chief defense counsel, he instructed Kamigaki to exercise adequate caution and be sure not to do anything that would arouse suspicions. Munakata likely testified this way in consideration of the fact that my notes would later be submitted to the court as evidence.

While I was forced to stand during his interrogations, Kamigaki would sometimes leave the room. On one such occasion the assistant who sat in on the proceedings unexpectedly spoke to me.

"The prosecutor's gone to have a cigarette and won't be back for a few minutes. It's OK for you to take a seat. When I hear his footsteps, I'll let you know and you can return to where you were."

Up until then, this assistant always just sat like a piece of furniture, never saying a word. Now, he spoke very kindly.

"Simple bribery carries a maximum sentence of three years. In your case, Mr. Ezoe, the sentence would probably be suspended; but even if you did receive a jail sentence, the system allows for you to be released on parole after serving a third of your time. This being your first offense, if you did go to jail, after about a year-and-a-half you would be out. Isn't it better just to let things pass that way rather than enduring such painful things here?"

When I mentioned this to Hino on his next visit, he warned me to be careful. "I wouldn't follow that assistant's advice if I were you. Don't you realize he and the prosecutor are teaming up?"

Life in Detention

The daily routine in the detention center was lights-off at nine P.M. and wake-up at seven A.M., seven days a week. Even if you were not sleepy, you had to stay in your futon the full ten hours. On average I would sleep only seven hours. My interrogations ended a little before nine P.M., and then I would have spent the next three hours in my futon before I finally became drowsy enough to fall asleep.

The guards would peer into the cell every five or six minutes. I imagine they did so because on rare occasions an inmate, unable to endure his incarceration, would attempt to take his own life. As the guards wore rubber-soled shoes, you couldn't hear them approaching. There were times when, lying in my futon, I would suddenly open my eyes and meet the gaze of a guard peering in at me. It gave me the creeps.

Every morning at seven o'clock we had roll call. After that, electric shavers were passed out and we had three minutes to shave. Then came breakfast. No clocks or watches were permitted, perhaps to prevent any coordinated uprisings, so I'm not sure of the exact time, but generally we had about five or six minutes between the time our food arrived and when they came to collect the tray.

I'm a very slow eater, as I've said. Not having enough time, I could manage to eat only about a quarter of each meal. To supplement my calorie intake, I would mix the sweet-bean candy that I received at visitations into my rice, and afterward have some chocolate.

Since I was in the hospital when I was arrested, Kamigaki expressed concern and said to tell him if I wasn't feeling well. The first two days, I was strong and told him I was fine, but on the third day I grew anxious and had the guard take me to the infirmary. The infirmary was staffed by a young doctor and a male nurse.

I told the doctor my stomach wasn't functioning properly. He placed his hands on my stomach, pressed very lightly, and began moving them over my stomach ever so slowly back and forth and to the left and right. A few moments later, a growling noise began and my stomach resumed normal functioning. At the same time, my circulation improved and my body became warm. I gradually felt calm again.

"Here in the detention center, there's no physical intimacy whatsoever," the doctor began. "And when we feel nervous or lonely, our digestive functions can be dulled. Sometimes the functioning of the digestive tract, or of our organs, improves simply by placing hands on them. Please feel free to come anytime and I'll give you treatment like I just did."

He sounded kind and sincere, and after that I started to visit the infirmary three to four times a week for such treatments. No medication was involved.

About a hundred days after my arrest, I saw a female nurse in the infirmary. I felt my heart jump as though I'd seen something taboo. I'd seen only men until then.

At the time of my arrest, I was undergoing dental care for an implant, so when I learned there was a dental facility within the detention center, I had the guard take me there during lunch break. The dentist on duty was a gentleman around seventy years of age. No sooner had he shined a light into my mouth and peeked in than he declared, "You've got a decayed tooth here. Let me pull it for you right away." As he began making preparations to do the job, I voiced my refusal. I returned with the guard to my cell.

Bathing at the detention center was permitted twice a week. It was no leisurely affair. The allotted time was very short: only fifteen minutes from the time you left your cell until the time you had to get back. The first time I went for a bath, I was washing my body and shampooing my hair when the guard announced I had three minutes left. Totally flustered, I rushed to wash off, soaked in the tub for about a minute, and wiped myself off. I returned to my cell feeling as chilled to the bone as before.

One day, during the lunch break I heard a low voice coming from two or three cells down. I could not make out exactly what was being said, but it sounded to me like someone reciting Islamic prayers.

The guard on duty immediately came running. "DAMARE!!!" he yelled. "Chobatsu da zo!"

The prayers continued.

"Call somebody who speaks English!" he shouted to another guard.

In no time six or seven guards rushed to the scene. "BE QUIET!!! SHUT UP!!!" one yelled.

But the prayers just went on. I imagined the offender didn't understand English, either.

I was eager to see what might happen next, but the guards just shrugged their shoulders.

"Don't waste your breath," one suggested. "He won't stop. He's a Muslim."

The next thing I knew, the guards had taken off back to their posts. No further fuss was made, and the prayers continued for a while longer. I began to wonder what on earth could happen at interrogations when someone couldn't even understand simple English, let alone Japanese.

I later learned that attorneys with experience in such matters typically advise foreigners who don't know much Japanese to speak in their native tongue during the investigation phase. Apparently when someone speaks in his native language, without an interpreter present there can be no real conversation between the prosecutor and the suspect, which makes it impossible to take written statements. As a result, foreigners who get arrested often get off without being indicted.

In the case of Muslim inmates, what happened during Ramadan? How did the detention center deal with concerns that arose from religion and eating habits?

The most stressful part of being in detention was not being able to get in any physical activity. Except for brief exercises in the morning and again at three in the afternoon—impossible if you are in interrogation—you have to sit still the whole time you are in your cell. Without physical activity, your legs lose their strength. In my case, I was also worried that if I didn't get any exercise, my digestive system would shut down.

Besides people like me under investigation, the Tokyo Detention Center was also home to convicted felons serving time, and they were made to perform a variety of menial jobs: handing out meals, cleaning the inner courtyard, and so on. They do so with great vigor and efficiency. I, being prohibited from any real physical activity within my cell, found myself envious of them.

On one occasion, I began doing squats. No sooner had I started than a young guard came rushing over and began reprimanding me.

"Stop! Any more moving around like that and you'll be punished!"

I asked my lawyer just what sort of punishment they meted out in such cases. He said they put you in a cell with no window. And if you persist in disobeying even after that, they sometimes put you in handcuffs.

On days when the weather was nice, around nine in the morning we were allowed to go, under guard, to an outdoor recreation area for about fifteen minutes. The area was shaped like a fan partitioned into 10 separate zones. At the point where the "ribs" of the fan would meet at the base, a guard was on duty. We were each assigned to a section about fifty square meters. I would run wildly in circles like a dog in this "cage," practically bouncing off the walls.

In my cell the walls were too close for comfort. Through the bars on the window, all I could see was a piece of sky. When your range of vision is restricted like that for days on end, a person can become emotionally unstable. I remembered from psychology class how if you kept one rat in a cage and if you let another rat run free, the caged rat generally died before the other rat. I began to think that I was like the caged rat.

The way I saw it, life in a detention cell denied a person human rights. It didn't matter whether you were guilty or innocent.

One day, toward the end of February, the guard escorting me back to my cell from the interrogation room struck up a conversation.

"I'll finally be getting out of this place the end of next month," he began. "I've been here since 1961. I've reached retirement age, so I'll be leaving here ahead of you, Mr. Ezoe."

Together we got in the elevator. When we alighted at the fourth floor, through the window I could see a red neon sign in the distance.

"Red lights are pretty, aren't they," I remarked.

"That's a a pachinko parlor," the guard responded. "Everyone in here always longs to see bright colored lights. Go ahead, take your time. I'll wait while you look."

He was very kind. I stood there gazing at the red neon sign for some time. It was a feast for my tired eyes.

From this guard I learned that unmarried guards lived in a dormitory on the grounds of the detention center; if guards were married, they lived in government housing on the site. Family members carried passes to enter and exit the site, and children commuted to school from the center.

The job of a guard—monitoring detained suspects and convicted criminals—was a monotonous one performed in a place with no heat or air-conditioning. And like their charges, they had to eat their lunches every day in silence. Being a guard was no easy business, either.

Staring Contests

From the time I was a young married man, whenever my wife and I had an argument, she would give me the silent treatment. Even if I said something conciliatory in an attempt to pacify her, she would remain silent and never change her opinion in the matter. As the years went by, she became all the stronger for it, and I had a hard time suppressing my feelings. If we argued in the morning, I would be so upset throughout the long train trip from Zushi to Tokyo that I would find myself unable to concentrate on reading the morning papers.

The relationship between Prosecutor Kamigaki and me was very similar: here, too, the one who remained silent had the upper hand. Faced with no response whatsoever to his questions, Kamigaki must have found this suspect sitting there before him maddening. As the interrogations proceeded, I came to understand what may have lurked behind his outbursts.

On this particular day, we sat glaring at each other. After our silence had gone on for some time, Kamigaki sought to break the deadlock. "Let's just chew the fat a bit," he said, and he instructed his assistant to make me "a fine cup of tea."

He then addressed me in a sedate tone: "I've got a son who graduates from high school this year, who's studying for his college entrance exams. I'd like to give him some words of encouragement from time to time, but ever since I became involved in your case, I haven't gotten home before midnight even once. I live far away, in Urawa, and every day I have to leave home by seven A.M. For two months now I haven't had a chance to talk to my son the way a parent should. You've got a daughter who's studying for her entrance exams, too, don't you? It's painful for both of us not to be there for them."

I involuntarily found myself moved by what he was saying, almost to the point of tears. I suddenly felt a rapport with him. We drank our tea and the atmosphere was no longer so tense.

"Shall we get back to the subject at hand, then?" he said. "When you provided the shares, you were expecting something in return, weren't you?"

"As I've told you any number of times, I had no intent of that sort in mind."

When I resumed my silence at that point, Kamigaki's irritation returned and he started to shout. He tried different ways to get me to open up, but I refused to say anything. By this time he might have been tired: he just stood in silence and stared directly into my eyes. I stared back into his.

I suddenly recalled the game I played as a child where two people try to outstare each other. Unlike the game, which usually ends in one person breaking into laughter, outstaring Kamigaki left a bad aftertaste. A strange sensation came over me, but the staring contest continued.

At lunch time, the guard came to escort me back to my cell. In the intervening hour before the afternoon interrogation began again, both the prosecutor and I managed to cool down a bit. The afternoon session started with Kamigaki once more trying to chat.

"You know, the food you eat in your cell and the food I eat in the dining hall are prepared in the same kitchen. So what we eat is quite similar. Pretty bad, isn't it?"

Normally I eat very plain food. When I was still working, I would often have a meal of instant noodles while conducting a meeting with employees, so I actually thought the food in the detention center was fairly tasty. I didn't say this, though.

In my notes, I made almost no record about the food I was served in detention, but this is what I recall:

Breakfasts often consisted of hot rice and a raw egg or *natto* (fermented beans). I'm very fond of rice with raw egg, and I would take the egg and mix it into the rice, adding the *wakame* seaweed-flavored miso soup as a sub-stitute for soy sauce. I thought it was delicious. Saturday breakfasts were generally Western-style. The standard fare was a heated soft bun, butter and jam, and a small carton of milk. This was almost the same as what I normally ate for breakfast at home.

Lunch would typically be hot rice mixed with barley and ramen noo-dles. The amount was always sufficient. I prefer my food relatively bland—as do most people who, like me, hail from the Osaka area, so I found the detention center food over-heavily flavored and too salty. When we were served *soba* (buckwheat) noodles, I would water down the broth by mixing it with the water in which the noodles had been boiled, which I requested. When we had ramen, I would water that down, too. In the beginning they didn't give me enough time to eat everything, but then I found out it was possible to ask for additional time.

The evening meal was often pork miso soup containing different ingre-dients. They would also often serve two of my favorite fish dishes: salt-grilled mackerel pike and salmon. We received them still warm, and they were very good. We also often had Chinese spicy tofu (bean curd) and Indian curry. The latter was savory and delicious.

About once a week, for dessert they would give us *shiruko*, a sweet por-ridge of azuki beans served with a *mochi* rice cake. One of my attorneys told me since no alcohol is allowed in the detention center, many inmates have cravings for sweets instead. The *shiruko* was sweet and delicious.

My only difficulty with the food was the absence of raw vegetables, which I was very fond of, especially with salad dressing. We weren't served anything unless it had been cooked. Otherwise, both in terms of quantity and quality, the food was quite satisfactory. They must have had an excel-lent dietitian and cook.

Two of my defense counsels, Shozaburo Ishida and Masanori Ono, were also in charge of the Lockheed scandal, and they told me that from the day former Prime Minister Kakuei Tanaka was arrested, the food budget at the Tokyo Detention Center substantially increased.

I Finally Give in and Sign

Picking up where I left off:

The prosecutor's interrogations reached an impasse. Kamigaki would try to get me to admit I had passed bribes. I would deny my actions had constituted bribery. He would start shouting. I would go silent. He would go silent. Then we would just stare at each other, seemingly forever.

When the conversation turned casual, Kamigaki would again tell me how he was being reprimanded by headquarters for not getting me to sign a written statement. The one who was especially annoyed by his "dawdling" was Yusuke Yoshinaga, who, according to Kamigaki, had a reputation around the Public Prosecutors Office for being a frightening boss.

"C'mon, consider my position in all this," the prosecutor pleaded with me. "I don't get home every night till after midnight. I'm here early every morning. Assistant officers get paid overtime, but not us prosecutors. The assistants make more than me!"

On another occasion he would adopt a different tactic:

"You know, if you keep refusing to cooperate, your detention will just drag out longer and longer. It won't be easy to take, you know. You'll be taken from here to the courthouse every week tied up with rope. The charge against you is just simple bribe-passing, not bribery to solicit favors from NTT. What's more, no money was involved, only shares of stock. I'll put plenty of what you're contending into the statement so you'll have ample chance of making an argument for yourself in court. You'll be convicted but with a suspended sentence. Cooperate with me in drawing up a statement, and I'll see that you get out on bail early. Headquarters has already agreed to that."

Once, he brought up the American court system:

"In the U.S., court trials are like battlefields. In Japan, courts are places where apologies are made. You admit what you've done, you say you're sorry, and you're granted extenuating circumstances. Your attorneys are likely telling you not to sign any statement that goes against the truth, but if you stick to that stance, you'll only see a lousy outcome. Think of me as your attorney. Trust what I say."

I had read in the newspapers and seen on television how a defendant in a trial was granted extenuating circumstances and got a suspended sentence because he admitted his guilt and apologized for what he had done, so I allowed what Kamigaki was saying was probably true. In my case, though, I wasn't about to admit having committed an offense I hadn't committed, so I stuck to my denials. That brought on further threats: "You keep to an attitude like this and headquarters will put out a directive to have Ida arrested. You can bet on it."

I realized only too well if I continued to deny any wrongdoing forever, the special investigators indeed might have no choice but to arrest Ida. Hearing threats to that effect yet again, I began to feel pangs of anxiety.

Toshihiko Sasagawa, Recruit's legal counsel in its Osaka office, visited me with the following advice: "Manual laborers, gangsters, and people like that can endure a long detention, but people who are high-strung like you, Mr. Ezoe, take a long time to return to themselves after being detained for a long period. From what I see in the press, even if you're found guilty, the crime wouldn't be very serious: you would likely get a suspended sentence. Your lawyers appear to lean toward the side of human rights and may be telling you not to sign anything contrary to the truth, but the outcome in most cases is the same: you'll only come to feel what you did was in vain. You'd be better off signing the statement and getting out on bail as quickly as possible. Make it easy on yourself."

I knew full well that during the Lockheed affair, former Prime Minister Tanaka hadn't signed a single statement yet he was given an unsuspended prison sentence on the basis of statements taken from, among others, his driver (who later committed suicide), his secretary Toshio Enomoto, and Marubeni president Hiro Hiyama.

In my case too, I could be found guilty even without a written statement. Were that to come to pass, I could very well, as Sasagawa suggested, end up feeling that my staunch denials were all in vain.

In the end, on March 4, no longer able to resist for fear of Ida's arrest, I signed my name to the written statement the prosecutor prepared. As a result, I was indicted on charges of having passed bribes to Shikiba and Hasegawa.

Fresh Arrest Warrant

Two days after my indictment, on March 6, the guard came to my cell after dinner and unlocked the door. I was taken from Kosuge to the Public Prosecutors Office in nearby Adachi ward, where I was served a fresh arrest warrant.

The warrant had Shinto's name on it. I was stunned.

I later speculated that the special investigators wanted to arrest Shinto from the outset as he was a man of great prominence. However, since he denied all wrongdoing and Kozo Murata, his secretary, steadfastly maintained he acted completely at his own discretion, they were unable to make an arrest. With no other alternative, they arrested Shikiba and Hasegawa in order to buy time until they could arrest Shinto. Their strategy was probably to arrest Shinto and Murata subsequently and achieve written statements from them.

At 8:54 P.M. I was taken back to the interrogation room at Kosuge and subjected to further questioning from Kamigaki, who this time railed at me angrily. Once again, I denied what he was accusing me of and fell silent.

I was again made to stand facing the wall. My eyes began hurting, the wall took on a yellow tinge, and my legs became painful from standing too long. From time to time, Kamigaki would come close by my side.

"You're a sly devil, you old fox!" he'd yell into my ear. "Always thinking of yourself and never considering my position in all this!"

The outburst made my eardrum hurt, but I endured.

I had signed a written statement concerning Shinto during my voluntary interrogation by Prosecutor Munakata. The gist of that statement was that in providing the shares of Recruit Cosmos stock to Murata, my actual target was Shinto. When I signed it, Munakata had a satisfied look on his face.

"This'll do just fine," he had said.

When I told Kamigaki all this, his comeback was harsh: "There's no connection between Shinto and Murata. That's why we decided to say you phoned Shinto directly. You called him and spoke with him directly."

"I did *not* telephone Shinto."

"Stick with that attitude of yours, and I'll cancel all visits with your attorneys. I'll consider arresting them, too!"

In spite of his threats, I stuck to my denials.

During Hino's next visit, I asked him about the prosecutor's threat to arrest him and my other attorneys.

"Relax!" he reassured me. "In prewar days there was a case of legal counsel getting arrested—that was in connection with the Teijin scandal—but since the war there has never been any instance of an investigative attorney being arrested."

After our long standoff, Kamigaki allowed me to take my seat again.

"I graduated from a regional college," he said in a conciliatory, almost congenial tone of voice, "and I've had to fight hard to get where I am today. These past four months, I've lost a lot of sleep conducting this interrogation. But when you take that attitude of yours, it puts me in a tight corner, headquarters constantly harping at me. After we make an arrest, it's the interrogating prosecutor's job to get a written statement that will enable the court to find the defendant guilty. I know you must be having a rough time here, but this is rough on me, too, you know. I'll make the statement vague enough to allow you to fight your case in court. Please, for both our sakes, just sign the statement for now and then take your fight to court. Please!"

He was practically begging me.

At the time, Kamigaki was suffering from severe pain in his lower back. "It's just killing me," he said. "I'd like to go see a doctor, but I can't until I can get a statement out of you. Come on, help me out, please!"

In the face of his words of desperation, I suddenly felt tears run down my cheeks—tears of empathy for the man who was my prosecutor.

"The prosecution decides what sentence to seek at the time of indictment. In your case, neither did Recruit receive any favors from NTT, nor did NTT suffer any damages. This is a case with no victim. We can ask for a light sentence at the time of your indictment, and the sentence we ask for is the same as what the prosecutor will ask for in court when making his closing argument. If you don't believe me, ask Hino. This is a case involving shares of stock, not money. I'll include your side of what happened in the statement, and headquarters has already agreed to let you out on bail quickly. Sign it. Please."

After all the scare tactics he used on me, here was Kamigaki talking to me as though it was coming straight from his heart. I suddenly found myself in a quandary as to what to do.

Prosecutor Munakata Comes to See Me

On March 13, during the afternoon interrogation session, Kamigaki announced that Prosecutor Munakata would be coming to see me that evening.

"It's rare for Mr. Munakata to come here," he said, then added, "While he's here, I'll leave the room." He spoke of Munakata, who was his superior, with deference of a kind I had not seen in him before.

As promised, when word came that Munakata had arrived, Kamigaki left the interrogation room. His assistant stayed behind until Munakata's assistant arrived.

A few moments later, Munakata appeared.

"We managed to get here giving the media the slip. I'd like you to cooperate in our investigation of Shinto. No harm will come your way, I promise."

"You've already taken a statement from me at the Shiba Grand Plaza," I replied. "I testified that when I handed over the shares to Murata, I had Shinto in mind; it was not just a transfer to Murata. Didn't you tell me that would be sufficient?"

"That's true, but now Murata's saying he did everything on his own and Shinto's saying he didn't know anything. We can't make a connection between the two of them, which is why I'm here—with a request that you cooperate with us."

"I merely spoke with Murata on the phone. I don't know anything about what may or may not be between him and Shinto."

"Won't you just please cooperate with us in this?"

Munakata then proceeded to ask me a few questions about NTT, before shifting the topic to the transfer of shares to Vice Labor Minister Kato. "If you aren't including Kato in your list of share recipients, you'll have to prove nothing took place between you."

"Didn't you yourself say it's impossible to give 'proof of the devil'?"

"All along Tatsumi has said he acted under instructions from you."

All I could think, upon hearing this, was that Munakata was lying.

Masao Tatsumi had joined Recruit in its third year, so he was practically a founding member. We eventually parted ways over a minor disagreement, and he was the only managing director whom I ever developed a rift with.

At the time, Recruit was one of four major magazine publishers—the others being Diamond-Big, Disco, and Mainichi Communications—which, at the request of the Central Employment Measures Council, were exercising voluntary restraint regarding the timing of the distribution of job-information magazines to university students. When Mainichi Communications started to distribute its magazines before the agreed-upon schedule, Eiko Kono, Recruit managing director of advertising operations, went to Tatsumi, who was in charge of business operations, and argued that if Mainichi Communications was distributing its magazines early, so should Recruit. Tatsumi then made the decision that Recruit distribute its magazines before the agreed-upon date as well.

I was subsequently summoned by the presidents of Diamond-Big and Disco, who vehemently lodged the complaint that Recruit, the industry leader, had broken the self-regulatory agreement entered upon. They demanded that Recruit take responsibility for its actions by transferring Tatsumi to another post.

After mulling the issue at length, I called a meeting of the board of directors. There, after debating the matter for quite some time, we ultimately decided that, with due respect to Tatsumi, it would be best to transfer him to Cosmos Life, a Recruit affiliate, in the position of company president.

The matter wasn't so easily laid to rest, however. At issue was a requirement calling for Tatsumi to return his Recruit shares in tandem with his transfer to his new position. Due to a misunderstanding on the part of the person in charge of company stock, the situation surrounding reversion of his shares created bad feelings between Tatsumi and Recruit. In the end we had our legal counsel, Seiji Shimodaira, intervene, and a settlement was reached whereby Recruit would provide Tatsumi with a deposit until other retiring employees sold off their shareholdings. A memorandum of agreement was signed, but the rift between Tatsumi and myself remained at the time the events in question had taken place.

Under such circumstances, there was no way I could have chosen Tatsumi to act as my messenger in the transfer of Recruit Cosmos's shares.

"I didn't give Tatsumi instructions of any kind," I told the prosecutor. "I know Kato well. I hosted a party to celebrate his appointment to the vice-ministerial post, and he once took me out to dinner in Akasaka. If I were going to give him shares of stock, I'd telephone him directly."

Earlier, when Kenzaburo Hara was serving as Labor Minister, Kato was his secretary, and he had asked me to offer support to Hara, contending that Hara was destined to become speaker of the House of Representatives. In those days I had already made a lot of money from Recruit Cosmos's initial public offering, and while the amount being requested of me was substantial (the *Asahi* article dated February 10, 1989, described it as "absurdly large"), I couldn't refuse and purchased tickets to a fundraising event for Hara. It was to thank me that Kato had treated me to dinner. That was back in 1986.

I explained all this to Munakata. The prosecutor was not pleased. "If you drag this out, it'll invite political chaos," he argued. "The Prosecutors Office has decided to bring this investigation to a close quickly, so I'm asking for you to cooperate with us. The longer you hold out, the longer the media will keep reporting on this affair, and the wider the scandal will spread. The LDP—the party you support—will weaken and the political situation in this country will become unstable. If reports about politicians persist, we'll have no choice but to prepare cases against them. That's the way things work."

"Why, just because something gets reported in the press, do you have to make a case against someone?"

"What the papers write is public opinion. If the Special Investigation Department fails to bring a case against someone for what's written up in the press, it loses its public esteem."

All along I imagined the reason new reports about my political donations kept appearing in the press was because the Public Prosecutors Office was making announcements to reporters at their regular meetings based on the materials they seized, or because Munakata or Kamigaki was leaking information bit by bit. Now, though, from the discomfort discernible in Munakata, I had the impression it was the special investigators who were actually in a bind because they were under pressure from the media.

"Holding out like this won't do you any good, you know," the prosecutor went on. "Please, cooperate with us in preparing a statement. We know very well that Recruit didn't receive any favors from Shinto. We'll make sure no harm comes your way from all this."

With that Munakata left the room. No sooner was he gone than Kamigaki returned.

"What did you say? Prosecutor Munakata said he won't let any harm come your way, didn't he? You could be out of here right away. Please, out of respect for Munakata, cooperate with us in drawing up a statement."

On March 16, when I entered the interrogation room the prosecutor was unusually congenial.

"I've got some good news for you. Your daughter got into the college of her choice."

"How do you know that?"

"I wanted to do something that would cheer you up, so I did some checking around."

I was flabbergasted to think investigators would go that far.

"Your daughter really persevered, didn't she, getting into the college of her choice despite her father being written up like a major criminal. I'm very happy for her. So what do you say? Isn't it about time we wrapped up this case?"

Kamigaki's tone was so friendly, so completely different from before, that I was overcome by mixed emotions: joy and chagrin. I bit my lip.

Two days later, my attorney brought a letter from my daughter informing me of her good news. He held it up to the clear acrylic panel that separated us in the visitation room, to let me read it. Tears welled up in my eyes.

When I finished reading the letter, he asked me how the interrogation was going.

"Is the prosecutor still making you stand up?"

"Lately I've been allowed to stay seated."

"What's he asking you about now?"

"The connection between myself and Shinto."

On my way back to my cell I noticed the cherry tree in the inner courtyard was beginning to blossom. Seeing this unexpected sign of spring amid the concrete surroundings of the detention center, I felt lighthearted in a way I hadn't felt in a long time.

Suspects under arrest aren't allowed to write or receive letters, but when I arrived back from the visitation room to the interrogation room, Kamigaki announced he had received permission from his higher-ups to suspend part of the restrictions imposed on me.

"Go back to your cell and write your daughter a letter," he suggested, handing me some paper to write on.

I was very grateful for this special consideration on his part. I returned to my cell and wrote letters to my daughters, my wife, and my cousin.

My Relationship with NTT's Shinto

The main point of dispute in my interrogations relating to NTT was whether I had actually approached Shinto directly about the Recruit Cosmos shares, and not gone through Murata, his secretary. From the outset, during voluntary questioning, I said I approached Murata with Shinto in mind but that I had not directly phoned Shinto to discuss the matter with him.

I was one of the six members of the "Shinto School," the name given to a group of Shinto supporters, all owners of their own enterprises. We would hold regular meetings at a restaurant in Shimbashi, and it was at one such gathering that something Shinto said made a particularly strong impression on me.

The year was 1981, and in line with the privatization initiative of Yasuhiro Nakasone, it was decided Nippon Telegraph and Telephone Public Corporation would be privatized. Hisashi Shinto, then chairman of Ishikawajima-Harima Heavy Industries, was chosen to serve as the public entity's president in the run-up to its privatization.

"Mr. Nakasone told me I could bring others from Ishikawajima-Harima along with me, but I knew that if I did that, people would think we were acting like an occupation army and the privatization process wouldn't go well. So I told Mr. Nakasone I'd come alone. I'm terrible with money management, though, so in the end I decided to bring along just one person, Kozo Murata, who had long managed my finances. But once we were at

NTT, a lot of politicians' secretaries started coming to Murata for help in getting NTT's sibling companies—telephone exchange manufacturers and the like—to purchase tickets to their fundraising events. It was a practice that had been around for a long time."

Shinto paused for a moment and then continued: "I told Murata, 'Don't do it.' But if it was absolutely impossible to decline, then I told him to take the money out of my personal funds. If we became indebted to our sibling business partners, cost reductions would be impossible."

Shinto's salary as president of NTT wasn't all that large—about the same level as a postal vice-minister. I was moved by what he said, and this was my motivation for transferring shares in Recruit Cosmos on to Murata. So long as I let Murata know what I was doing, I thought it didn't matter whether or not that information was passed on to Shinto. I telephoned Murata and left all the details to Hiroshi Kobayashi at First Finance.

When news of the share transfer broke on December 14, 1988, Shinto, at that time chairman of NTT, immediately stepped down, stating that he had entrusted his bankbooks entirely to his secretary Murata. When I heard that, I made the conclusion that Murata must have handled the shares at his own discretion. I became all the more convinced of this each time Kamigaki repeated that the Prosecutors Office wasn't able to make any connection between Shinto and Murata.

The prosecutors seemed to be having difficulty building a case against Shinto in spite of having arrested him, for they kept pressing me to change my story and say I phoned Shinto directly and talked to him about the shares. When I refused repeatedly, insisting that I had talked with Murata—not Shinto—Kamigaki flushed with anger.

"It won't hold water if it's Murata!" he shouted.

Kamigaki then talked about documents prosecutors had confiscated from my office showing that I had entertained Shinto at a restaurant. "You wanted favors from him, I bet."

I responded that I had once told Shikiba that Recruit, being a Type II telecommunications carrier, which was not allowed to have its own circuits, had purchased circuits from NTT and was then selling them cheaper than NTT, and that must have irked NTT. Shikiba had reassured me that the matter was of no concern to NTT, and he suggested that I meet with

Shinto to confirm this was the case. This was the occasion I had dinner with Shinto, and Shikiba was present there too.

I had arrived at the restaurant first, and took my seat in the corner of the private room I had reserved. When Shinto arrived, I offered him the place of honor at the table.

"No, no," he said. "Recruit is NTT's customer. It's you, Mr. Ezoe, who should sit in the place of honor."

"You being my senior, that would be disrespectful to you," I said. "Please, sir, please take the seat of honor."

He was persistent, however. "Even when I was at Ishikawajima-Harima, I never sat in the place of honor. In fact, I was never entertained by any of the steelmaker or other companies that we bought from."

At Recruit too, I had banned entertaining prospective clients in order to get work from them. On the contrary, I had always encouraged my employees to become the kind of sales personnel that our clients would want to entertain. So I felt an affinity to Shinto's way of thinking.

In the end, the proprietress persuaded Shinto to take the position of honor, and when Shikiba arrived, we proceeded to have our meal.

Shinto said he had heard about my concerns. "You know, Mr. Ezoe," he began, "we're a private company now. For many years we just rested on our laurels as the only carrier in the business; but today, unless we see the emergence of new competitors, our employees won't undergo a change of mentality; that'll happen only when they're faced with pressure from outside. The existence of competition will drive them to start focusing on cost cutting; so please, by all means, give us all the competition you can."

When we were through eating, Shinto excused himself. "I'm afraid I have to change my clothing to attend the funeral of an employee," he said. "When I was at Ishikawajima-Harima, if an employee lost his life while on the job, I would always stop whatever I was doing and attend his funeral. At NTT before I arrived, if an employee died on the job, not even the branch manager went to his funeral, let alone the president. I thought this was disrespectful to the deceased, and once I started attending funeral services, branch managers and other management staff started doing the same."

With that, he had changed his apparel and took his leave.

Kamigaki, hearing this explanation, showed no interest whatsoever.

Brought Down to My Knees

At 6:18 P.M., on March 18, no sooner had my nightly interrogation begun than Kamigaki suddenly left the room. After twenty minutes he came back, flinging the door open and then slamming it behind him. I got the feeling this wasn't going to be our usual *tête-à-tête*.

The prosecutor walked straight to my side.

"You lied to me!" he bellowed into my ear. "Shinto just confessed and said you phoned him directly. All this time you've been lying to me! In all my years, I've never dealt with a liar like you!"

No sooner were the words out of his mouth than he gave my chair a powerful kick. The impact sent the chair reeling sideways, practically propelling me out of it. Stopped by none other than the prosecutor himself, who with great agility moved around to the opposite side to "catch" me, I had the feeling he had planned the whole thing.

"Stand up!" he roared. "Over there, by the window!" I did as he ordered and stood by the window, putting us face to face.

"Get down on your knees and beg for forgiveness!"

He was seething to the point that I thought he was going to punch me in the face. Too frightened to resist, I got down on my knees and, just as he demanded, placed the palms of my hands down on the floor in front of me, bowed my head until it was practically touching the floor, and asked to be forgiven. The longer I maintained that posture, the more I began to feel like he had me under mind control.

"You phoned Shinto—you've just forgotten. Do you remember now? Once it comes back to you, I'll let you return to your seat."

Everything I had said up until then had been true. But now, gripped with fear, I was, sad to say, beside myself. "Yes, now I remember," I mumbled in a tiny voice.

At that point Kamigaki began dictating a statement for the assistant officer to write down.

> *I apologize deeply for having lied to the prosecutor. I was lying when I said that I had never contacted Mr. Shinto directly and that I gave the shares to Mr. Murata.*

No longer having the will to resist, I signed the statement as I was told. When I finished, the prosecutor looked pleased.

"That's what I wanted," he said half to himself, and with the statement in hand he rushed out of the room.

He was gone nearly two hours. When he finally came back, he looked quite pleased with himself.

"OK, that's it for today. You can leave."

The whole experience was like a nightmare. When I was taken back to my cell, it seemed colder and starker than usual.

After I was released, as I pored over my notebooks from my incarceration alongside related newspaper articles from the same days, my eyes came to a halt on a headline in an evening edition of the *Mainichi*: "Ezoe Made Share Offer Directly to Shinto. Bribe-taking Case Now Sure to Stand."

The article reported this information had come to light in the course of the investigation and from testimony made by parties involved in the case. The date it appeared, however, was March 14—four days *before* I had been made to beg for forgiveness and sign the prosecutor's statement. The whole scenario had been cooked up by the prosecutors!

Could Shinto really have signed a statement saying I had phoned him? This was a doubt that continued to gnaw at me from that time forward.

After the trial relating to the "NTT route" got under way, Shinto's statement prepared the same day I had been forced to beg for forgiveness was made public. In it Shinto testified that he "had heard [about the shares] from Murata, my secretary, who had been contacted by Ezoe." There was nothing whatsoever to the effect that I had phoned him directly.

My attorneys, after my release, believed that this is probably what happened: Kamigaki told me Shinto had sworn that I had called him as a way of getting me to sign my statement, and that Shinto in turn had been told that I had signed a statement to that effect as a way of getting him to confess. Conducting an investigation in this way is illegal, they said, but there are times when a prosecutor, frustrated at not being able to get a statement out of the accused, resorted to such tactics.

It was also after my release that I learned that Murata, during his twenty days in detention, had not signed a single statement. My lawyers said it was practically unheard of, except perhaps in cases involving public security, for prosecutors to arrest someone and not get even a single statement out of him. It became clear to me just why Shinto placed so much trust in Murata.

After his indictment, Shinto insisted on his innocence and chose to fight his case in court.

Since Murata had not signed any written statements, his testimony in court would stand as evidence. If he were to take the witness stand and testify that he had done everything at his own discretion, Shinto could be found innocent—an outcome the prosecution feared. I learned from Shinto's defense counsel that Murata did not appear at Shinto's trial.

The possibility existed that the statement I had signed, admitting I had called Shinto directly, could be used as evidence to find Shinto guilty—and this weighed heavily on my mind. When I appeared as a witness at his trial, I greeted Shinto with a deep bow, but I wasn't able to look him straight in the eyes.

The Media and the Special Investigators

In the course of my interrogation, Kamigaki seemed to be an avid reader of the daily reports in the press. While the prosecutors provided information to the media, I had the feeling they themselves were vulnerable to what and how the press reported.

In a casual moment, I once asked Kamigaki why he so often asked me things based on what was in the media. His response was that there are at most only about thirty special investigators, whereas the number of reporters working for the press, TV stations, weekly magazines, and the like was twenty or thirty times more.

"We don't have enough people. We don't have the means to go looking for crimes—and even if we did, we wouldn't find any. The only option we have is to monitor various suspicious activities reported by the media, choose the ones where we think we can make an arrest, and build a case against them. In Recruit's case, we were been able to build a case because the media kept reporting on it."

So the media act like an investigator, and the prosecutors do the inter-rogating. A structure like this might be good in terms of raising judicial efficiency, but from my experience it seemed that if public prosecutors rely on the media to build their cases, the media had become a "third power."

"You say you don't have enough people, but when you undertake a house search, you're always shown entering a place as a horde," I responded.

"Prosecutors are mixed into the group, but most of the people you see are assistant officers."

"What about the police? There are plenty of them."

"Police officers have limited capability when it comes to investigations. Special investigators don't count on them."

"What about all the district prosecutors found in every prefecture?"

"Special investigators are selected from the most capable of the district prosecutors. It's the special investigators who take charge of cases that dis-trict prosecutors find difficult to prosecute."

"So prosecutors are basically a two-tiered hierarchy?"

"You could look at it that way."

If what Kamigaki was saying was true, then the thirty-odd prosecutors belonging to the Special Investigation Department hold rank over some 2,500 district prosecutors and about 250,000 police officers nationwide. That couldn't be good for the morale of the local prosecutors and police.

For my own experience, I knew that prosecutors with the Special Inves-tigation Department live busy lives. Interrogations go from morning to night, with no breaks on weekends. It's a demanding job, so demanding that if it were a company in the private sector, it would violate Japan's Labor Standards Act; but that act doesn't apply to career officials with this country's central ministries and agencies.

Back at the home office, the prosecutor directing the investigation—in my case, Munakata—and the chief public prosecutor above him reviewed the written statements passed up to them and gave instructions on what kind of statement to take next and from whom.

The interrogating prosecutor who received those instructions must then struggle to get the statement he had been instructed to secure. If the time of detention—forty-eight hours plus twenty days—were drawing short and the suspect continued to deny the charges, the prosecutor was in a bind. To get the statement he needed, sometimes the prosecutor resorted to threats. It was hard on the suspect being threatened, but I wondered if it might actually be harder on the prosecutor who had to make the threats.

I always thought being a public prosecutor, being in the business of exposing all the world's evils, was a laudable profession. Now I understood it was a job that put strain on an individual both physically and mentally. When Kamigaki spoke in an unguarded moment of wanting to quit and become a lawyer, he was probably telling the truth.

Long Detention or Early Release?

In my voluntary interrogation of January 9, I put my signature on a statement Munakata penned stating I had no involvement in passing shares to Kato. I also maintained to Kamigaki that everything was as put forth in that earlier statement. He must have grown weary of trying to corner me, and on March 24, with an air of agitation, he conceded. "OK, if you insist, I'll draw up a statement, in the form of questions and answers, presenting your position."

> *Q: Who chose Takashi Kato to be the recipient of the 3,000 shares, who decided on the number of shares, and who approached Mr. Kato?*
>
> *A: I had no involvement either in the selection of the recipient or in the decision on the number of shares. I also did not instruct anyone working under me to negotiate in the matter. I did not select Mr. Kato; the accusations being made against me are false.*

I signed this statement, too. No sooner had I done this then, to my astonishment, the prosecutor burst into laughter.

"I can't believe you signed this!" he said, gloating. "By signing this denial of any implication, you'll never get out on bail now. You'll stay in detention and go to court from here. The courts have formal authority over releasing suspects on bail, but they won't let anyone out unless the public prosecutor agrees to it. If you don't believe me, ask your attorneys."

"Why won't I be let out on bail?"

"Two reasons: destruction of evidence and fear you'd flee."

"First of all, I wouldn't flee. And second, any evidence there might be has already been seized, so there's nothing to destroy."

"That's the way things operate around here."

I felt like I had been trapped.

"Do you know Osamu Takita, the activist charged with leading that deadly attack on the Ground Self-Defense Forces headquarters way back in 1971?"

"I know his name from the newspapers, yes."

"A sentence was passed down in his case the other day. The guy's been in detention so long, he ended up spending more time in custody than the sentence he was given. When they released him, he said he felt like Rip Van Winkle. What do you think will happen if you stay here and go to court through your entire trial? When it's finally over and you do get out, you'll be cut off from both your company and your family—and all because of the statement you just signed."

I felt an icy tingle down my spine.

After a lengthy silence, Kamigaki finally continued, "Tomorrow's Saturday, so government offices are closed. As a special favor I'll grant you a thirty-minute visit with your attorney. Ask him whether or not what I'm telling you is true. See what he's got to say."

When Hino arrived the following day, March 25, he brought news of his own.

"I was called to the Public Prosecutors Office today and just met with Prosecutor Munakata. He told me if you continue to persist in saying you didn't choose Kato to receive the shares, you'll be kept in detention for a long time. But if you say the statement you signed was wrong and make a new statement to correct it, they'll let you out on bail straight away."

"How long would I be detained?"

"At least until your trial starts. There've been people who've been through that who say they'd have clawed their way through the walls if they could've gotten out that way, it was so tough on them. Munakata told me if you give the court a statement at your first trial session or anytime thereafter, co-signed by your attorney, saying you admit you knew the profits that would be made by the recipients of the shares you offered them constituted a bribe, they'll let you out on bail. Doing so, of course, would render you guilty. But if instead you just stick to your denials, there's a possibility you could be in detention for a very, very long time."

"If I signed the statement Munakata's suggesting, would it still be possible to fight the charges in court?"

"The case against you is a hopeless scenario to begin with. The notion that they could convict with what they have on you is ridiculous. There's ample latitude for you to fight your case in court. If you're let off on even one of the charges against you, you'll get a suspended sentence. I think its well within reason to expect you can get off on one or two of the charges. It's up to you to decide whether you'd rather deny all charges and fight to win a not-guilty verdict resigned to a long detention, or get out on bail quickly and wage your battle in court. I, for one, think it would be better for you to get out on bail as soon as possible."

If I signed the statement, I would be admitting my guilt. If I stayed in detention for years on end, I'd end up a physical and mental wreck. After mulling over my options, I decided to sign the statement, take an early release on bail, and fight my case in court.

A Statement Is Prepared; I Sign

That afternoon Kamigaki entered the interrogation room in an upbeat mood.

"So, did Hino tell you to keep denying all charges and stay here until a sentence is passed?"

When I didn't have a swift response, he went on, "You want to become like Rip Van Winkle?"

Obviously, he knew what I was thinking.

"I'll do as you say," I finally said, which made him visibly pleased.

"So, you've come to see my point. This is a case that has no victims. You'll get off with a suspended sentence. Getting out on bail as early as possible is for your own good."

At that point he began dictating a statement for his assistant to take down:

To be honest, my recollection of the matter surrounding Mr. Kato was extremely vague. The human conscience is a strange thing: while in one corner of my mind I had a memory of having included Mr. Kato in my list [of share recipients], I simultaneously had no clear recollection of how I made contact with him—neither of having approached him directly myself, nor of having had someone contact him for me. But my defensive instincts toward the investigation kicked in and I was unable to admit this. In court, you either win or lose. Feeling that acting as I did would be my way of making amends to those upon whom I brought this trouble, I became firmly set in the conviction that I had not included Mr. Kato in my list and that I had given no instructions, and this conviction heightened to the point that it became my memory as I have it now.

At this point Kamigaki glanced my way. "I think we should retract your previous statement and have you apologize. If you apologize, they'll grant you extenuating circumstances and you'll get a lighter sentence. Now that you're on your way toward getting out on bail, you must be relieved. Let's put your attorney's name in here, too."

Then he picked up where he had left off:

The fact of the matter is, however, that I did list having given 3,000 shares to Mr. Kato. All along I rudely told the prosecutor that if any proof existed that I had done what he suggested, then I was being framed and the accusations against me were false. I wish to take this opportunity both to offer my apologies and to retract what I said earlier.

Kamigaki said putting in my attorney's name would guarantee my release on bail; but after my release one of my attorneys told me that a statement prepared in discussions with Hino would add to its credibility but in court would actually work to my disadvantage.

I could have kicked myself.

The next day, March 26, the prosecutor looked perturbed.

"Headquarters blasted me last night. They said your statement didn't get to the point. We'll have to do it over again."

He wrote up a new statement and had me sign it. Then suddenly he seemed to recall something.

"Oh yeah, Headquarters also chewed me out for not connecting you to Tatsumi."

He then appended the following two sentences:

> *Normally it would have sufficed for me to telephone Mr. Kato, but in fact I did not phone him directly. From the perspective of hindsight, I think what is closest to the truth is that I asked Mr. Tatsumi to intervene.*

I signed the statement.

After my release on bail I read an article about Osamu Takita that had appeared in the *Asahi*. The verdict in his case was passed down on March 2, 1989, and the article, which appeared the following day, stated that Takita was released after spending six-and-a-half years in detention after his arrest. He was quoted as feeling "like Rip Van Winkle."

The article stated that Takita was sentenced to five years in prison. This much of Kamigaki had said was true.

My Third Arrest

The next day, March 27, was my final day of interrogation—or so I thought. I was indicted on a charge of passing a bribe to Shinto. I was promised early release on bail. I looked forward to finally being able to get exercise to my heart's content, and I was excited at the sense of freedom that was soon to be mine again.

"Would it be possible to allow me to have visitors again starting tomorrow?" I asked the prosecutor. "I'd like to read what's in the newspapers."

"I'll see what I can do. I'll ask Headquarters." The tone of his voice was quite friendly.

During the interrogation that evening, though, Kamigaki's attitude underwent an abrupt change.

"I'll be coming as usual tomorrow. Be prepared to be interrogated."
I felt every ounce of strength drain from within me.

The following day, after dinner, the guard came to my cell and ordered me out. I was taken to the Public Prosecutors Office in Adachi ward, where I was shown an arrest warrant—my third—this one on a charge of having passed a bribe to Kunio Takaishi, former vice minister of education.

Although the charge was "simple" bribery, the content of the arrest warrant was far more complicated than the others had been. It consisted of one extremely long sentence entirely lacking in punctuation. Unable to decipher where the subject ended or what the predicate began, I was hard put to understand the reason for my arrest. More importantly, I had never imagined I would be arrested in connection with Takaishi in the first place.

Some news reports, citing the fact that a transfer of shares to Takaishi had occurred, saw the Ministry of Education as having authority over Recruit. But as a publisher of information magazines, Recruit neither had to be authorized by nor needed to report to that ministry. The authorities under whose aegis Recruit operated as a distributor of employment and school-entrance information magazines are the nation's local boards of education, and if any entity served in a "supervisory" role, it is these boards or their presidents. What's more, since information magazines of the kinds published by Recruit, which were targeted at high school students, are distributed free of charge only to those who want them, this was an area over which the Ministry of Education had no authority. And besides, freedom of the press is constitutionally guaranteed.

After my release on bail, I learned that on the very day I was arrested a notice had been distributed by the Elementary and Secondary Education Bureau to the boards of education nationwide on the subject of "improving academic and career counseling in high schools." Its main points were as follows:

1. Counseling and assistance regarding academic advancement or employment to students approaching graduation should be provided

based on sufficient understanding of each student and maintaining close contact with each student's guardian(s).

2. Guidance counselors should deepen their understanding of each student's individual abilities, aptitudes, interests, etc. based on systematic and ongoing observation as well as materials gathered by other means.

3. Guidance counselors should provide students with appropriate and abundant information and materials concerning their future path options. To do so, all teachers should make every effort to cooperate in collecting and providing such information according to their assigned roles and duties.

It was surely no coincidence that a memo of this kind was issued on the exact day I was arrested. At my trial session of January 10, 2001, the director of the Elementary and Secondary Education Bureau, Sumiichi Furumura, gave the following testimony: "Given that questions from the budget committee would reach us after February 10, as bureaucrats we knew we had to take measures of some sort before that. . . . The matter had become a serious social issue. With so much being written in the press, people were beginning to suspect that Recruit was colluding with the schools. That was the impression the press was giving anyway, so we felt it was necessary to detach ourselves once and for all, and that's why we sent out that memo."

I was stunned that the memo was issued the very day of my arrest, but when I heard Furumura's testimony in court, I understood his situation. He needed to issue the memo so that, when questioned in the Diet about Recruit, he would be able to present the instructions the bureau was providing.

That memo, however, was a mere notice sent out to the boards and offices of education at the prefectural level; it wasn't legally binding. I thought it would be impossible for the court to find me guilty based on such a memo.

Change of Interrogators

After returning to the detention center, I was taken again to the interrogation room. However, instead of Kamigaki, I suddenly found myself in the presence of a new interrogator.

"The name's Shoji."

Tamotsu Shoji was a small man with an air of integrity about him. No sooner had he introduced himself than he put two blank sheets of paper down on the table and handed me a pencil.

"You've really caused an uproar, you know," he said in an unexpectedly blunt manner. "I want you to sit there and write down exactly the sort of trouble you created for all the people whose lives you've disrupted. And, I want you to write how much you regret the whole thing. Go ahead, apologize!"

I just sat there.

"You've caused a major uproar! Now write an apology!" he shouted. "What do you think the employees back at Recruit think of you now? Not to mention the new employees? Go ahead! Write a goddamn apology!"

With each word, his fury had escalated, and by this point he was banging his fist on the table.

I just kept silent.

"Write an apology, damn it!" he kept repeating.

I just sat there and didn't say a word.

He had probably had ample experience dealing with people like me. Before long he appeared to have reached the conclusion that further shouting would get him nowhere.

"OK, go back to your cell and think the matter over carefully," he said by way of final warning.

In the news there were occasional reports of how a suspect initially admitted the charges against him but later denied them. I began to think it was common practice in interrogations to intimidate suspects on the day of their arrest.

Mine wasn't the only prosecutor with a habit of raising his voice during interrogations. Whenever I was escorted to the bathroom, I would hear shouting coming from more than half the interrogation rooms.

Of the three prosecutors in charge of my case, only Munakata did not resort to such tactics. In fact, there were occasions when I was unable to make out what he was saying because the sound of his voice was drowned out by the shouting or table-pounding of the prosecutor in the next room.

"That guy's certainly loud, isn't he?" Munakata once remarked. "I've never conducted an interrogation that way."

Munakata's style was to open up to the person he was interrogating as a way of getting him to open up in return. Then, just at the critical juncture he would alter his tone of voice, rattle the suspect, and wrest a statement out of him. This ploy was much more frightening than being bombarded ceaselessly by someone yelling.

One afternoon, the interrogation rooms were unusually quiet. When I asked Prosecutor Shoji about this, he told me the Public Prosecutors Office was showing some people around the facility. I wished they would come every day.

The next day, March 29, beginning with the morning interrogation, Shoji spoke in a normal tone of voice, and taking a different strategy from the previous day, he began with small talk.

"Now that I've been assigned to interrogate you, the press comes to my home every day. They even wait for me at the train station," he told me as if in strict confidence. "Don't worry, though: I won't tell them anything about what goes on here. I have no interest in making a big name for myself as a prosecutor—the job involves too much moving around, plus you have to live in government housing, which is no pleasure. For my next transfer I'm putting in for Kyoto. After that, if they tell me to move again, I plan to quit and become a lawyer. My wife wants to live in Kyoto."

He struck me as a sincere man. At one point he even appeared genuinely interested in my welfare and expressed sympathy toward my situation. "Are you doing OK?" he asked. "You must be quite worried about your children. In big cases like this, the family of the accused has to live with the windows shut and the blinds closed. Your family didn't do anything, but they're victims in this, too."

In the interrogation session that evening, he told me Kano, the man formerly in charge of the Public Employment Service Division at the Ministry of Labor, was released on bail that day after admitting to his crime.

"If you don't admit to any wrongdoing like you've been, you won't get out on bail," he said, as if this were something I didn't already know. "You'll be kept in detention a long time and go to court from here. Think it over carefully and decide which would be to your advantage."

He didn't stop there, however. "You should admit what you did was a crime and bring this investigation to a close swiftly, before you cause any more trouble to the people at Recruit than you've already done. For your own sake, too—that way you could rehabilitate yourself as quickly as possible. In this case, neither you nor Recruit has gained anything. You've been arrested, and then indicted. Once you're indicted, there's no avoiding a guilty verdict. But in your case, even if you're found guilty, you'll get a suspended sentence. Holding out to the very end isn't to your advantage, if you ask me."

He repeated arguments like this over and over again in his attempt to convince me to admit to guilt.

On March 30, at eight A.M., I was taken from my cell and, like before, roped to other suspects heading to the courthouse. As we waited for our bus to arrive, I noticed the cherry trees on the grounds of the detention center were in full bloom, their petals dancing in the gentle breeze. I thought it was the most beautiful display of cherry blossoms I had ever seen in my life, and it gave my heart a lift.

After arriving at the courthouse, I was once again placed in a solitary cell in the basement with no view at all. When I was called into the courtroom, the judge informed me of my right to remain silent and then told me a decision had been made to keep me in detention.

In my interrogation that evening, I was repeatedly grilled as to why Recruit employees frequently entertained the Ministry of Education's senior curriculum specialist. I was told the materials seized by the prosecutors revealed that he was entertained by Recruit at restaurants, bars, and golf.

"We found nearly a hundred instances of entertainment, so it had to be company policy," Shoji pronounced. "And that makes you responsible."

"It wasn't company policy. I don't even know the person who was involved, and I have no knowledge of such entertainment."

"If it wasn't company policy, then press charges against the employee for embezzlement."

"Why don't you arrest the ministry official for bribe-taking?"

"Investigative policy is decided by the higher-ups. We don't get told what policy they set."

I later asked my attorney why the curriculum expert Recruit entertained wasn't arrested. He said he imagined the official made a deal with the public prosecutors whereby they wouldn't arrest him if he cooperated in their investigation. But on that day, my attorney told me the special investigators had secured backup from other district prosecutors and increased the number of prosecutors working on Recruit's connections with politicians. This meant the investigation was far from over—a prospect that propelled me back into gloom.

My stomach continued to bother me, and about once every three days I would go to the infirmary during lunch break for treatment. I was weighed and discovered I had actually gained two kilos.

"Did you normally drink?" the doctor asked me.

"Almost every night."

"You've been making up for the lack of alcohol by eating lots of sweets, I would guess?"

"You're right. Lots of sweet-bean candy and chocolate."

"It's no wonder then. Everyone who comes here who used to drink or smoke on the outside ends up gaining weight. Lack of exercise doesn't help, either."

His words made me wonder how much longer my current situation, this lack of freedom, would continue. It made me all the more depressed.

It was around this time that I noticed the notebook in which I was writing everything down would occasionally be someplace in my cell other than where I had left it. Blue markings were also added every few pages. The authorities were checking what I wrote.

The detention center and the Public Prosecutors Office aren't under the same jurisdiction, but they may in fact be connected. Up until this time, besides writing what had happened during my daily interrogations, I also wrote about private matters, my mental anguish, or things that would likely work against me if read by the prosecutors.

From this day forward, I no longer wrote such things.

A Compromise Is Reached

Even before I was arrested there was wide coverage in the media about my alleged unsavory connections with the Ministry of Education.

Among the materials seized during their search of Recruit, the prosecutors found a document written by Yoshiki Katsuno, head of the business department that handled the promotional advertising of educational institutions, addressed to the Recruit board of directors. The document called for, among other things, Recruit to set high value on its relationship with the Education Ministry.

Elsewhere, in the minutes of a meeting of the board of directors held in Nagoya, prosecutors found a quotation taken from a memo that was prepared by the head of my secretariat, Toshihiro Ono. It quoted me as saying that Recruit's work was inseparable from educational administration and that Recruit should set high value on its relationship with the Ministry of Education. I also said if Recruit were requested by the ministry to have someone serve on a ministry committee, we should acquiesce and have someone in a managerial position fill the post.

The special investigators appear to have concluded on the basis of this that they could build a case on the grounds that Recruit sought to get on close terms with the Ministry of Education out of a desire to garner favorable treatment.

"Recruit provides information on employment opportunities and education," I told Prosecutor Shoji. "The magazine *Career Guidance* is distributed free to high schools and *College Management* is distributed free to universities. While it's true that people from the Ministry of Education are occasionally asked to contribute articles to both publications, Recruit's operations neither have to be approved by the ministry, nor does the company report to it. I believed, though, that as far as possible operations involving advertising by educational institutions should fall in line with ministry guidelines."

"Then why did your employees need to entertain the ministry and accept an appointment on its committee? The reason you passed shares to Takaishi was because Recruit wanted to maintain a cozy relationship with the ministry, wasn't it."

"Having an employee serve as a committee member was something the ministry requested. As for the transfer of shares, I'd known Mr. Takaishi a long time and he'd decided to run for a seat in the Lower House. The shares were my way of supporting him."

"Recruit receives student rosters from high school teachers, doesn't it?"

"Some high school students want to continue on to college while others want to get a job after graduation. The majority of schools have a mixture of both, and in order not to discriminate between those who want to continue their education and those who want to work, the schools have their guidance counselors conduct a student questionnaire. Based on this, Recruit mails the appropriate information magazine—on education or employment—to their homes."

Shoji, likely having no further rebuttal, decided to launch his assault in a different direction. He began insinuating that the motivation behind my passing shares to Takaishi was to express my appreciation for being appointed to the Curriculum Council.

"Your becoming a member of the Ministry of Education's Curriculum Council would make Recruit appear trustworthy in the public's eye. It would also be a feather in your cap."

The fact of the matter, however, was that the ministry official in charge of the council had come to Recruit and presented its request through my secretary, Ono. I had turned it down. Takaishi then telephoned me and asked me to reconsider.

"I told him I was a complete outsider when it came to elementary and secondary school education, and said I'd be of no use to them."

Takaishi was persistent. He asked me to accept, even if I never attended any meetings. I finally acquiesced.

The Curriculum Council was chaired by Kenichi Fukui, winner of the Nobel Prize in chemistry. Among the council members were such celebrities as Aiko Sato, a highly prolific author; Ryosuke Hatanaka, opera singer and professor at Tokyo National University of Fine Arts and Music (now Tokyo University of the Arts); and Wakako Hironaka, a well-known commentator on educational, social, and cultural issues.

At the council's very first meeting, Fukui opened with the following remarks: "I'm not an expert in education. My specialty is chemistry, and chemistry is the only thing I know. I ask that you offer me your guidance and advice concerning what we can do to improve education in our schools."

Hatanaka was the first to speak up: "In elementary and secondary education, cultivating an appreciation of culture and the arts is very important, as is physical education. But once students reach high school, music and physical education become electives, and teachers in those areas are made to feel as though their jobs are somehow less important than those of their peers. I'd like to see this situation changed."

"I agree," I said. "In the United States kids in junior high and high school actively participate in sports, music, and other club activities, and having been a YMCA or Boy Scout leader works in their favor when they apply to college. It's really only after they get to university that they devote themselves to studying."

As the room remained silent for some time, I decided to continue: "Here in Japan, the required curriculum at agricultural and commercial high schools is no different from at regular high schools; guidance counselors at both recommend to their students that they go on to college. I find this very strange. If that's the case, then what's the point of having these schools?"

The next day I was paid a visit by someone from the Ministry of Education's Elementary and Secondary Education Bureau. "The statement you made yesterday drew a very angry response from groups representing the nation's principals of agricultural and commercial high schools," he said. "We'd appreciate your understanding of the situation and not saying anything to fuel dissension."

He then proceeded to lecture me for nearly an hour, during which I was reminded of the strength of the Japan Teachers Union. It was clear that the ministry was in a position of weakness in dealing with the educational institutions under its supervision. There was definitely something wrong with this picture.

At the subsequent council meeting, I told the members about my own educational experiences: "When I was in high school, I took a class in German taught by a native speaker. Later, the first time I went to Dusseldorf, when I got in a taxicab and told the driver in my halting German where I wanted to go, he looked back at me and said, 'You learned German from a German, didn't you?' From my own experience, I think we should consider hiring Americans to teach English conversation in our high schools. That would largely do away with the need for college students to go to English conversation schools in addition to attending their college classes."

The following day I was visited again by someone from the ministry: "If we hired Americans, our own teachers of English would rebel," he said. "These statements of yours cause us a lot of trouble, you know."

Once again I was subjected to a lecture that went on for almost an hour. As a result, I decided to absent myself from most council meetings.

I related all this to Prosecutor Shoji, but he was unimpressed. In the end, I succumbed to his tenacious probing of my intentions, to the point that when he prepared a statement saying I had become a member of the Curriculum Council in order to burnish my reputation—and by extension, Recruit's—I signed it.

Besides my position on the Curriculum Council, I also accepted an invitation from Takaishi to join the ministry's University Council. The council was newly formed in response to a report issued by the Nakasone administration's Ad Hoc Council on Education. It was chaired by Tadao Ishikawa, president of Keio University. Other newly appointed members included: Soshitsu Sen, grand master of the Urasenke School of tea ceremony; Jiro Kawake of Oji Paper Company; Jiro Ushio of Ushio Incorporated; and Ken Moroi of Chichibu Cement. Only Ishikawa was an expert in university education. This led me to think the government preferred to put well-known people on its councils rather than specialists because the former are probably more easily swayed to act in ways reflecting the government's intentions.

I have long had an interest in reforming Japan's universities. In the days when Eiji Toyoda was president of Toyota, at the suggestion of Isao Amagi, an advisor to the Ministry of Education and an authority on higher education, Toyota and Recruit together funded the establishment of the Institute of Higher Education (now, the Institute for Development of Higher Education), a foundation chaired by Amagi. The institute had its offices in Recruit's former headquarters building. Directors, besides myself, included Ikuo Amano, a professor at the University of Tokyo, and Ryoichi Kuroha, a former member of the editorial committee at Nikkei. Higher education in Japan lags behind education in the West, and I had my own views on reform. So when I was asked by Takaishi to join the University Council, I accepted.

Shoji heard me out and made no attempt to probe any further.

At the time I sold the Recruit Cosmos shares to him, Takaishi was returning to his hometown, Fukuoka, every weekend to put together a support group in preparation for running for a seat in the Diet. Though faced with a bribery charge, he was confident of his innocence and decided to run in the Lower House elections taking place before his trial began. The Education Ministry was supporting his candidacy from behind the scenes. This was only natural given that bills relating to the ministry had a greater chance of passage when former ministry bureaucrats were in the Diet, especially when they were on or even chairing an educational subcommittee. Ministry officials would stay in contact with such politicians and make their "requests" known.

I had joined Takaishi for dinner or a round of golf perhaps two or three times a year. Shoji questioned me about one particular occasion when we dined together at a restaurant in Asakusa in the company of, among others, Kakuji Yanagawa, a member of the House of Councillors who originally headed the Ministry of Education's Physical Education Bureau. Shoji wanted to know who was present and what was talked about, but as the dinner in question took place more than ten years earlier, all I could reply was that I didn't remember.

From the time I was young, on weekdays I never had dinner at home. I was always out with other people. Saturdays I would work, and Sundays I played golf. The only time I had dinner with my wife and children was on Sundays. Many of my dinner engagements had no specific purpose other than getting to know someone better. Shoji, though, seemed to think there had to be a purpose behind every such encounter. If I footed the bill, it constituted entertainment—and entertainment, he contended, equated to asking the party I entertained to do something for me in return. He thus kept asking me what purpose was behind each meal I had ever had with Takaishi.

The same was true of our weekend golf outings. Shoji kept asking me what objective I had in mind, and I kept replying that Takaishi and I merely played golf together; there was nothing more to it. But again, if I said I paid the golfing fee, the prosecutor would come back and say, "So it was entertainment!" And he alleged that if it was entertainment, there must be some motive behind it. From the way he harped on this, it was apparent we held completely different views on such matters, likely attributable to the difference in our situations in life. It was a gap that was not to be easily bridged.

Out of curiosity, I later asked my defense counsel about this. I was told that when prosecutors go golfing, they always split the bill, and when they go drinking together, it's generally to a place they all know well and everyone pays his own way.

On April 15, three days before I was scheduled to be indicted, Shoji spoke to me in an atypically calm tone of voice. Unable to get a statement out of me, he seemed to be cornered. Our interrogation sessions were going on until after ten every night. This was well after the nine P.M. lights-out at the detention center.

"When you're in detention for a long time, stuck in a cramped cell by yourself with nothing to do, it can make a person go crazy. When I was questioning a guy in Otsu accused of murdering his father, he kept denying any intent to kill and was detained for quite a long time. Eventually he received a suspended sentence and was released, but two days later he committed suicide. If he'd listened to me, admitted his intent to kill, and then served some time in prison, he'd have been rehabilitated while serving out his sentence and then gotten out on bail—in which case I don't think he would have killed himself. Spending a long time in detention is harder on a person than being in prison. If you keep this up, you could end up having a breakdown, too."

I'm high-strung by nature and not very good at being alone. I was more than aware that I might undergo a complete change of personality if forced to remain in that tiny cell of mine over a long period of time. Listening to Shoji, I felt more and more anxious.

The following day he spoke along the same lines. He must have sensed I was wavering.

"Remain in detention for a long time, and your entire personality will change," he warned, this time in a very ominous tone. "You'd be better off signing a statement now and then fighting your case in court. What I'm saying is only for your own good."

The more he repeated himself, the more I came to feel that perhaps he was right. I myself was becoming more and more desperate to get out of my present situation. I decided I really had no choice but to sign the statement he would draw up concerning my intentions toward Takaishi.

My Fourth Indictment

On April 18, Shoji announced he was preparing the statement in a way that would allow me ample leverage to argue my case in court.

"Why don't you go with the option of getting out on bail quickly and fight your case in court? My boss says it's negotiable. We don't want you ending up like that guy in Otsu, do we?"

I had already signed any number of statements allegedly enabling me to get out on bail quickly. Sadly, by this point I no longer had the strength to resist. I decided to go along with Shoji's suggestion and negotiate. He wrote up a statement as I watched, and when he was finished I signed it.

"This should do it," he said half to himself. "I'll go phone the boss and get his approval." Within fifteen minutes, he was back.

"The boss says this won't do. It's too weak." With that, he started drafting a new version. Again, I watched as he wrote:

> *I also had in mind a desire to maintain the same favorable relationship with the Ministry of Education in the future as we had enjoyed in the past, for the benefit it would bring in terms of advancing Recruit's business.*

I tried to contain myself and remain as calm as possible. "Takaishi had already decided to leave the ministry and go into politics. I had no intent whatsoever to have him do any favors for me," I said.

I could see the anger rising in Shoji.

"Come on now, we've come this far. You're not going to fight me on this now, are you? Just sign it and let's get this finished!"

He wasn't about to yield, and I didn't have the wherewithal to do combat. I signed.

"This should satisfy the boss," he piped, not so much to inform me as to bolster his own confidence. Once again he left the room.

Within thirty minutes, he was back again, this time with an even sterner look on his face.

"He said it's *still* too weak! You know what he said? He said, 'When the hell are you going to stop dithering and get this job done? We don't have all night! Remember, there's a party on tonight.' He was so riled, he sat down and drafted the statement himself. He said once you sign it, he'll negotiate to get you out on bail as soon as possible. Oh, yeah, he also said if you don't sign it, you'll be in detention until the cows come home. It's up to you."

By this point, the prosecutor's face was on fire, the hair on his head standing on end. An eerie silence filled the room for some time. He then began again, this time in a less rankled tone.

"You know that 'party' the boss mentioned? It's to celebrate winding up preparing our case against you. I'll give it to you straight: I'm the guy they're celebrating, so if I don't show up, there won't be any toasting. I'm running out of time here. The boss said he won't do anything harmful to your case. So please . . . Please sign the thing and let me be on my way."

"Party? You mean you'll all be drinking at the Public Prosecutors Office?"

"Right. We kick off with a toast—with beer. The star of the evening is the prosecutor in charge of the indictment. That's me, so I can't be late. Please! Just sign the statement!"

Ours was a strange relationship: the prosecutor entreating the accused.

"OK," I said. "All I ask is that you confirm one more time that Munakata guarantees I'll get out on bail as quickly as possible."

Shoji flew out of the interrogation room to call his boss for a third time.

"He said he promises you'll be swiftly released on bail," the prosecutor announced upon his return, still puffing from his sprint.

Hearing his assurance, I signed the statement.

"Thanks! You can go back to your cell now," he blurted. With that, he rushed out of the room, my statement firmly in hand.

In questioning conducted in Kyoto on September 28, 2001, I asked Shoji about his interrogations at the detention center.

Defendants in a trial have the option of questioning the prosecutor who conducted their interrogation, but usually they don't. They don't because in most instances, since interrogations take place behind closed doors, it turns into a contest between the two sides—one side claiming something was said and the other side denying it, the defendant alleging he was threatened and the prosecutor saying no threats were made. The courts aren't fond of such bickering.

My attorneys advised me not to question Shoji. I did so anyway. I did so because I wanted the court to understand what goes on behind those closed doors in the hope that I would get a fair judgment. I assured my counsel I would be careful not to lose control of my emotions. They advised me not to go longer than fifteen minutes. So I limited my questioning to the circumstances surrounding how I was threatened and coerced into signing that statement after the prosecutor brought up the case of the man in Otsu who was accused of murdering his father—the one who committed suicide two days after getting off with a suspended sentence.

I began nervously but with determination, keeping one eye on the judge to see how he might react.

"In that case in Otsu where the accused was charged with murdering his father, didn't you believe it would have been better if the defendant had been sent to prison?"

"Yes, I did. If he'd been sent to jail, then I could have been there when he got out and offered him some encouragement. It's a case I have deep regrets over."

"So you're saying you agree it would have been better if he'd not received a suspended sentence?"

"For what the defendant did, I thought he deserved a suspended sentence. But I kept feeling remorseful because if he went to prison, I could have given him the encouragement he needed when he got out."

"You related all this to me in the course of your interrogation, didn't you?"

"No, I didn't."

"If I didn't hear it from you, then how would I know about it?"

"Just when, and in what context, are you saying I told you this?"

"You talked about the Otsu case any number of times."

"That's impossible. Tell me the exact date and in what context I supposedly said all this."

"It was when you told me to sign the statement or I'd never get released on bail."

"And just when was that?"

"April 18, for one."

"You're saying I talked to you about the Otsu case on April 18?"

"Yes, when you were preparing the first draft of that statement saying Recruit needed to maintain a favorable relationship with the Ministry of Education in order to ensure that its business would go smoothly. You said I would be guaranteed to get out on bail if I signed it. After a number of revisions, I did."

"That's not the way it was at all. This story of yours doesn't make sense in too many places. That's not what happened at all."

His responses were riddled with contradictions. The only way I could have known that Shoji was in charge of the Otsu case, or known his feelings toward the perpetrator of that crime, was by hearing it from the prosecutor himself. Shoji also appeared to be astounded when I came up with the precise date of April 18. I figured he did not know about my notebooks and was totally taken by surprise and flustered to learn of their existence.

Moral Wrong vs. Legal Wrongdoing

After I signed the final version of my statement, I was led back to my cell. Not long after the guard locked me in, I had an unexpected visitor: the "floor manager" who manned the guard station at the center of the corridor along which the cells are located. The floor manager's duties were to monitor the movements of both the inmates and the guards.

He unlocked the cell door, stepped in, leaned over and in a hushed voice said, "If you think it's you who decides when you'll get out of here, you're making a huge mistake. When you get too eager to get out, you start going along with anything the prosecutor tells you to do. For your own good, stop thinking about when you'll get out of here. Focus on finding some enjoyment in your everyday life here. Got it?"

I was flabbergasted to see the floor manager showing concern this way and offering me, a suspect, his advice. He must have observed how dejected I was and thought it was from having signed a statement accommodating to the prosecution. A man of about fifty, he no doubt had extensive experience in his job and seemed to know how an interrogation was going judging from the volume of the prosecutor's voice wafting from the interrogation room and the expression on the face of the accused when he passed his station every day.

A copy of my formal indictment was delivered to my cell in a plain brown envelope. It consisted of one inordinately long sentence containing a string of adverbial clauses. Reading it, again I didn't have a clue as to the reason I was being indicted.

In Japan there is the concept of moral evil that traces its origins to Confucianism. Moral evil is a moral hazard separate from wrongdoing in the legal sense. Legal wrongdoing is a transgression against the very minimum of social norms. Wrongdoing in a moral sense spans a wider range than transgression in a legal sense.

The media reports do not differentiate between moral wrong and legal wrongdoing. Special investigators build a case on what the media choose to report in the most sensational way. This, I think, is why public prosecutors also confuse moral wrong and legal wrongdoing.

The media aren't to be blamed for confusing the two types of wrongdoing in their reporting. This is just the way it is in Japan, a country influenced by Confucianism—a fact not necessarily to its detriment. How legal wrongdoing is understood, however, varies from one generation to the next and from one person to the next.

The courts, however, should make a strict distinction between the two and judge wrongdoing based on the law. Otherwise Japan could no longer exist as a country that is ruled by law. If the courts pass verdicts influenced by media reports, eventually their authority will be eroded and the people will lose faith in their country's judicial system.

The "Political Route"

At the Kosuge detention center inmates are not permitted to read newspapers or magazines. The radio is often playing, but turned off whenever the news is broadcast. Except for visits from my attorneys—fifteen minutes twice a week—my only source of news was what I heard from the prosecutors.

This was how I heard about the introduction of the sales tax and learned of the death of Noboru Goto, former president of the Japan Chamber of Commerce and Industry. It was also from Munakata that I learned that Prime Minister Takeshita decided to step down. When he told me he had read this news in the morning papers, I noted what I thought to be a faint smile on his face. Gradually I came to depend on him and his successors as my source of information.

Agriculture, Forestry, and Fisheries Minister Kato

After my interrogation regarding Recruit's connections with the Ministry of Education got under way on March 28, Prosecutor Munakata resumed coming to Kosuge.

"Mutsuki Kato used Recruit's helicopter to travel to Appi," he began, "and based on what we gather from the press reports, we've decided to bring him in. We assigned Kamigaki to the case and sent him up to Iwate, so now your interrogation will be handled by Prosecutor Shoji."

Munakata proceeded to offer up the information that Kato—Minister of Agriculture, Forestry, and Fisheries at the time in question—had a spate of gossip written about him in the weeklies, and he said the Special Investigation Department was eager to nab politicians of his ilk.

Mutsuki Kato was a bigwig in the Fukuda faction, whom I knew through Shintaro Abe. Over dinner one night he told me his ministry was working to enact what came to be known as the "Law for Development of Comprehensive Resort Areas," commonly referred to as the "Resort Act." "Now that Japan's become affluent," Kato had remarked, "it's time for the people of this country to start enjoying more leisure."

The suspicions surrounding Kato reported in the press had to do with the cancellation by his ministry of its designation of forested watersheds at Appi Highland, which was a protected forest in Iwate Prefecture.

In Europe, people work all year in anticipation of enjoying their holiday vacations. In Germany and Austria, during the winter ski season schools close for two weeks, starting with the northernmost states and progressively moving southward. Some companies also shut down for winter holidays. There are also many people who after retirement spend long periods of time at ski resorts.

Ski resorts in places like Europe, the United States, and South America are designed to be enjoyed in short- or long-term stays, rather than as destinations for day trips. I was eager to build a large-scale ski resort of that kind here in Japan, and this was my incentive for developing the Appi Highland Ski Resort.

In response to a report by the 1st Ad Hoc Commission on Administrative Reform released in 1964, the Forestry Agency in 1973 issued a directive banning, in principle, the creation of new "forestry operations" within national forests, as a way of preventing uncontrolled development of Japan's woodland resources. Coinciding with this initiative, the agency drew up a plan for developing forested recreational areas. The plan called for the development of ten specified recreational areas, with all other development of such kind to be banned. Appi Highland was the only one of ten designated areas for development as a recreational area.

Construction was initiated in April 1980. Financing came from both the public and private sectors, including the Hokkaido-Tohoku Development Finance Public Corporation, Iwate Broadcasting Company, Iwate Nippo, and local municipalities. The hotel's guest rooms were all sold as condominiums, a format common overseas. The venture got off to a successful start, with all rooms attracting purchasers and all facilities operating in the black.

I was very proud of the Appi resort. It had the most extensive network of ski trails in Japan, its seven hundred rooms were completely sold out, and operations were robust. I thought that if Kato, as Minister of Agriculture, Forestry, and Fisheries, were to come and observe how successfully its development was carried out, it might help in promoting implementation of the Resort Act.

At the time, the Tohoku Shinkansen ran only as far as Morioka, so whenever I or someone involved in the project wanted to visit Appi, we used Recruit's helicopter. When Kato's secretary contacted me and said that the minister decided to accept my invitation, I arranged for him to be taken by the company helicopter. He went and came back the same day, accompanied by another person from the ministry. Neither I nor anyone from Recruit escorted him.

Because of this one occasion when he made use of Recruit's helicopter, coupled with the fact that I passed on shares of Recruit Cosmos to him, the media reported I must have asked Kato to cancel Appi Highland's status as a protected forest.

Kato visited Appi in February 1987. All felling of trees in the forests at Appi were completed by the time the resort opened for business in December 1981. Plans existed to expand the cableways and the hotel facilities, but these were all matters under the jurisdiction of the Ministry of Transport, not the Ministry of Agriculture, Forestry, and Fisheries. In 1987 there were no favors I could have been interested in asking from Kato. So when Munakata told me the Public Prosecutors Office intended to arrest Kato, I was confident they could never build a case against him.

I subsequently learned that when Kamigaki went to Appi, he made inquiries concerning the discussions the former Minister of Agriculture, Forestry, and Fisheries had in his meetings there. In the end, no case was brought against Kato.

"Negotiations"

In those days almost every week I attended a breakfast or dinner gathering for politicians surrounded by their supporters. At no time, however, did I ask a politician to do anything related to Recruit's business. For that reason I assumed that even if investigations were carried out, none of the politicians to whom I passed on shares of Recruit Cosmos would be charged with bribe-taking.

My confidence was irrelevant; Munakata and the Prosecutors Office had other things in mind. "Back at headquarters, we've been discussing how to build the case against some of the politicians you've been involved with. Now that so much has been written in the press, we can't just let things slide without nailing somebody," Munakata told me.

The logic of the argument repulsed me. "I've never asked any politician to do anything for me," I said.

"I hope you'll cooperate with us here—from a broad perspective, shall we say."

"What do you mean?"

"It's important that the public gets the impression our investigations are being carried out without any bias. We've already made our decision: we'll arrest Kato and one other person from the LDP and one person from an opposition party. I hope you'll just accept this as something that can't be helped."

I shuddered at the very notion that public prosecutors would decide to arrest someone based on how it should appear in the press.

"Every night," Munakata went on, "reporters hang around my house asking me when we're going to nab Kato and whether we intend to grab Nakasone too. The credibility of the Public Prosecutors Office rests on this case."

At this point he leaned over until we were mere inches apart, looked deep into my eyes, and continued in a lower tone of voice, "You see, we'd like to do some, well, 'negotiating' here. Say we don't arrest you on this one. We really wouldn't want to do that to you because, surely, if you were sent up on a fourth indictment, it would hurt your, well, public standing. So say we skip the indictment and just interrogate you on a voluntary basis. That way you'd be able to meet with your attorney every day—which would be to your advantage, I might point out. We'll just ask you about your political connections voluntarily, I'll draw up a statement, and you can sign it. We'll make sure you get a light sentence and get out on bail quickly. Don't forget: it's the public prosecutors who decide what sentence to ask for when making an indictment. Negotiate with us, and we promise no harm will come to you."

"If I signed a statement about a politician, it would cause him trouble."

"The political situation is still in turmoil. We'd like to settle this once and for all and be able to declare the investigation over. It's all been decided and agreed on: you'll get out on bail quickly. Since you've already been indicted on charges of passing bribes to four people, you won't avoid a conviction, but if we can bring politicians into this, we'll seek a suspended sentence for you. The sentence sought when submitting an indictment and the sentence sought by the prosecutor in his closing argument are identical. Ask your attorney. I'll grant you a visit with him tomorrow."

The next day, April 15, was a Saturday, but as Munakata had promised, I received special permission to meet with Hino for thirty minutes. I related what the prosecutor had said to me. He confirmed that it was true.

"The sentence the investigating prosecutor asks for at the time of an indictment is carried on by the prosecutor who substantiates the charges in court," he explained. "We aren't privy to it, but from what I hear, the sentence being sought remains unchanged in virtually all cases."

In the next interrogation session Munakata picked up pretty much where we had left off.

"This case of yours, technically it's bribe-passing, but in your case, what took place was a transfer of stocks. Recruit didn't actually gain anything from that, so we can ask for a lighter sentence. Won't you cooperate with us so we can bring this case to a close?" He spoke in what seemed to be an earnest tone.

"If I cooperate, it'll cause a great deal of trouble to the politicians involved," I repeated.

"If you insist on sticking to an attitude like that, we'll have to arrest you again and bring you down once and for all. We might have to bring in Ida, too—and what would happen to Recruit if its president got arrested?"

His earnestness had now shifted to exasperation disguised as threat. I kept silent, assuming that if they seriously intended to arrest Ida, they would have done so already. The silence went on.

"Think it over carefully. Which would be better for you? To be arrested for a fourth time and stay in detention for who knows how long, or to submit to voluntary interrogation, have the indicting prosecutor seek a suspended sentence for you, and get out on bail early? After all that's been written up in the press, the special investigators would lose face if all the politicians involved here got off scot-free. We've already decided to arrest some politicians, and it's my job to carry that decision out."

Whatever gets reported in the media inevitably comes to form public opinion, and special investigators have to respond to that opinion. Yes, that was why the media was the "third power." That was what he was saying.

"Avoiding a political vacuum is something we both want, isn't it?" By this point the prosecutor seemed to be close to his wit's end. "What I'm asking you to do is the best option for both of us."

He did have a point here. Ever since my arrest, the Diet had been at a standstill because of the scandal. He was also correct in pointing out that I had already signed statements admitting that I had passed bribes to four people. Even if I stuck to my ground now, I would surely end up getting indicted again, meaning all my effort would ultimately be for nothing.

I came to realize the situation was already at a point where I had no viable alternative but to submit to Munakata's "negotiations."

Katsuya Ikeda

Munakata said the prosecutors had decided that the opposition-party lawmaker they would arrest would be Katsuya Ikeda, a member of the Komeito, the Clean Government Party (CGP).

Besides the fact that I had passed shares of Recruit Cosmos stock to Ikeda's secretary—his younger brother, Yuzuru—in the materials seized, the investigators found faxes Katsuya Ikeda sent to Recruit. Among them was a stenographer's record from his questioning in the Diet concerning the issue of high school students applying for more than one job simultaneously.

"When we found this among the materials, we literally jumped for joy!" Munakata showed a wide, self-satisfied grin.

Katsuya Ikeda long ago decided to devote his career as a lawmaker to addressing problems associated with Japan's hiring practices. At his request, Recruit had submitted materials to him relating to student job-seeking for his use in preparing questions to bring before the Diet. This was done with my knowledge.

As for the passing of Recruit Cosmos shares to Ikeda's secretary, however, I knew nothing. This was something I was unaware of until it was reported by the media. When Munakata brought up the subject, I insisted repeatedly that there was no connection between the lawmaker and myself.

Ikeda had been elected from Tokyo electoral district no. 3. It was the same district in which Takashi Kosugi, a university classmate of mine, ran for office on the LDP ticket along with other Diet regulars such as Tokusaburo Kosaka and Michio Ochi. The district was famous for its closely fought battles among five candidates, all with experience in the Diet, and as there were only four seats up for grabs, in each election one of these known politicians would inevitably lose.

From Kosugi's very first run for the Lower House, I always backed him. There was no way I would give shares in Recruit Cosmos to Ikeda.

"I wasn't involved in any of this," I declared matter-of-factly to Munakata.

"Ikeda's questions to the Diet were prepared using materials provided by Recruit, which is why we intend to take him in. We know for a fact that Yuzuru Ikeda received the shares. If you yourself weren't involved, couldn't you, well, say that someone else at Recruit had recommended Ikeda to you and you had given the matter your approval? If we put someone in the middle here, it would get you a lighter sentence. We wouldn't indict the middleman, I promise."

"I've never even met Yuzuru Ikeda. How could I say there'd been a middleman?"

"Yuzuru Ikeda's said he's never met you, either. If there's nobody who could have acted as your middleman, we'll have no choice but to find a connection between you and Katsuya Ikeda. We'll still leave you leverage for arguing your case in court. But for now, why don't you just sign a statement saying you phoned Ikeda directly?"

When I didn't immediately succumb to this dubious scheme, Munakata took his ploy a step further.

"Ikeda said when he once gave a talk before bookshop operators in the assembly hall on the eleventh floor of the Recruit Building, he exchanged greetings with you."

Katsuya Ikeda, at the time referred to, was editor-in-chief of *Ushio*, a magazine with strong connections to Soka Gakkai.

"I would hardly approach someone I'd only exchanged greetings with about accepting shares of Recruit Cosmos stock."

My response appeared to reignite a fire in the prosecutor. His face suddenly turned a brilliant red. "You mean you're *still* going to put up a fight!?"

I said nothing. Minutes passed somewhat awkwardly without either of us saying a word.

"Tell you what I'm going to do," he finally began. "I'll make the entire statement vague enough so you'll have ample leeway to fight your case in court."

With that, he began drafting a statement.

"I'll say you telephoned him."

"I told you, I didn't phone him."

"Yuzuru Ikeda's already said he never met you. We'll have to go with the story that you called Ikeda yourself. I'll say your memory is vague and you don't remember whether you called him at his office or his apartment in the lawmakers' housing block."

Apparently Munakata didn't know that members of the Diet elected from Tokyo aren't assigned government housing.

He proceeded to draw up a statement and passed it to me to sign. I saw no alternative but to go along with him. This is the gist of what it said:

> *I can't remember exactly who it was—probably an officer either from Recruit or from Recruit Cosmos—but someone suggested that I provide 5,000 shares of Recruit Cosmos stock to Katsuya Ikeda, a lawmaker affiliated with the Komeito. I think it was that officer who also specified the number of shares. As I recall, someone subsequently reported back to me that a phone call had been made to Mr. Ikeda—I'm not sure if it was to his office or his official apartment—and he had agreed to accept the shares in his younger brother or a secretary's name. I had never met or even heard of this "Yuzuru Ikeda" before, so I absolutely did not have it in mind to give him— nor did I ever give him—stock in Recruit Cosmos.*

If Katsuya Ikeda sold off the 5,000 shares after Recruit Cosmos went public, he must have made about 10 million yen in profit. Passing the shares to him was, as in other instances, done to receive favors beneficial to Recruit's operations, and I deeply regret my actions.

In preparing the list of who should receive Recruit Cosmos shares, I placed part of the responsibility in the hands of the company's president Tomoyuki Ikeda, senior managing director Norio Kozakai, managing director Masaaki Takashima, and Satoshi Shigeta, in charge of operations in Kansai. They drew up a list of about thirty potential recipients, selected from among various people involved in some way with Recruit Cosmos's business operations, clients, and such.

In constructing condominiums, projects are often held up by the opposition of local residents, and in not a few cases a settlement is reached only through intervention of a politician. Ikeda represented Tokyo's Setagaya and Meguro wards, areas prone to opposition movements of the kind, and Recruit Cosmos may have put him on its list as a politician who could potentially help them out in resolving such local disputes in the future.

In my next interrogation, on April 20, Munakata opened the session with a slight smirk on his face.

"You made political donations to Katsuya Ikeda, didn't you?"

"That's utterly impossible. Lawmakers belonging to the JCP and Komeito don't accept political donations."

"Your Cosmos Life paid consultant fees to a company affiliated with Ikeda, a company called Seiga. When we pressed your secretary Ono on the subject after his arrest, he said he'd reported the matter to you and you'd approved it."

"Cosmos Life is a subsidiary of Recruit Cosmos. I have no say whatsoever in how Cosmos Life operates. Furthermore, this is the first time I've ever even heard of Seiga."

"There were five payments made to Seiga, but we'll go easy on you and indict you only on one, a payment in the amount of three million yen.

That's as far as we're willing to go. Here again, I'll write the statement to be vague—you know, saying things like 'This is the way I *think* such-and-such happened,' or 'My memory isn't very clear on this point.'"

By now, the prosecutor's smirk had transformed to a look of menace, a rush of blood turning his face a fiery red. There was no way to fight him. I meekly signed the statement, which was to the following effect:

> *Starting in December 1985 Cosmos Life made payments to Seiga at Ikeda's request. I heard about this from Mamiya or Ono—probably Ono—and gave my approval. I don't know how the payments came to be increased from two million yen to three million yen.*

With this statement the prosecutors could have indicted me on a charge of having passed bribes totaling fifteen million yen, but they indicted me on only one of the five payments, in the amount of three million yen. They may have done this to balance things out with the amount of my donations to Chief Cabinet Secretary Takao Fujinami (on this more later) or perhaps because Yuzuru Ikeda wasn't a state-paid secretary.

After my trial began, I questioned my secretary Ono about all this. He replied that Seiga was a company run by Yuzuru Ikeda that provided building and condominium management services. The company had asked for work connected to properties under Recruit Cosmos's management, but he'd turned Seiga down. Then Yuzuru Ikeda himself started coming around and kept making his request—to the point that Ono ultimately gave in and paid him off in the form of consultant fees.

Former Prime Minister Nakasone

On April 24, Munakata shifted the focus of his questioning to former Prime Minister Yasuhiro Nakasone.

"Nakasone's refusing to testify before the Diet. There must've been something between the two of you."

He seemed eager to dig as deep as he could into this one.

"There was nothing whatsoever."

"Do you have any idea why he'd be refusing to testify?"

"None."

"You visited the prime minister's official residence, something that would never happen under normal circumstances with the president of a company. What was your purpose in going there?"

"I didn't have any special purpose. I went because I was asked to come."

"You didn't go to ask for something related to the Ad Hoc Council on Education?"

"The council is an advisory panel to the prime minister. If Recruit were going to ask for something concerning the agreement on student job recruitment, wouldn't I go to somebody on the council, not the prime minister?"

The prosecutor's temper was slowly but surely flaring up.

"Nakasone's trying to avoid having to testify, so there must be something he doesn't want to be asked, wouldn't you say? We checked his daily schedule printed in the newspapers, and it seems he met you on three occasions—once for golf in Zushi, once at his official residence, and once at the summer home of a business bigwig in Karuizawa. Starting tomorrow, I'll ask you what you two talked about."

The next day Munakata lost no time in asking me what had transpired when we played golf in Zushi.

"The fact of the matter is I didn't even play in the same group as Mr. Nakasone. I was in the group after his."

"Then how'd you get together with Nakasone?"

"A member of my group, a prominent businessman, was close friends with the prime minister, so after golfing we met up in the clubhouse bar, eight of us in all, for a few beers and small talk. That's all there was to it."

"That's *all* there was to it?" The prosecutor looked both amused and ready to pounce further.

"I was hardly the only one there. A lot of people were around. What's more, the bar is in an open space connected to the clubhouse restaurant—not the kind of place where one would try to ask for favors secretly."

Apparently another prosecutor had already gone to the club and checked the records to see who I had played with that day, and also checked the layout of the clubhouse.

Munakata never mentioned the golfing occasion again. Where his interest lay was in my visit to the prime minister's official residence.

Call from the Prime Minister's Secretary

On March 2, 1985, I visited the prime minister's official residence, alone, and met with Prime Minister Nakasone. About a week earlier I had received a phone call from his secretary saying that the prime minister wanted to hear my views on educational reform and suggested we discuss matters over lunch at his residence.

Nakasone had been addressing the issue of reforming Japan's education system, and it was at his instigation that the Ad Hoc Council on Education had been established. The main target of the council was to amend the country's overweening emphasis on academic credentials.

About six weeks before my visit, on January 21, I had been invited to give a talk before the council committee charged with reforming higher education. On that occasion I spoke on the topic of academic credentials and hiring, making reference to materials produced by the Japan Productivity Center comparing workers' lifetime wages based on a breakdown of their academic backgrounds.

I began by citing statistics indicating that the average lifetime wages earned by a high school graduate in Japan equated to 81 percent of the wages of a college graduate. This income gap, I pointed out, was noticeably smaller than the divergence found in other countries. I then noted that in Japan the percentage of high school students going on to college had risen to the point that college graduates were having a more difficult time finding jobs than high school graduates, with the result that it was increasingly common for college graduates to take jobs as policemen, firemen, and the like.

In the public sector, I cited the fact that a college graduate who rose to the position of vice finance minister was earning about 2.5 times more in his lifetime than a high school graduate who worked his entire career as an employee of a tax office. Meanwhile in the private sector, a college graduate who eventually became president of a bank earned four-to-six times more in his lifetime than a high school graduate who spent his complete career within a bank's rank and file. Here again, the disparity between the two was far less than in the banking industry of the United States or Europe.

As to major business corporations, I pointed out that employment opportunities were open to all high school and college graduates, and I noted that in the Kansai area in particular, many officers at big companies—Sumitomo Bank, Sanwa Bank, Matsushita Electric Industrial, Sanyo, and Sharp, to name a few—were high school graduates.

By way of conclusion, I expressed the view that compared to the situation outside Japan, there was no discrimination based on academic credentials needing to be amended, and I said I saw no need for even more social homogeneity than already existed. I qualified those remarks, however, by offering that if discrimination did exist in this country, it was in the work and authority delegated to "career track" bureaucrats vs. those accorded to "non-career track" civil servants. And I said that more than rectifying Japan's alleged discrimination based on academic credentials, what industry—and by extension, Japanese society as a whole—was demanding was reform of the nation's universities.

Shortly thereafter I received a phone call from an old acquaintance, Takemochi Ishii, a professor at the University of Tokyo who was serving as head of the Council on Education's committee assigned to study the question of how to vitalize the nation's educational functions. Apparently the negative view I took toward the argument that the nation's "credentials-oriented society" needed amending came up at his committee meeting, and he requested that I come and speak along the same lines as my earlier talk. I agreed and gave a similar speech before his committee on February 27.

It was immediately after that that I received the phone call from Prime Minister Nakasone's secretary.

Lunch with Prime Minister Nakasone

On March 2, wearing a new suit and tie and carrying the materials I used at the two committee talks, I went to the prime minister's official residence. I arrived five minutes before the appointed time.

Upon entering the building, I was somewhat taken aback. In contrast to the edifice's stately exterior—reminiscent in many ways of the façade of the original Imperial Hotel designed by Frank Lloyd Wright—the interior was somewhat decrepit. In the entry hall, warmth was provided by a gas heater, a relic that had long disappeared from most ordinary Japanese homes.

I was escorted into a somewhat small tatami room. In the center was a low table, on either side of which was a flat cushion. The walls showed signs of wear and were completely without adornment. There was no artwork, no flowers. It was altogether stark. It saddened me to think this was the best Japan could muster for the residence of its prime minister.

Within a few moments, a refined lady, dressed in an elegantly understated kimono, entered the room.

"I'm Mrs. Nakasone," she said, setting a cup of green tea onto the table in front of me. "Thank you for taking the time out of your busy schedule to come here today."

I nodded politely, and she withdrew. Moments later Prime Minister Nakasone entered and took his seat on the cushion opposite me.

As my invitation had been for lunch, I had been entertaining notions of the fine fare that might be served. When Mrs. Nakasone returned after several minutes carrying a large tray, however, what she placed before us were two plates of curry rice, garnished with a Japanese substitute for chutney.

I'm very fond of curry, but who would ever have imagined that was what I would be served for lunch at the prime minister's! Even more disheartening, the curry lacked any aroma. It had probably come directly out of a package.

Japan in those days ranked second worldwide in the amount of economic assistance it provided to the developing countries. Among the nations receiving Japan's official development assistance (ODA) were some whose leaders lived in magnificent buildings worthy of the name "palace." Yet here was the official residence of the prime minister of Japan, the assistance provider, not only without a chef of its own but also lacking service staff. Surely the prime minister must receive a considerable number of visitors. At the very least his official residence should befit a nation of this stature.

Part of the role of the prime minister of Japan, it seems, would be to invite ambassadors of different countries to the official residence as a way of opening diplomatic avenues. Wouldn't service staff be necessary at such times when the prime minister was fulfilling official duties?

For a long time, it was common practice for the prime minister to discuss matters, over drinks, with the reporters assigned to cover him. Occasionally, when there was a deadlock in the Diet, a veteran reporter might actually intervene between the ruling and opposition camps. Surely a maid ought to be on hand to serve drinks at such times.

I had spoken with Nakasone on a number of occasions. I was, as I've said, a member of a group supporting the prime minister—known as the Sanno Economic Study Club—which I had joined at the invitation of Hajime Tsuboi, chairman of Mitsui Fudosan. This, however, was my first time meeting Nakasone one on one. He lost no time in getting directly to the point of our lunch.

"Education is vital to the future of this country," he began, "and I'm eager to undertake full-scale reforms of our educational system. But radical reforms aren't possible if all you do is listen to what the officials at the Ministry of Education tell you. This is why I wanted to hear your views on the matter."

He paused briefly, took a spoonful of curry, and then continued: "Just the other day I was talking to members of the rock band Yokohama Ginbae, and they suggested we should do away with the first-stage exam all college applicants are required to take and make it possible for anybody to take the exams for places like Todai [the University of Tokyo]. Mr. Ezoe, what's your opinion about this?"

Much as I was impressed to hear that the prime minister would lend an ear to the views of members of a popular rock band, I wasn't entirely in agreement with their suggestion. "There was a time when it was possible for anybody to take the exams for Todai," I said. "But in those days, competition to enter college became so fierce, it led to the scourge of 'examination hell.' Would-be university students were forced to sit through two rounds of entrance exams, and those not making it into college were compelled to go to college prep school and try again. This was followed by the introduction of scholastic aptitude tests and proficiency tests before those were superseded by the 'common first-stage exam' in place today."

I paused to have a spoonful of curry.

"In other advanced nations, students have to take a common test prior to their university entrance exams: in the United States, it's the SATs, and in Europe, the baccalauréat in France, the Abitur in Germany, the Maturità in Italy, and so on. In the case of the European exams, if a student does not pass, he won't be qualified to receive a high school diploma, so he's barred from taking university entrance exams."

The prime minister, who'd been listening attentively, responded, "I'm wondering if it wouldn't be better to eliminate the first-stage exam."

"Michio Nagai, when he was Minister of Education, suggested that instead of everybody trying to get into Todai, they should target a wider range of colleges. If everybody aims for Todai, I think the educational system will become skewed."

I took a deep breath and then tried to explained myself in greater detail: "In the West, students get guidance counseling starting from junior high school, and from secondary school the emphasis is placed on vocational education. In Germany, where the tradition of the Gymnasium is strong, students take great pride in receiving a vocational education. In France, there are cases where a chef wins the coveted MOF—a Meilleur Ouvrier de France [One of the Best Craftsmen of France] award—or even the nation's highest honor, the Légion d'honneur. In Japan, the rate of entrance into university is higher than in other developed nations, but in terms of return on investment, going to a university in Japan brings fewer rewards."

Nakasone pondered what I had said for a few moments. "Don't you think the common first-stage exam is eroding equal opportunity in education?" he then asked.

"I think what a student learns in high school greatly affects how much he will get out of his studies once he's at university. For example, how much a student majoring in English literature will learn depends on how much English he learned in high school; and how much a math major will learn depends on how much math he studied in high school."

The prime minister listened to my every word, but the expression on his face was anything but congenial. I didn't let that stop me, though. "May I offer up my views on educational reform?" I asked.

"Please."

"I think educational reform is very important, but more than amending this country's inordinate emphasis on academic credentials, I think it's more important to reform our universities. In the West, universities teach practical knowledge. In Japan, in courses on business management, for example, students learn about management theory and the history of management, or about the theories espoused by different management experts, but they don't learn the things they need to know in the real world, like preparing balance sheets or profit-and-loss statements."

I tried not to sound imperious but was eager to make my point. "To cite another example, students studying architecture in Europe spend a year working as an architectural intern, and in the United States six months. I myself have a license to teach, and in my case on-the-job training lasted only two weeks. Standing before a class for two weeks isn't enough to learn how to teach a class. Teaching a class is no easy job, what with every class dividing up into several groups. Trying not to let anyone fall by the wayside while simultaneously striving to elevate the overall level of learning is very hard. I think at least six months of on-the-job training is necessary to gain the needed experience."

I sensed myself running on a bit too long for comfort, but I still had more on my mind. "In other countries, even if a student gets into a top university, he can't graduate if his grades are poor. Here in Japan, once a student successfully passes the entrance exam and gets into a university, he can graduate no matter how bad his grades are. If there's a form of discrimination that needs amending, it's the discrimination that exists between career-track and non-career track bureaucrats."

To this, Nakasone nodded. "There does seem to be discord between the career and non-career bureaucrats, I agree."

I then launched into my final point. "Another problem, I think, is the quota system used for university departments. At places like Todai, Kyoto University, and Kyushu University, even now there continues to be more slots available to study agricultural science than business administration. Students who study education and graduate with a license to teach have no guarantee of ever finding a job, given the falling birthrate. Meanwhile students in engineering courses are in high demand by industry. I think what Japan needs is rectification of its university departments."

"I see," the prime minister said, the expression on his face still showing no emotion.

"Japan has less wage discrimination based on academic background than other countries." This was my final observation, and for reference, I handed the prime minister the materials I'd brought with me—the information prepared by the Japan Productivity Center. I thanked the prime minister for lunch and the opportunity to have this conversation, and took my leave.

Once outside, I was surrounded by reporters eager to hear what I had discussed with the prime minister. Wary of what the media might turn my comments into, I made no response and got into my car. Inside the official residence there had not been a single service staff. At the entry gate, however, seven or eight security guards were milling around on duty.

The leaders of this country embrace the ideal that all Japanese citizens should enjoy the same level of education and the same standard of living. But in a market economy, disparities inevitably develop. Japan is a nation where there are only minor disparities in education or earnings, and few people fall by the wayside. Its leaders—and not just Prime Minister Nakasone—base their thinking on the ideal view of a state espoused by Marx.

These were the thoughts that drifted through my mind as I was driven back to my office after my momentous meeting with the country's leader.

Our Meeting in Karuizawa

Munakata next asked me about the time I met Nakasone in Karuizawa.

The meeting had taken place on August 8, 1987, at the summer home of a relative of his, a prominent business leader. According to the newspaper record of the prime minister's daily appointments, I arrived at 6:01 P.M. and spent about twenty minutes conversing with Nakasone in the company of Keita Asari. In this instance too, I had gone to see the prime minister after receiving a phone call from his secretary.

Keita Asari was the founder of the Shiki Theatre Company. He was the first Japanese to direct an opera—which was "Madame Butterfly"—at La Scala in Milan, and he on frequent occasions has been invited to direct operas at the Salzburg Festival. He is the only Japanese to have undertaken opera direction at numerous theaters outside his native country.

I myself attended a performance of his production of "Madame Butterfly," a production that drew on elements of Japanese culture and scenic ambience: his use of *kuroko*, the "invisible" black-clothed stagehands familiar to kabuki, and of traditional dance viewed as shadows cast on papered lattice windows. In the climactic scene where Butterfly dies by her own hand, four out-of-sight stagehands manipulated strings from the four corners of the stage, causing a crimson-red blood stain to spread gradually over a white cloth. This dramatic staging elicited audible sobs from the audience.

At the time, Asari was serving Nakasone in an advisory capacity. It was on Asari's advice that the prime minister had begun to pour his passion into the construction of the New National Theatre, and this appeared to have been what the two were discussing when I arrived.

I myself was serving as chairman of the Japan Opera Foundation, formed from the fusing of two opera companies, the Fujiwara Opera and the Nihon Opera Kyokai, and I was on the council overseeing preparations for the establishment of the nation's second national theater. This was likely why I was invited to Karuizawa that day.

Earlier I had visited the Ministry of Education to petition for the new theater's creation. The response I received was myopic. "Do you see any kabuki theaters being built in New York or Paris or Rome?" the official had retorted. "Opera is something for the affluent echelons of Europe. Surely it would be odd for us to use Japanese taxpayer money to build a theater for a foreign performing art, wouldn't you agree?"

Without the vigorous effort taken by Asari to persuade the prime minister, there would never have been a new national theater, a dream long embraced by Japanese opera performers.

When I joined in, Nakasone and Asari seemed to have already finished their discussion of the new theater. We began chatting on random topics. Nakasone had already declared that when his current tenure as prime minister ran out, he planned to step down.

Asari got the conversation going with a question on many people's minds at the time. "Rumors are flying around that you'll be succeeded by Mr. Takeshita, Mr. Abe, or Mr. Miyazawa. Care to tell us your thoughts?" Asari spoke with a big smile on his face.

I don't know if Nakasone knew I was a fan of Abe, but he turned to me and offered the following remark. "Mr. Abe's a fine man both in character and in vision. He has the charisma to attract people to him. I think he'd make a good prime minister."

Before I had a chance to become excited at the prospect, the prime minister continued: "As a politician, though, the task I've most given myself over to is restoring the nation's fiscal health. Now that JNR [Japanese National Railways], NTT, and Japan Tobacco and Salt have all been privatized and shares have been sold, the nation's fiscal picture has improved each year to the point where we're almost at our goal. Mr. Takeshita has many years of experience as Minister of Finance and knows his economics. If he becomes prime minister, the country's fiscal health will be restored."

He paused briefly, then shifted his focus. "Now that Japan has joined the ranks of the world's leading nations, foreign diplomacy is going to be more and more important. Mr. Miyazawa's fluent in English and has the ability to get along well, in English, with political leaders in America."

At this point his tone became somewhat philosophical. "I went into politics with the aim of one day becoming prime minister, but the role of the prime minister as one imagines from the outside is very different from the reality that awaits you when you actually become prime minister. In this country, the bureaucracy puts up formidable obstacles that prevent you from doing things the way you'd want. My first year or so, I had quite a difficult time and did a lot of worrying. Everybody has his own way of being a good leader, and in the case of the prime minister, it's something you can learn only after you take office. In that respect, I think Mr. Abe, Mr. Takeshita, and Mr. Miyazawa all have what it takes to be a good prime minister."

His initial comments functioned like a smokescreen obfuscating what he was really intent on saying in his final remarks, which I found very interesting. I guess it's part of the job of being prime minister to be able to operate that way.

Just around this time, Takeshita had spoken out about the need to improve the nation's ratio of direct to indirect taxes. Nakasone may have had in mind the expectation that if Takeshita were to become prime minister, he would introduce a sales tax.

Munakata listened to my account of these exchanges at Karuizawa but, perhaps because Asari was present the whole time of the conversation with Nakasone, he showed little interest in pursuing the topic any further.

Ihei Aoki's Suicide

On April 25, Prime Minister Takeshita announced he was stepping down.

The reports in the evening editions of the dailies—which I was finally able to read after my release on bail—were almost unanimous in their sentiment that the move was to be expected and had come "too late." Takeshita's exit was prompted by the allegations of his involvement in the Recruit scandal at a time when he was already being roundly criticized for having introduced the sales tax.

The following day, during the afternoon visit with my attorney I learned that Takeshita's former secretary, Ihei Aoki, had committed suicide.

I didn't know Aoki well, having met him only on two occasions: once when he requested I purchase tickets to one of Takeshita's fundraising events, and once when he came to express Takeshita's gratitude for my having done so. I was never interrogated, not even once, concerning Takeshita or Aoki.

From the moment I heard this disturbing piece of news, the question kept gnawing at me: Why had Aoki chosen to take his own life? After my release, I asked my defense counsel about it, and one of my lawyers suggested that Aoki had probably been investigated over the "gold screen scandal."

The gold screen scandal, since as far back as 1985 or 1986, had generated strong media interest for the alleged light it shed on financial institutions, their backroom dealings, and the shady involvement of politicians. The Prosecutors Office, however, had been unable to build a case. When the backroom dealings perpetrated by Heiwa Sogo, a mutual bank on the brink of failure, were investigated, attention focused on a folding screen covered in gold leaf.

Here is how the deal worked. Say a powerful businessman with political connections buys an art object—like a gold screen—from an art dealer for 100 million yen and offers it as a gift to a politician. Later the art dealer might buy it back, working through the businessman, for 80 million yen. The politician is left with 80 million yen and the art dealer reaps 20 million yen in profit. Since no money actually passes between the businessman and the politician, building a criminal case is extremely difficult.

In the case at hand, rumors were rampant that Takeshita was on the receiving end of the transfer of a gold screen that was eventually purchased back from him at a highly inflated value, all funded by Heiwa Sogo, whose interest in the deal was in having Takeshita, Minister of Finance at the time, assist the ailing bank and keep it afloat. Aoki, as Takeshita's aide, was privy to everything that had transpired.

According to *The Justice Trap*, a book on the Recruit scandal written by the journalist Soichiro Tahara, Aoki was grilled incessantly about the incident because the Prosecutors Office, not content with Takeshita's merely leaving office over the Recruit scandal, was apparently intent on putting the former prime minister behind bars. The day before he took his own life, Aoki reportedly telephoned one of Takeshita's supporters and said that he was being pushed to reveal every detail he could muster. Physically exhausted and mentally drained, Aoki suggested, with desperation, that the evidence against Takeshita was quite solid, and Aoki was unsure how much longer he could maintain silence of his full knowledge of the deal.

The day Aoki took his life, Munakata did not come for my regular interrogation. During our next session the following day, April 26, he wasn't his usual self.

"It really puts us in a bind when the person we're investigating commits suicide," he said.

My interrogation that day was unusually subdued.

The LDP's Connections with the Prosecutors Office

After my evening interrogation session, I returned to my cell around nine o'clock. Fifteen minutes later, the guard reappeared and took me back to the interrogation room, where Shoji was waiting.

"What I'm going to ask you now has nothing at all to do with your case," he began.

This was puzzling.

"I'm going to show you a list of ten politicians. For each person on the list, I want you to tell me, yes or no, whether you or any of your affiliate companies ever made a political donation to this person or bought tickets to any of his fundraising events. And please, tell the truth."

"I've been telling you the truth all along."

"I'm doing this on orders from headquarters. They want it back by ten o'clock, so we don't have much time. Please, I need your answers right away."

The list contained these lawmakers: Takeo Fukuda, Toshio Komoto, Shin Kanemaru, Masaharu Gotoda, Seisuke Okuno, Tatsuo Tanaka, Yohei Kono, Seiroku Kajiyama, and Michita Sakata. The tenth name was someone I had never heard of, and as I had forgotten it by the time I wrote in my notebook the next morning, I have no record of who it was.

I imagined it was a list of candidates picked to join the new cabinet being formed after Takeshita's resignation. The upper echelons within the LDP must have thought they would face a prickly situation if Recruit or any of its Group companies had bought tickets to fundraising events from any of them.

For each name on the list, I said that I didn't think any party tickets had been purchased, but I added that any number of such tickets had been bought without my personal approval, so I couldn't say absolutely that no purchases had been made. The one exception was Yohei Kono.

Immediately after Kono had quit the LDP and founded his New Liberal Club, a certain journalist asked if I wouldn't join Kono's support group, suggesting I read an article Kono had written in the current issue of *Chuokoron* magazine. "He's a very knowledgeable man," the journalist noted, encouraging me to meet with Kono directly. I subsequently did meet Kono, in the company of this journalist, for dinner in Akasaka, and agreed to join his support group. I met him only on that one occasion, but must have continued paying my "dues" to the group.

I knew that if I were to reveal all this, Kono's chances of joining the new cabinet would be over. So I just replied in his case as I did in all the others, that I just "wasn't sure."

It was 9:50 when I got back to my cell. From this episode I came to understand the connections between the LDP and the Public Prosecutors Office.

Desperate to Nab Nakasone

As my interrogation stretched into May, Munakata became increasingly adamant about "nabbing Nakasone." He kept pressing me for evidence that could be incriminating.

"When you visited Nakasone at the official residence, what did you take him?"

"Material put together by the Japan Productivity Center corroborating that there's very little wage discrimination in Japan based on one's academic credentials."

"Surely that's not all."

"That's all."

"You must have asked him to include the matter of the student recruitment agreement in the Ad Hoc Council's recommendations."

"I never discussed that issue with the prime minister."

"Oh, really? According to press reports, there are suspicions you were involved in it."

As the questioning continued, the voltage rising every moment, Munakata's face became increasingly flushed. I tried to explain that insofar as Recruit was concerned, it would be advantageous to have no agreement. That way Recruit would be able to provide students with information freely, all year long, which would be good for the company's business. My argument fell on deaf ears.

"If the agreement were rescinded," I persisted, "it is private colleges away from the main urban centers that would suffer. Students at well-known colleges are unofficially recruited for employment during their junior year, and once their place of employment is set, they work part-time at the company that's hiring them or travel overseas. They no longer attend classes. If there were no recruiting agreement, students at the famous schools would all get hired first, putting students at local colleges or newly established colleges at a disadvantage, and the hiring gap between colleges would get wider. That's why four organizations representing private colleges—like the Japan Association of Private Universities and Colleges and the Association of Private Universities of Japan—are going through the Ministry of Education and asking the Nikkeiren [Japan Federation of Employers' Associations] to abide strictly by the agreement. If anybody

were to ask for the agreement to be included in the council's recommendations, it would be the four associations, not Recruit."

I explained the background to the issue in great detail, but Munakata
showed no interest. The prosecutors had seized the materials I was refer-
ring to when they searched my office, but apparently Munakata had not
seen them.

"The Prosecutors Office has already decided to bring Nakasone in," he
responded, his annoyance abating. "It doesn't have to be about the council.
Anything you can give us will do."

"I have nothing to offer you."

"Nothing at all? Isn't there anything you can think of we could nab him
on?"

It amused me to think how the tables had turned. Here was the prosecutor asking his suspect for suggestions.

The newspapers at the time were filled with articles relating to Nakasone,
mostly on the growing likelihood that the former prime minister would
be called into court to testify. When I read these pieces after my release, I
understood why Munakata had been so eager for me to pin something on
Nakasone: The prosecutor was under heavy pressure from his superiors.

The intentions of the Public Prosecutors Office should be predicated
upon statements made by the suspect and those involved in the case at
hand; charges would then be pressed accordingly. Yet, here were top echelons in the office forming their intentions based on media reports, and
then forcing its prosecutors, like Munakata, to figure out how to induce
a written statement out of the accused, namely me, that fit their plans. A
clear case of mistaking the means for the end.

In growing desperation, Munakata shifted to a different tact. "Your
appointment as a special member of the government's Tax Commission—
that must have worked nicely to your advantage. Did you ask Nakasone
for that appointment?"

"Konosuke Matsushita, the 'god of management,' once said that the
entrepreneur's greatest rewards are for his business to serve in the public's
benefit, for it to generate earnings, and to pay taxes to the nation. My being
appointed to a committee seeking to introduce a sales tax is something my

business clients would resent. It would hardly qualify as a reward."

Again, my argument fell on deaf ears. Munakata seemed to be of the opinion that the sole reason people work is to reap rewards.

Chief Cabinet Secretary Fujinami

The special investigators appeared to have given up trying to pin anything on Nakasone. They were now turning their attention to Takao Fujinami, the former chief cabinet secretary.

"We checked out this guy in all the dailies and weeklies, and we didn't find anything negative about him at all. He seems to have a good reputation," Munakata said to me.

"Fujinami's an outstanding individual," I said.

"We want to go after the politicians with the bad reputations. I don't want to go after Fujinami, but if we can't pin anything on Nakasone, we'll have to go after Fujinami."

My connection with Fujinami could be traced to Jiro Ushio, who had approached me with a request to join him as a key member of Sazanami-kai, a group he was forming in support of Fujinami. He said that when he was head of the Japan Junior Chamber (JC), he had become acquainted with Fujinami, who was head of the organization's Mie chapter, and he had supported him ever since he'd run in his first election. I acquiesced and became one of Sazanamikai's three key personnel, alongside Ushio and Yotaro Kobayashi, president of Fuji Xerox and a man I greatly admired as a business leader.

The more I heard him speak at meetings of Sazanamikai, the more I came to respect Fujinami as a man of few words and a man of integrity, an upstanding politician who fulfilled his duties studiously. I once invited him to speak on the political situation before the board of directors at Recruit. He was also quite renowned as a haiku poet.

In my position as one of his key supporters, I made donations to Fujinami twice a year, each in the amount of five million yen. This was before he became chief cabinet secretary in 1983.

I had already been questioned as to why I had given Fujinami shares in Recruit Cosmos, and Munakata had drawn up a statement on April

15—the gist of which was I had known Fujinami for a long time, respected him as a politician and human being of outstanding character and knowledge, and in giving him the pre-flotation shares hoped to make him happy.

On April 27, however, Munakata entered the interrogation room visibly upset. "The boss chewed me out on this. He said a statement like this won't do." He then looked directly into my eyes and began speaking in a grave tone. "You've visited Fujinami's official residence, haven't you?"

Yes, I had gone to his residence after he became chief cabinet secretary. At the time, there was a move afoot to push forward the date for announcing the final list of those who had passed the national exam to become high-ranking civil servants. Private industry, however, including the likes of the Nikkeiren, were of the opinion the announcement date should, if anything, be pushed back along with the gentlemen's agreement on student recruitment.

Under that agreement, October 1 was the earliest date students could visit prospective employers and November 1 was the date after which companies could make their choices. The results of the civil service exam were released on October 15, and the government agencies at all levels were free to start making their picks at any time thereafter. As a result, Yoshinobu Matsuzaki—senior managing director at the Nikkeiren and head of the Central Employment Measures Council, the body that put the gentlemen's agreement in place—was worried that if the current schedule were allowed to continue, sooner or later encouraging the private sector to uphold the gentlemen's agreement would become impossible.

As the situation was, immediately after the results of the first-stage college entrance examinations were released, the major government agencies were losing no time in trying to attract successful students through announcements, posted at the University of Tokyo, of briefings on employment at, for example, the Ministry of Finance or what was then the Ministry of International Trade and Industry. This was earlier than the timetable for students to start visiting potential employers in the private sector under the gentlemen's agreement—a situation prompting criticism directed at the Nikkeiren that the public sector was being given favorable treatment over the private sector.

At the time, I was serving as a special committee member at the Nikkeiren, and I had gotten to know Matsuzaki quite well, aided in part by the fact that we both hailed from Saga Prefecture. We would often discuss the gentlemen's agreement over dinner or a game of Go.

A rule mandating when employment-information magazines could be distributed was not in Recruit's best business interests. Nevertheless, we cooperated, voluntarily keeping to the distribution timetable in the belief that initiating an earlier start of students' job-seeking activities would be harmful.

After hearing Matsuzaki's concerns, and not being well versed in matters relating to the civil service exams, I thought to ask Fujinami how the issue might be resolved. I believed that Fujinami, in his position, and knowledgeable of the workings of government agencies, would be able to tell me precisely where I should go to discuss the matter. Surprisingly, when I posed my question, Fujinami appeared stumped.

"Hmm. Where *would* be best . . . I wonder if, maybe, you should go to the National Personnel Authority. . . . Hmm."

Later that day, I went to see Matsuzaki to report the outcome of my inquiry. He made a note of what I said in order to relay the information to Kazuo Inoue, a subordinate:

> Mr. Ezoe thinks it would work well if August 2–19 were shifted to after October 1st. He said Mr. Fujinami replied he would consider it if a petition were submitted by an appropriate source.

This note, which came to be referred to as "the Matsuzaki memo," was submitted as evidence by the prosecution at my trial session of November 2, 1990.

Munakata twisted my actions around and contended that pushing back the date for announcing the successful civil service examinees was tantamount to preventing the early selection of civil servants, and he asserted that the purpose of my visit to Fujinami was to request prevention of such early selection. The statement he drew up relating to this read, in part, as follows:

I requested of Mr. Fujinami that he do something about the early selection of civil servants. I said early selection of civil servants was a social problem and the major reason the gentlemen's agreement on student recruitment wasn't being abided by. "Isn't there anything that can be done?" I asked him. "The public sector gets preferential treatment over the private sector, and I'd like to see the public side do what's proper. Can't something be done about the early selection of civil servants?" In view of having asked favors of him regarding the gentlemen's agreement, I provided Mr. Fujinami with 10,000 shares in Recruit Cosmos, as I stated previously.

In his interrogation of me on May 6, Munakata was practically pleading with me: "I'll make the statement vague enough so you can fight your case in court. Just sign it and I promise we'll lighten the sentence we ask for when you're indicted. Yoshinaga, my boss, is as tough as they come, the scariest guy in the Public Prosecutors Office. Please, I beg you, just sign the statement!"

He seemed eager to avoid any further chaos in the political situation. In the end, I signed a statement to the following effect, aware all the while of the trouble it would cause Fujinami.

Continued adherence to the gentlemen's agreement and the elimination of early recruiting of civil servants were vital to our company's operations. For that reason, between 1984 and 1985 we devised and carried out plans to approach various quarters with the aim of maintaining abidance of the agreement.

Insofar as Recruit itself was concerned, it would have been better for there to be no such agreement. I thought the part about eliminating early recruitment of civil servants contradicted the part about approaching various quarters with the aim of maintaining abidance by the gentlemen's agreement, but I went along, kept my mouth shut, and signed.

The following evening, May 7, Munakata seemed frustrated. He announced that he wanted to re-work my statement.

"I'll make you a deal. It involves three things: we'll say you were thanked by Ikeda; we'll say you telephoned Fujinami directly and didn't go through his secretary, Eiji Tokuda; and we'll leave Nakasone out of this. How about it?"

When I showed no reaction, he continued: "We asked Tokuda ten times about this, but he said he never received a phone call from you. My boss is on my back to get some connection between you and Ikeda and Fujinami. Please, help me out."

He seemed to be under a lot of pressure. "Just these three things," he kept repeating. "We want to get the political situation back to normal as fast as possible."

Again, silence reigned for an awkwardly long time. When he eventually spoke, what he had to say took me by surprise.

"You know how, at the end of a French movie, the word 'FIN' appears to tell you it's over?" he said.

"Yes."

"Well, that's what we've got here. 'F' as in Fujinami, 'I' as in Ikeda, and 'N' as in Nakasone. All you have to do is go along with those three things, and we can bring this Recruit investigation to a 'FIN.' How about it?"

The prosecutor had a sharp wit. He was also frank, sincere, and good-natured. I sympathized with all the agony he was going through, to the point where I was no longer in a frame of mind to put up resistance. I decided to go along with him, and he rather gleefully drew up a statement along the following lines:

> *I telephoned Mr. Fujinami directly at one of his offices—I don't recall which—and told him that Recruit Cosmos would soon be going public in the OTC market, and I was hoping he would hold 10,000 shares in the company. I told him I would send Ono, my secretary, over to see his secretary and provide him with the details.*

I signed the statement.

During my trial, I directly questioned Munakata about this on June 11, 1993. Long after, on February 27, 2003, as my trial was approaching its end, the *Asahi* ran an article about the exchange in court, which it described as "fierce."

The former Recruit chairman contended the statement was prepared against his will. In reference to the twenty million yen in total provided to former Chief Cabinet Secretary Fujinami, he also claimed that he told the prosecutor the money was a political donation made twice each year.

"That's not the way it was at all," Prosecutor Munakata replied. "You pleaded with me not to make any mention of bribery, saying it would destroy Fujinami's chances of becoming prime minister in the coming century. You got down on your knees and begged me."

Ezoe noted that during the interrogation Prosecutor Munakata made a play on the word "FIN," the word that appears at the end of a French film. He stated that the prosecutor suggested "FIN" in this case stood for the initials of [former Chief Cabinet Secretary] Fujinami, [former Lower House lawmaker] Ikeda, and [former Prime Minister] Nakasone, and he said if he went along with the prosecutor's scenario it would bring the Recruit scandal to its "FIN." Prosecutor Munakata rebutted by saying he did seem to remember mentioning something like this in the course of an informal conversation, but he had no recollection of having said anything about the Recruit scandal coming to an end.

At the next court session on June 16, however, Munakata testified as follows: "What I said is that if you take the initials of Mr. Fujinami, Mr. Ikeda, and Mr. Nakasone, and add to them the 'E' of Ezoe, you get 'FINE'—which is the word that appears at the end of an Italian film. I also recall having commented that if you remove the final 'E', you get the end of a French movie."

In court Munakata also testified he had been aware that I was writing into notebooks in my cell. He knew I submitted my notebooks to the court, and I figured he probably made that statement thinking that when I was given the chance to question him toward the end of my trial, he would then be able to account for any discrepancies between his contentions and what I had recorded in my notebooks.

A Compromise Is Reached

Now that my detention dragged on into May, life in my cell became difficult in yet another way. First, the warmer weather brought out cockroaches in droves. Perhaps they were attracted to the sweets I kept near my bedding. At night as I lay awake I would hear them scurrying about, and on occasions one would actually make a mad dash across my neck. To make matters worse, the arrival of early summer also brought out swarms of mosquitoes, likely from the nearby Ayase River. My cell having no windowpane meant they had free access to my room. Cockroaches were bad enough, but mosquitoes bit—and the itchiness was terrible. To combat these nuisances, every day after lunch an inmate, under the watchful eye of a guard, would enter our cells and spray a disinfectant. This would serve as an effective repellent only briefly, and by lights out the mosquitoes would be back in full force, ready for their evening feast. Itchy and unnerved, I found it impossible to get a good night's sleep.

As my interrogation went on, Munakata kept pressing me.

"We've established you provided shares in Recruit Cosmos to many LDP politicians, and after taking the investigation this far, we can't just put the matter to rest and say nothing happened. OK, if we can't pin anything on Nakasone, we'll settle with nabbing Fujinami. Say we draw up a statement contending that your aim in giving the shares to Fujinami had been 70 percent political donation and 30 percent a token of appreciation, and then let you fight your case in court. Would you go along with that? If the answer's no, there'll be no end to this investigation."

When Kamigaki questioned me on my connections with NTT, he pressed me to go with a statement that my intent was 50/50, and said I could fight my case in court. This time, with Fujinami, the balance was 70/30.

Munakata was sitting with his left elbow on the table. He slowly slid toward me and spoke in a voice just above a whisper. "Or, you could let us put into the statement that the political donations you gave to Fujinami twice a year had been a 'thank you.' The statute of limitations on bribe-taking is five years; on bribe-passing, three years, so your time's already up. Plus, we'd keep the amount to just twenty million yen; we've decided to eliminate the donations you made before the end of 1984."

The scenario put together by the Prosecutors Office was that after I had gone to ask favors of Fujinami at his official residence in 1984, I had begun making donations to him out of gratitude. But, I pointed out, the fact of the matter was that I had been making donations of five million yen twice a year to Fujinami, starting from when I became a key member of Sazanami-kai, before Fujinami became chief cabinet secretary. Munakata persisted in asserting that no record existed of my contributions prior to visiting Fujinami at his residence.

I kept silent.

The prosecutor, a scowl on his face, fell silent as well. This standoff went on for an uncomfortable while before Munakata began again. "We'd like to be able to call this investigation to a close as quickly as possible. As I've said time and again, in our indictment we'll ask for a suspended sentence and we'll let you out on bail swiftly. Won't you cooperate with us on this?"

I said nothing. The prosecutor seemed to grow more desperate.

"The Diet is in a stalemate and the political situation remains in turmoil. We must avoid a political vacuum and simply can't let this investigation go on any longer. You want to avoid a political vacuum, don't you? We're of the same mind on that."

We *were* of the same mind on that point, but if I went along with what he wanted, Fujinami would get indicted. If I didn't go along, then the political void would continue.

Perhaps Munakata detected my vacillation. He lowered his voice.

"Ever since we started investigating Fujinami, the press has been hounding me nightly, asking when we'll be nabbing him. They're making it really hard on me, you know."

This was no longer the hard-driving prosecutor I had faced at the outset.

"Please, won't you cooperate with us?" he pleaded, wiping the sweat from his forehead. "After all, what we're talking about here wasn't a transfer of cash but of stocks, and stocks go up and they also go down. In our indictment we'll ask for a suspended sentence."

Initially the prosecutors had insisted whoever received shares in Recruit Cosmos would have been sure to make money hand over fist. At the time I was arrested, however, the stock was trading below three thousand yen—a level guaranteeing that anyone who sold at that point was in for a loss.

I declined Munakata's offer. By this point, the prosecutor had little energy left to fight any more battles.

"If that's the way you want it, we'll have to issue another arrest warrant on you. Ida will be arrested too, you know."

Both of us knew by this point that the likelihood of arresting Ida was virtually nil. The exchanges between us had obviously reached an impasse, and with nothing new left to say between us, Munakata seemed stuck. Again, silence prevailed between us.

The only way to break the deadlock, I admitted to myself, was to agree to sign the statement for now and then fight my case in court.

"OK, I'll go along with you. So long as you prepare the statement so I can fight my battle in court, I'll sign it."

The prosecutor seemed visibly relieved.

"Thank you. I'll put in your contention that the money given to Fujinami was political donations."

He immediately set to writing up this statement:

> As far as I am concerned, the funds I provided were political donations given at mid-year and again at year's end. If it is suggested that they were partly intended as an expression of gratitude for favors I requested, this cannot be denied; but my true feelings were that Mr. Fujinami is destined to become a future prime minister, and I felt more strongly that I wanted to give him financial support in the hope that his political ambitions would be fulfilled. I acknowledge that the funds were, to a small extent, a token of my gratitude as well.

I signed it.

"OK! That's great! Thanks!"

Munakata seemed very pleased indeed. He picked up the signed document and hastened out of the room.

That was May 13.

After my trial got under way, my defense counsel went to the Public Prosecutors Office to seek disclosure of the accounting records they seized from Recruit. It took more than a month but they finally succeeded in locating a receipt for the purchase of tickets to Fujinami's fundraiser in 1982 and records relating to the five million yen donation I made to him in November 1983.

Obviously the prosecution must have seen these items, too. All the same, while knowing the facts, they had concealed them and instead fabricated a scenario under which, after asking Fujinami for favors, I allegedly began passing bribes to him in the guise of political donations starting in early August 1984.

In the course of my trial, my attorney was quick to pick up on what had transpired. "The reason they left out your donations made in 1983 and before was because there would have been no bribery motive to attach to your donations around that time," he said.

This was how the prosecution invented "crimes."

Fifth Revision—and a Sixth

The evening of May 14, Munakata entered the interrogation room with a look of mild embarrassment.

"The boss was on my tail again. He said we need to state clearly what the benefit for Recruit was. This boss of mine, when he looks over the major statements taken in a case, if he doesn't like what he sees he makes us do it over again. He ordered me to add the sentence, *We at Recruit are put in a very difficult position as well.* So please, let's do that."

The prosecutors often pressed me to redo a statement because "the boss said so," and in court I had the opportunity to get a glimpse at how the prosecutors conducted their interrogations in line with what has been decided by their superiors.

At my court session of June 11, 1993, one of my lawyers, Mamoru Wada, posed this question to Munakata: "From what we gather, it appears you and the other prosecutors pressed the accused to make oral statements while showing him written statements you already had in hand. Is this so?"

Munakata replied matter-of-factly: "There's a traditional way special investigators go about their job. In order to conduct an interrogation as unaffected as possible by what others have said, the prosecutor doesn't receive the written statements made by others but rather is informed only of what his superior chooses to tell him. In the current issue of *Seiron* magazine special investigator Tsutomu Hotta is quoted as saying this is the way special investigations have traditionally been carried out, and he laments that because that's the case, prosecutors involved in investigating major cases don't know anything other than what they learn through their own investigations, which, he says, makes it very difficult for them to conduct investigations. He is absolutely correct."

Munakata went on to say that prosecutors conducted their interrogations so as not to be affected by the statements made by others, but he himself had told me when his boss looked over written statements, if he didn't like what he saw he forced the prosecutor to do them over. It seemed to me that what actually happens is that the chief prosecutor purposefully collates the statements taken by the various parties involved in such a way as to make sure the court will arrive at a guilty verdict.

I refused to go along with Munakata's request to add this single sentence.

"The Prosecutors Office goes and conjures up some scenario without listening to the accused's side of the story, and then coerces him to make a statement matching it. Isn't that doing things backwards?" I said.

Munakata by this point was in no mood to back down.

"We're already at the final landing stage here. If you put up a fight now, we won't get anywhere. Please, let me make the statement include a bit more of a nuance of you requesting favors. We won't ask for a heavy sentence—the boss has already agreed to that."

"Even if the gentlemen's agreement were abolished, it wouldn't affect Recruit in the least. The ones who would be hard-put are the universities."

"Don't start bringing that up again now. I'll make the statement so it includes your side of the story. Please."

Without waiting for any more rebuttals from me, Munakata began revising the original draft of the statement. When he was convinced he had made the revisions he needed, he began reciting the new text for his assistant to take down.

After we had made small talk for some time, I asked Chief Cabinet Secretary Fujinami, who oversaw the government agencies, whether it wouldn't be possible for him to take measures of some sort to prevent the early selection of civil servants.

"The reason I've come to see you today," I began, "has to do with student recruitment. Although the Ministry of Education has issued its directives, the Central Employment Measures Council given its instructions, and there's a gentlemen's agreement in place, the government agencies are ignoring such conventions and making their selections early on, and this early recruitment of students to join the civil service is a major factor why the gentlemen's agreement affecting the private sector isn't being obeyed. This is both a social problem and we at Recruit are put in a very difficult position as well, and I wondered whether there isn't something that could be done about this. The way things stand now, the public sector is being given preferential treatment over the private sector, and we'd like to see the public sector do what's right. Isn't there anything you could do to prevent the early recruitment of civil servants? I'm here to ask for your help."

Munakata showed me the statement and urged me to sign it. Feeling like I had no real choice in the matter, I signed it. He seemed quite satisfied.

"Great! This should get the boss's approval!"

And with that he left.

On May 17, though, he showed up looking thoroughly worn out.

"We need to do the statement about Fujinami over again," he announced. This would make for our fifth redo.

"When I showed the last one to the boss, he gave me hell again. He said it's still too weak and we have to make it clearer what you gave him was intended as a thank you."

At the start of my interrogations, I had been scared of Kamigaki. But he in turn was scared of Munakata, and now I saw that Munakata was scared of his boss. It struck me that the Special Investigation Department had the same kind of entrenched hierarchy as the Japanese military did during the war.

"I thought you said the last statement would be OK."

"We're on our final landing approach here. Takeshita's announced his resignation, and it won't sit well if we can't declare an end to our investigation even after he's left office. Surely you can see my point."

Now the blood was clearly rushing to the prosecutor's head, and he began to lose patience. Earlier, Shoji had shown me that list of people who were probably candidates to join the new cabinet after Takeshita's resignation. The prosecutors must be in a frenzy. Munakata began trying to drive me into a corner.

"Neither you nor Fujinami intended any wrongdoing here, so even if Fujinami is found guilty he won't have to serve time. I'm an expert in bribery cases and have even written a book on bribery crimes for the Public Prosecutors Office's internal use. Fujinami didn't demand you give him either the stocks or the donations, so when we indict him we'll ask for a light sentence. I'll also put your side of the story into the statement and ensure that when you're indicted, we'll ask for a suspended sentence for you."

As he spoke, he placed the newly revised statement in front of me.

> *The crux of the matter is the money was intended in two ways. First, it was intended as a political donation to Mr. Fujinami. Second, it was intended as Recruit's expression of gratitude to Mr. Fujinami in his position as the Chief Cabinet Secretary for his response to our requests to take steps concerning the early recruitment of civil servants and other matters.*

I said nothing.

"We'd like you to cooperate with us here—from a broad perspective. Please."

By this point, from our ongoing conversations behind closed doors I understood all too well that Prosecutor Munakata himself was a sincere man but that, because of his position, he had to get a statement out of me even if by coercion.

I signed as he requested, for the seventh time.

Two days later, May 19, Prosecutor Shoji appeared with the draft of a summarizing statement.

"Is this OK?" he asked rhetorically, pushing the statement in front of me. "If there are any mistakes, feel free to make changes."

My statement of April 30, about my conversation with Fujinami, had said I discussed with him whether it might not be possible to push back the announcement of successful candidates taking the exam to become high-ranking civil servants, and also where I should go and what procedures I should follow to make such a request.

In a statement subsequently prepared, my visit to Fujinami was specified as having taken place in mid-March 1984, and the focus of my discussion with him had shifted to preventing government agencies' early recruitment of students. However, the content of my request as recorded in that statement lacked specificity, and it could potentially be construed that I had not requested specific prevention measures.

In the new statement Shoji had drawn up, the passage concerning the circumstances under which I had visited Fujinami now read as follows:

I requested of Chief Cabinet Secretary Fujinami that something be done to prevent the early recruitment of students to become civil servants, and also that the date for announcing the successful candidates of the civil service exam be pushed back.

I revised this to read:

I requested that measures be taken to prevent the early recruitment of students to become civil servants—specifically, that the date for announcing the successful candidates of the civil service exam be pushed back.

Whereas I wanted to stress that the "specific" matter we discussed during my visit to Fujinami had been the deferment of the exam results, Shoji deleted that part, perhaps thinking it would contradict my earlier statements.

When I tried to have the original wording restored and wrote "stet" next to the passage in question, Shoji reacted immediately.

"You can't change that," he said brusquely, and he struck out the offending "stet." That "stet" in my handwriting—and not the assistant's—stands as clear indication of my true intent in the matter. Ultimately, my "stet" was deleted and the final statement read as the prosecutor wanted it to:

I requested that measures be taken to prevent the early recruitment of students to become civil servants.

In order to make a case of bribe-taking stand against Fujinami, the prosecutors had demonstrated a request for favors was made relating to his official duties. If, as I said, what we discussed had been the schedule for announcing the results of the high-ranking civil service exam, that, being under the jurisdiction of the National Personnel Authority, would lie outside Fujinami's official purview.

This seemed to be the reason special investigators concocted a scenario that pushing back the date for announcing successful civil service candidates was tantamount to preventing the early recruitment of candidates, and that my purpose in visiting Fujinami was an alleged attempt to request prevention of such measures.

Freedom to Read Newspapers and Letters

On May 22, the ninety-eighth day after my arrest, I was indicted for passing bribes in the indictments filed against Fujinami and Ikeda. When the guard handed me the indictment document, I attempted to read it, but like before, it was written in a manner that defied comprehension.

It was around this time that my lawyers' request to lift the ban against my receiving or send out written materials was approved, so I was allowed to read newspapers in my cell. I was also able to receive and send out letters, subject to censorship.

I applied for subscriptions to the *Asahi* and the *Nikkei* (*Nihon Keizai Shimbun*, the Japan Economic Times), and both dailies were delivered to my cell starting the next day. Being able to read a newspaper for the first time in a long while, I felt buoyed by the hope that my anxieties from being cut off from all information would now dissipate.

I also received any number of free newspapers issued by religious groups. I could imagine how some people, feeling desperately alone in their cell, might be induced to become believers.

I also received some seventy to eighty letters that had been held since my arrest. They had all been opened, with critical parts blacked out. Nearly all the letters were from other detainees at the same facility, many suggesting we write to each other on a regular basis. Not a few began by describing the reason they were arrested.

Some of these letters contained heartfelt messages of encouragement. "As far as I can tell from reading the newspapers," one read, "it doesn't seem like Recruit received any favors from any politicians. Under the law, you are innocent. Let's both fight our cases."

From these letters, I came to realize there were many others who were going to court from the detention center bolstered by belief in what we had all been taught in school: *in dubio pro reo*—"When in doubt, favor the accused."

"Negotiating" My Release

On June 4, Munakata entered the interrogation seeming somewhat preoccupied.

"Who's going to be your trial lawyers? Same guys you have now—Hino and Tada?"

"I think so."

Kyuzaburo Hino, the head of my defense team, was at that time serving as chairman of Shinpokai, a group of legal professionals who had graduated from Chuo University. Munakata and my other attorney, Takeshi Tada, were also members of this group, a situation that seemed to make it easy for them all to discuss matters informally. During the investigation stage, Hino was my main attorney, and he visited the Public Prosecutors Office about twice every week and spoke with Munakata. The prosecutor seemed to think he would be able to negotiate with my lawyers during my trial also.

"As a condition for letting you out on bail, I want you to sign this."

Munakata drew up yet another statement, this one admitting my guilt in all charges against me, starting from violation of the Securities and Exchange Law. He pressed me to sign it, saying that if I did, he would release me on bail two days later.

I no longer had the energy to refuse, plus my attorneys had told me that statements taken after an indictment have no legal force, so I signed it.

"If you put up a serious fight, your trial in the lower court will take ten years."

At first I couldn't tell if he was offering advice or being flippant.

"You'll probably have three court sessions or so a month. While you're on trial, you can't do anything. It's up to the court to reach a verdict, but we've lightened the sentence we're asking for at the time of your indictment and you'll likely get a suspended sentence. So if I were you, I wouldn't put up too much of a fight."

Two days later, June 6, Munakata entered the interrogation room accompanied by Kamigaki.

"Thank you for cooperating in the investigation. As promised, we're letting you out on bail today."

With that, Munakata extended his hand, a big grin on his face. Kamigaki followed suit.

Seeing the happy expressions on their faces, I took their hands in turn and gave each a firm handshake. I felt unspeakably relieved.

Both prosecutors were no longer the menacing ogres I had suffered during my interrogations but now just smiling, friendly faces. The ease with which they underwent such dramatic change in their attitude reminded me of Dr. Jekyll & Mr. Hyde.

Perhaps, as part of their profession, interrogating prosecutors necessarily put on two faces: one kind and sincere, the other frightening and mean. It occurred to me that among them there may be some who, serving too long in their profession, truly do undergo changes in character.

My Release

At just after four P.M., on June 6, 1989, I was released on bail. The amount was unusually high: two million yen. I had been in detention a total of 113 days.

In the room where I was first disrobed, I changed into the shirt, necktie, and suit taken from me at arrival. I then headed toward the door, walking past the infamous checkpoint where I was forced to "dance the can-can."

"There's a huge crowd of photographers out there," Hino cautioned me. He then asked if I wanted to address the press. I said no.

As I stepped out the door, I was greeted by the familiar phalanx of flashing cameras as when I entered. Hino provided a shield enabling me to proceed, and with his help and much effort I finally made it into the waiting car.

As we pulled away, we were closely followed by a number of vehicles from TV stations. Overhead we were tracked by helicopters. The only way there could be helicopters on hand was if the Public Prosecutors Office informed everyone in advance of my impending release.

I cringed at the thought of again becoming a spectacle.

The TV vehicles and helicopters were relentless in their chase. We made a complete circuit around the Metropolitan Expressway, exited, and then drove to the Hotel New Otani. We stopped at the lower level of the two-story parking lot, I got out, ran up one flight of stairs, and got into a different car, enabling us to elude the TV cameras beyond that point.

From the New Otani we drove to a condominium owned by Recruit Cosmos in Moto-Azabu.

III

AFTER MY RELEASE

"**T**okyo District Public Prosecutors Complete Investigation of Recruit Affair"
    Thus read the front-page headline in the *Asahi* on May 30, 1989, capping a report on a press conference that was held by the chief public prosecutor, Yusuke Yoshinaga.

According to the article, the investigation into the Recruit scandal involved the questioning of some 3,800 individuals, searches of approximately eighty locations, and the seizure of some nine thousand pieces of evidence. Starting from the date that charges were brought against lawmaker Yanosuke Narazaki, the investigation had gone on for roughly 260 days and engaged fifty-two prosecutors and 159 assistant officers—a scale unprecedented in the history of Japan's judiciary. More than a dozen prosecutors from other district offices provided back-up support to the investigation.

The article went on to state that the Public Prosecutors Office had concluded, in light of the fact it was shares of stock that traded hands, the passing of the shares—even if they were assured of rising in value—was not subject to the Political Funds Control Act because, among other reasons, the timing of the acquisition of money "as a political donation" was not certain. This view, depending on interpretation, could be construed as saying no illegal act occurred. It could also be taken as an indication the Public Prosecutors Office deemed the provision of the shares did not engender uniform profits for the recipients, and indeed there were instances when losses were incurred.

The same press conference was also mentioned in *Tokyo chiken sosabu no uchimaku* [The Inner Workings of the Tokyo District Public Prosecutors Office's Special Investigation Department], by Yuji Yamamoto, published in November 1989. Yamamoto, a former *Mainichi* reporter, quoted the chief public prosecutor as saying the investigation was "extremely long and more difficult than any [he] ever previously experienced." Munakata was cited as having described the case as both "profound in depth" and "broad in scope." "For those of us who served on the front line," Munakata said, "the job was time-consuming and filled with difficulties."

But in Yamamoto's words, "The conclusion of the investigation into the Recruit affair was clearly different. In spite of its being the biggest bribery scandal since the Lockheed affair, the special prosecutors were left with the empty feeling their job was incomplete—a feeling visibly reflected in the glum demeanor of Mr. Yoshinaga and his colleagues at their press conference."

The special investigators interrogated approximately three thousand Recruit officers and employees, with some officers undergoing interrogation nearly a hundred times. Some employees were targets of interrogations that dragged on deep into the night, even on weekends—interrogations so severe that in some instances their family members were led to believe the person actually engaged in wrongdoing. Other employees, compelled to undergo questioning until the wee hours of the morning for days on end, opted to live in business hotels. They endured physical exhaustion and mental fatigue, and their recovery from the ordeal was lengthy.

Seiichi Tateoka and Shunjiro Mamiya, arrested on suspicion of violating the Securities and Exchange Law, were ultimately cleared, but they were detained and interrogated for more than twenty days. From what I have been told, even after they were released, they would regularly break out into cold sweats and talk deliriously in their sleep, and it took them about two months to return to normal.

Among the items the special investigators seized were employees' appointment books, floppy disks, and other personal items, disrupting their work and interfering with their private lives. Everything was gradually returned to them by the time the trial ended, but it was no easy task going through all the boxes, sorting things out, and returning them to their rightful owners. The eighty locations investigated included not only Recruit offices, but in some cases the homes of employees as well.

During my interrogations at the detention center, Prosecutor Munakata would sometimes just chat, and on one such occasion he allowed how impressed he was by Recruit's employees.

"Recruit's employees sure are strong. At most companies, if we threaten employees with arrest two or three times if they don't play along with us, they'll sign a statement even if it contradicts the facts. But Recruit's employees, if they think something's wrong, they insist it's wrong."

In fact, Recruit's employees were working harder than ever. Due to media reports on the scandal, Recruit could not advertise in newspapers or on television. Afraid that the company might go bankrupt under these circumstances, employees often slept in the office and worked on weekends to get their jobs done. As a result, in 1989–1990, the twenty-ninth fiscal year of the company, sales actually increased 23.6 billion yen—up 9 percent from the previous year. Operating profit increased 57 billion yen—up 12 percent from the previous year. My gratitude to Recruit's employees for their tremendous effort in times of tremendous hardship cannot be adequately expressed.

In a book published years later in 2001, Toshio Yahagi, a former Recruit employee who went on to open his own pub, wrote about those days:

> One day in June 1988, when I was 39, Recruit's 4,000 employees were suddenly plunged into a cataclysmic vortex, the likes of which we had never experienced before. The *Asahi Shimbun* came out with a splash report on the circumstances surrounding the provision of shares of Recruit Cosmos, which had just gone public, instantly creating a social issue of major scale: the so-called Recruit scandal.
>
> All the television stations rushed to put together special programs, and the scandal was their all-encompassing story for days on end. The dailies reported on the widening scandal in a big way too, together with commentary by pundits of every ilk. Open any weekly magazine, and out would pop the word "Recruit" in letters as big as could possibly fit on the page.

Practically every morning, TV crews would congregate outside Recruit's office building and stick microphones in front of us as we arrived for work. This went on for more than a year.

At the time, I was working in a department that did promotional work for educational institutions, and on repeated occasions I was questioned by the special investigators from the Tokyo District Public Prosecutors Office as someone who was potentially involved in the Ministry of Education "route."

I would wait at the reception desk at the Prosecutors Office in Kasumigaseki, and when my name was called I would walk down the long, dark corridor to the interrogation room on the fourth floor.

"You idiot! How long are you going to keep saying things like this?"

From the small rooms on either side of the corridor I would hear the prosecutors bellowing in anger and banging their fists on the table. Here before my very eyes, in real life, was the kind of scene I saw so often in TV dramas. The interrogation sessions would go on for seven or eight hours, day or night.

In my position, there was always the possibility that what started out as my questioning as a witness could at some point turn into my interrogation as someone accused, and that I could even get hauled off to jail. For a fact, one prosecutor threatened that if I kept saying what I did, he would shift to taking a written statement from me as a suspect "at any time."

Where does the truth leave off and slander begin? Where does business end and a crime begin? As I asked myself these questions, caught up in a whirlwind over which I had no control, I became a physical and mental wreck. This went on for days.

One night, when one particularly long and nerve-jangling bout of questioning finally came to an end, I was walking down the dark hallway when I saw someone whom I knew well through work coming up the stairs. I wondered if he was about to undergo the same kind of gut-wrenching interrogation as I had—the kind that feels like a drill is piercing your stomach—agony he wouldn't have to experience except for the reason that he did business with Recruit. Feelings of sadness, mixed with apology, drove me to hide in the shadows of the corridor, and after he passed without noticing my presence, I bowed low as I watched him proceed down the hall.

Across from the Prosecutors Office is Hibiya Park, a lushly green haven where many businessmen and office ladies take a break during the day. At night, though, after eight o'clock only faint white lights illuminated the paths. As I trudged slowly through the park, not another soul in sight, I found tears trailing down my cheeks—tears of vexation at having been forced to endure what I was going through, for reasons I couldn't rationalize. As I gazed up at the night sky, I suddenly felt I understood why many people implicated in bribery scandals end up taking their own lives. . . .

"No matter what people might say, we performed jobs of importance for the benefit of Japanese industry and the educational community." It was perhaps this sense of pride that managed to keep us going, barely, and not give in to the maelstrom in which we found ourselves.

I caused many employees and their families great pain—pain that no words of apology could mitigate.

Media Coverage—A Retrospective

After the first reports appeared about my having provided shares of Recruit Cosmos to Hideki Komatsu, Kawasaki's deputy mayor, the media all joined in the fray. Recruit staff kept all related articles in large files—twenty-seven in all. About half were from the *Asahi*. I had copies of all the material made so that I could pore over them before the start of my trial.

At first the reports focused on whether or not my selling of Recruit Cosmos shares constituted a violation of the Securities and Exchange Law. Then before long, when the issue of Recruit's having purchased the Cray supercomputer through NTT came to light, accusations flew that Recruit must have received some sort of favor from NTT. Next, the scandal widened to charges involving the Ministry of Education, the Ministry of Labor, and, in connection with the gentlemen's agreement on student recruitment, the Ad Hoc Council on Education. From there it eventually extended to the political arena—to former Agriculture, Forestry, and Fisheries Minister Kato, former Prime Minister Nakasone, and former Chief Cabinet Secretary Fujinami.

Various magazines entered the fray with special features on the scandal. The September 1989 issue of *Shokun* posed the question "Who really did anything wrong in the Recruit scandal?" The argument it raised was this: that the outcry to crack down on people who made a lot of money, all the while knowing they did nothing infringing on any laws, equated to the logic that it was perfectly acceptable to falsely accuse somebody who happens to be wealthy. Another special feature in the same magazine, in December 1989, was titled "Moral Yardstick for Measuring the Recruit Scandal." It concluded that while the whole affair was nothing to look favorably upon, there was something inherently askew in seeking the same rules for a professional wrestling match as you would for a grade-school field day.

The *Yomiuri*, in its regular column "Ronten" (Point at Issue), carried a series of articles on the Recruit affair by various pundits and commentators.

On May 24, 1989, Kotaro Tawara, a well-known, well-respected political commentator, wrote the following:

> In cases where, even if ultimately the indictment is suspended, unequivocal evidence exists and a party is subjected to investigation, or, even though the party in question goes scot-free while those directly connected to him are indicted, it is conceivable for some degree of responsibility to be called into question. The same may hold true in cases where no illegality was committed but evidence clearly shows that an act of impropriety has taken place.
>
> This, however, is as far as the matter should go. Although there may be people who, in response to mere suspicions cast upon them, say that they are solely to blame and thus take responsibility as a leader, the decision to do so is theirs alone; it is not something that should be forced upon them by others. How much more so when, despite the absence of evidence of any kind, an individual is called

on to take political or moral responsibility and personally attacked, based on speculation, guesswork, bias, or political machinations. This is clearly a political lynching, an act that is not permitted in societies governed by law.

As the investigation into the Recruit affair nears its conclusion, we hear calls not to let this "great evil" escape; or charges that the prosecutors are being too soft; or exhortations that the probe should next turn to questions of political responsibility. This is absolutely absurd. After the prosecutors—a group of experts specialized in what they do—were able to find no wrongdoing under law or by dint of evidence after investigating for half a year, the notion of then seeking to find wrongdoing as political propaganda is tantamount to calling a head of thick black hair bald—an act of outrage that is as destructive to law and order as graft and corruption.

The political commentator Taro Yayama, writing in "Ronten" on May 26, 1989, focused on the suspicions surrounding Recruit's purchase of the Cray supercomputer and the accusations that former Prime Minister Nakasone was involved in its purchase. Writing that the chief prosecutors fanned the media's flames by likening events to the Lockheed scandal, Yayama went on to say if indeed the events surrounding the purchase of the supercomputer were similar to the Lockheed affair, the comparison would hold water only if money was passed from Cray. In order for the shares provided by Recruit to Nakasone to qualify as a bribe, there would need to be evidence Nakasone exercised his professional authority on Recruit's behalf to a commensurate level. But, Yayama noted, insofar as the purchase of the supercomputer was concerned, Recruit was in a position to buy without any intervention by Nakasone. Why, Yayama asked, if no flow of money was revealed and therefore no evidence existed, did the media reports continuously contend Nakasone was guilty? Was the media manipulating public opinion even as the prosecution was leaking information to them?

In an article in the *Sankei* on May 24, 1989, the writer indicates that the prosecution had reached its legal limits, which suggests no wrongdoing by Ezoe under current laws.

News articles lashing out at Recruit or at me gradually vanished from around the time of my indictment. The number of highly critical magazine articles also diminished substantially.

Depression from Confinement

From the day after my release, I was tormented by indescribable loneliness. I was overcome with self-loathing for having signed statements betraying Shinto and Fujinami. Just as I felt before my arrest, I embraced the desire to do away with myself. Prosecutors Kamigaki and Shoji had kept saying that when a person is kept in detention for too long, he becomes mentally unstable—they were right.

To escape the watchful eyes of the media and any would-be assassins— a shot having been fired at my home the previous August—I remained in seclusion at the Recruit Cosmos condo in Moto-Azabu. One of my secretaries, Kei Sakuma, and a maid, who had taken turns attending to my daily needs, later they told me I would walk around in circles with a blank look on my face. My own memories of this time are vague at best, but I do remember waking with fear in the middle of the night, my bedsheets drenched with sweat.

Six days after my release, June 12, was my fifty-third birthday. Hoping to raise my spirits, about forty Recruit employees rented a club in Roppongi for the evening and held a party to celebrate the occasion.

My first taste of beer in a year—I hadn't had any since I entered Hanzomon Hospital—was somewhat bitter. I didn't drink very much that evening, but after not speaking with anyone for so long, I reveled in the opportunity to talk with everybody. The party went on until late into the night.

One thing on my mind ever since I was detained was that the students Recruit informally recruited might refuse to accept jobs with the company. At the party, Ginjin Aoyama, the hiring manager, told me he had been concerned too, but that in the end only about 3 percent of the recruited students had turned the offer down—it was no different from other years. He also recounted, with obvious pleasure, how the media were present in droves at the company's welcoming ceremony for its new employees, who all exhibited pride in joining Recruit.

I felt enormous gratitude to *all* Recruit employees, and humbled by their devotion and effort. Recruit's sales, I learned, had in fact increased significantly. And the company's telecommunications business was doing favorably as well, with sales up nearly 80 percent from the previous year. This area of business required that Recruit report to the Ministry of Posts and Telecommunications, and I was pleased to hear in spite of all the bad publicity about the scandal, the ministry did not give any special guidance to NTT and that NTT maintained its cooperative stance toward expanding Recruit's telecom business.

About a month later I left the condominium in Moto-Azabu and moved to Hikawa, a guesthouse in Akasaka I purchased from Shoichi Kajima of Kajima Corporation. My whereabouts were quickly discovered by the media, however, owing to the presence of two police officers standing guard out front. This made it difficult for me to go out, and I ended up staying cooped up inside.

Every day I would watch a laser disc that Pioneer's Seiya Matsumoto had given me: Bellini's "Norma," my favorite opera, with the soprano Montserrat Caballé, which was the only performance on the market at the time. I also listened to CDs—one being Hibari Misora singing songs originally made famous by Nat King Cole—but I was unable to escape a pervasive anxiety. I tried to cheer myself up watching videos of ballroom dancing and skiing, but getting back to my normal self proved elusive.

From time to time I would sneak out the back entrance and go to the home of Hiroshi Inoue, a psychiatrist. He would counsel me as we dined on a home-cooked meal prepared by his wife, and he provided me with sleeping pills and antidepressants. I apparently was more depressed than I was aware of, as Mrs. Inoue later told me that every three minutes or so I would let out a big sigh.

After a while Dr. Inoue indicated he found it difficult to counsel me because we knew each other too well, and he introduced me to Yoshio Kato of Toho University's Faculty of Medicine. According to Dr. Kato's diagnosis, what I suffered from was depression brought on by confinement. All combined, including the time I spent at Hanzomon Hospital and then at Kosuge, I had been in confinement for nearly ten months.

As he explained: "When a wild sparrow is caught and put in a cage, it first works itself up into a frenzy. After a month it adjusts and settles down to life in the cage. But suppose that the bird is released from the cage some-time later, it can't just fly the way it used to. It has to regain the ability to fly gradually. The same with you: you'll eventually return to your old self. How long it takes differs from one person to the next, but in three to six months you should be feeling like yourself again."

Dr. Kato then offered me two pieces of advice: one, to exercise regularly; and two, to focus on the future. He prescribed sleeping pills and antide-pressants, as Dr. Inoue had.

Hiroyuki Maishi, the president of Recruit She's Staff (now, Recruit Staff-ing), suggested I try meditation, offering to introduce me to a Zen temple. Meditation might help restore my peace of mind, I realized, but sitting still for long periods of time was too close to my experience of being confined in a cell. I appreciated his concern but declined.

Minoru Fujii, a close friend from university days, visited from Kyoto. A former professor at Kansai University who, at the age of forty, became a Buddhist priest, Fujii brought me *Tannisho*, a book with the sayings of Shinran, the founder of the Jodo Shinshu sect in the thirteenth century. "Read this over and over," he said, "and your mind will be set at ease." The book was short, less than a hundred pages, written in esoteric lan-guage that I found extremely difficult to understand. I did read it—twice—but failing to grasp what it was saying, I gave up.

After a time, to amuse myself and compensate for my lack of adequate exercise, I started playing golf again. On weekends, I would go to the foot-hills of Mount Fuji to the golf course at the Five Hundred Club, which I had joined on the recommendation of Noboru Goto when it first opened. Club members treated me quite warmly as they always had, and their sym-pathy for my situation brought me great comfort.

I also accompanied Hiroshi Okura, a close friend who was the founder of Noevir, to Akashima, in Okinawa. Amid the natural beauty, we dived and water skied, and I found myself letting go, truly enjoying what I was doing, and gradually, I began to feel the pall of depression lifting.

Back in Tokyo, my younger daughter visited frequently, always cheerful and reassuring. "Don't let things get you down," she would say.

To buoy my spirits, she would suggest we have dinner at a favorite Japanese restaurant in Ginza, where we could dine in privacy. Our conversation would often turn to the movies she was seeing—old movies I myself saw long before, like "Sabrina," "Roman Holiday," and "My Fair Lady," all starring Audrey Hepburn. These shared enjoyments gave great impetus to our get-togethers, and helped me greatly on the road to recovery.

The LDP's Crushing Defeat

Upon the doctor's recommendation of "a change of scenery," I decided to go golfing at Appi.

I disguised myself with a wig, hoping to avoid the media, and boarded the Shinkansen. I was also accompanied by a police escort, who was sitting in a seat not far away, in light of the shooting incident at my home.

By total chance, I found myself seated next to Ippei Kono, the president of Iwate Broadcasting Company, an old acquaintance. I could hardly pretend not to know him, so turning toward him, I said, "It's been a long time. I hope I haven't caused you any trouble."

For a moment Kono was perplexed, but then he recognized me. "Oh, Ezoe-*san*," he exclaimed. "You've been through quite a lot, haven't you."

We then chatted as the train whisked us northward.

The weather at Appi was clear, not a cloud in the sky. As I played a round of golf with people working at the links, surrounded by scenery so familiar—the lush green, the gently flowing river, and Mount Maemori looming—the tangled web of emotions that had been weighing heavily on me began to unravel, and I felt a calm sense of release. I was still unable to think clearly and didn't bother keeping score, but I felt thoroughly refreshed.

About a dozen local police officers were posted around the hotel—likely under instructions from the National Police Agency—but they appeared to having nothing in particular to do, so they were killing time, looking for any hapless speed violators who might come their way.

By coincidence, Yusaku Kamekura happened to be at Appi too, working

on the interior design for the new hotel tower under construction. When
completed, it would be the highest tower in the northern Honshu area.

Over dinner, he was quite candid. "I didn't know you were hanging
around with politicians like that," he began. "If I'd known, I'd have told
you to stop. I'm sure you thought giving donations to politicians would
bring about better government, but it doesn't work that way. Giving money
to politicians doesn't improve how they govern."

"I see that now. I acted rashly."

"Yes, you really did some very foolish things."

Ever since my stay at Hanzomon Hospital, not a day went by when I
didn't sorely regret how stupid I'd been. Unfortunately, regret doesn't erase
what has already been done.

"You caused political chaos and brought down the cabinet. In this country, besides crimes under the law, there's also such a thing as moral crime.
You're going to get a jail sentence, but probably a year-and-a-half at most.
Ezoe-*san*, you're still young. Do your time as soon as you can, get out, and
then get on with your work again."

Kamekura and I had known each other so long, he was one of the few
people who could say these things to me in earnest.

I returned from Appi on July 23, the day the Upper House elections were
being held.

Again I traveled in disguise, but the moment I alighted from the Shinkansen and stepped on the train platform, I was swarmed by a camera crew from
TBS, the Tokyo-based TV station that Iwate Broadcasting is associated with.

I managed to make my way to the exit and get into the car waiting for
me, but the photographers followed tenaciously. I had my driver take narrow back streets, enabling us to elude our pursuers eventually. By the time I
reached home, it was after eleven P.M.

I immediately turned on the TV to learn the election results. The LDP
was doing badly, winning just thirty-six seats, down from seventy-two
before the election. Meanwhile the Japan Socialist Party grabbed forty-six
seats. All throughout the campaign period, Takako Doi, the JSP leader, was
seen on TV daily railing against Recruit-gate. I expected that the JSP would
make a strong showing, but I never imagined it would be *this* strong.

The vote counting went on into the wee hours. When the final tallies were in, the LDP suffered an enormous defeat that brought a crash ending to its unchallenged domination of the Diet since 1955. In a victory speech, Doi proclaimed "the mountain has moved"; it was a scene that received huge coverage by the media.

The TV commentator was quick to point out that the impact of the Recruit scandal on the elections was far greater than anyone imagined. The anchorman reminded viewers that members of the House of Councillors were elected for terms of six years, with half the total number of seats contested every three years. What the latest election results meant, he suggested, was even if the LDP were to put in a strong showing in the next round of elections, it would have a hard time achieving a majority—something not likely to happen for another twelve years. Until this occurred, he said, the two houses would be controlled by different camps.

In between reporting the latest voting results, TBS kept broadcasting the film of me, in my wig, shot earlier in the evening. They were making a spectacle of me. I sat before the TV with my head hanging.

All I wanted to do was to vanish into thin air.

It was, just as the announcer on TV contended, another twelve years before the LDP was able to regain its majority in the Upper House. This was accomplished in the elections of 2001, when the party scored a resounding victory under its new president, Junichiro Koizumi, who campaigned for "structural reforms accompanied by pain" and promised he would "bust up" the LDP and its old ways.

In the interim, the LDP, unable to pass legislation on its own, for a long time failed to bring its policies to fruition. After the Takeshita Cabinet resigned, the prime minister position changed hands with dizzying speed: starting with Sosuke Uno (LDP: June to August 1989), to Toshiki Kaifu (LDP: August 1989 to November 1991), to Kiichi Miyazawa (LDP: November 1991 to August 1993), to Morihiro Hosokawa (Japan New Party: August 1993 to April 1994), to Tsutomu Hata (Renewal Party: April to June 1994), to Tomiichi Murayama (Japan Socialist Party: June 1994 to January 1996), to Ryutaro Hashimoto (LDP: January 1996 to July 1998), to Keizo Obuchi (LDP: July 1998 to April 2000), to Yoshiro Mori

(LDP: April 2000 to April 2001). The average term in office was a little over a year, not long enough for any of the prime ministers to implement policies they'd proposed. Drawing up supplementary budgets became an annual affair, and under the cabinet of Keizo Obuchi—the final remnant of the Takeshita faction—no fewer than four supplementary budgets were passed, resulting in a gradual buildup of the nation's debt.

I had made my political donations in the belief that without a stable administration there can be no economic development. In the end, my actions had the complete opposite effect. If destabilizing the political situation constituted a crime, then I was very guilty indeed. No amount of remorse could ever change that.

Both Sides Prepare For Battle

Shortly after I was released on bail, along with the personal items put into custody when I entered the detention center, I was given back my notebooks—something I did not expect.

One of Recruit's legal advisors, Katsuro Tanaka, recommended that I use my notes and write everything down in formal language while the details were still fresh in my mind. Then I should have it notarized and officially dated. The document would provide a record of what had transpired while I was detained.

I followed his advice and had one of my attorneys, Osamu Ishihara, come daily to record the circumstances of my interrogations throughout my detention and the contents of the statements I signed. He then had the records notarized. Recruit also had one of its lawyers do the same for company employees who had been interrogated.

Later, these actions proved effective when I petitioned the court for disclosure of statements taken from me by the public prosecutors on specific days.

My attorney indicated that I had two options: to fight my case in court, or to admit to wrongdoing and accept the punishment meted out.

"If your case also involved tax evasion, it would be different," he said, "but with simple bribe-passing of this sort, no defendant has ever actually been sent to prison. In the United States, when multiple bribe-takers are involved, the punishment stacks up proportionately; but in this country, any extra punishment is limited to 50 percent, regardless of the number of persons bribed."

He then qualified this optimistic outlook: "With the Recruit scandal, though, reporting has surpassed the coverage attracted by the Lockheed incident, making it the biggest news of its kind in postwar times. Plus, given how the media have been so critical of what you did, it's possible you'll have to serve time. Of course, you could admit to wrongdoing—in which case, even if you did get sentenced to jail time, you would probably get out on parole after eighteen months or so."

His argument did not stop there, however. "Then again, if you do choose to fight in court, you have seven bribe-takers here, and the court proceedings for each would probably take a year and a half at least, which means your trial would go on for ten years at the very minimum. During that whole time, you wouldn't have any freedom of movement and the expenses would be considerable. The choice is up to you."

I had not committed any wrongdoing. Moreover, Munakata promised the prosecutors would ask for a suspended sentence. The cost factor was a lingering worry, but I decided to fight my case in court.

In the meantime, my legal counsel, Katsuro Tanaka, Takeshi Tada, along with Fumihiro Sasaki, head of Recruit's legal affairs, were looking for lawyers to handle my defense in court. I was worried they might not find anyone willing to take on a case that had received as much media coverage as mine, but it turned out to be quite the opposite: many lawyers actually expressed interest in taking on my case *because* it was so big.

Ultimately I engaged the services of Shozaburo Ishida and Masanori Ono—both of whom were part of Kakuei Tanaka's defense team in the Lockheed scandal—and a number of others, including Teruhisa Maruyama, Junkichi Kuroda, Osamu Kasai, and Akinori Sakaeda—who were all human rights lawyers. I managed to elude the media vigil and met them in a Roppongi hotel.

"If I had been your attorney during the investigation, I would have advised you to stick to denying all wrongdoing," Ishida said with some regret. "In cases of simple bribery, without a statement admitting to a motive of bribery there can't be a conviction."

The others took a dim view of Kyuzaburo Hino's negotiations with the chief prosecutor. The fact of the matter, however, was it was extremely hard for a high-strung person like me to endure a lengthy detention and persist in making denials. I didn't say so in front of them, but I was actually quite grateful to Hino.

The meeting went well. I now had my defense team.

I was told the court was rushing to get the trial under way. Proceedings were set to start before the end of the year.

In typical court cases, evidence and statements secured by the interrogating prosecutor are handed to a different prosecutor charged with making a criminal case stand up in court. In my case, however, the Public Prosecutors Office set up a Special Trial Department headed by the chief prosecutor, and the interrogating prosecutors were directed to present the prosecution's case in court. To speed up the proceedings, the court decided to divide the trial into what came to be called three "routes"—which subsequently became four routes.

Hearing these special arrangements, I felt disheartened. If I were to face the same team of prosecutors in court as I had during my interrogations, I couldn't help fearing the trial would turn out just like the interrogations had.

Before long, some of my signed statements were disclosed to my defense team.

Ishida seemed impressed. "Kamigaki's very clever at taking statements, I see. It's to be expected, I guess, given how the court gives greatest weight to the statements secured by the public prosecutors."

I wasn't particularly interested in hearing this. "Don't you think some are vague, and open to interpretation, depending on how they're read?" I asked hopefully. "What about *in dubio pro reo?*"

"In principle that may be open to interpretation, but during actual trials, statements like these ultimately work in the prosecution's favor."

Once again it was driven home to me what they teach us about the law in school and what goes on in real life are two different things.

Advice from One Who Knows

One day in late autumn I met with Hiroshi Ito, who had been one of the defendants in the Lockheed trials.

I told him how during my interrogations at Kosuge I was coerced to sign the statements the prosecutor prepared. "I kept being told if I persisted in denying all wrongdoing, I'd never get out on bail and have to stay in detention throughout my trial."

"It was the same with me," he said. "They told me if I didn't confess, they would keep me at Kosuge and make me go back and forth to the courthouse in handcuffs, roped together with the radicals who committed the Asama-Sanso incident. The whole system is set up to work against you: the courts believe the statements you sign under threat are actually true."

In his lower court trial Ito denied all charges and was handed a jail sentence. He appealed and took his case to the High Court, this time admitting to the charges but offering an apology. He received a suspended sentence.

Hearing this was painful. I realized if I kept up my denials, I, like him, could end up with a jail sentence.

"Don't overreact to everything witnesses say in court," he advised. "Once your trial gets under way, the press will start writing about you again. The prosecutors actually give lectures to the legal reporters! During my first trial, every time the court convened—every time over six-and-a-half years—something always appeared in the press, and each time it was prejudiced in the prosecution's favor. Don't fret over what they write about your trial: it'll only wreck your health."

As I was pondering his advice, Ito suddenly asked me a question I would never have anticipated. "Ezoe-*san*, if I might ask, is everything going along OK between you and your wife?"

"No," I answered.

"In cases like this, the wives often start to feel like they're victims, too. In my case, I asked the proprietress here to talk to my wife and tell her things turned out the way they did only because of my job. It worked, and things improved between my wife and me. If you'd like, I could have a few words with your wife."

"Thanks for offering," I said almost apologetically, "but I don't think anything you could say would patch things up between us easily."

After dinner we played a game of Go. Ito held only a medium-level rank, but the way he played had the air of a true professional. As the game went on, I came to realize how this provided a release from everything weighing heavily on my mind and kept my mind off things. On the spot, I decided I would learn more about the game.

Several days later I joined a class offered by the Go Salon at the Hotel New Otani. It was taught by Chizu Kobayashi, a champion titleholder. Under her guidance I improved significantly over the course of the next two years.

Toward the end of that year, at the invitation of Isao Matsuoka, president of Toho, I attended his company's annual year-end party.

As he and I were engaged in conversation, we were surrounded by a pack of photographers all flashing their cameras our way. I practically had to crawl my way out of the room and into the elevator. To my great relief, the reporters and their photo crews were on hand to catch people in the entertainment industry and did not follow.

After that, and recalling what Ito told me about the connections between the prosecutors and the press, I made up my mind to talk to reporters myself—in the presence of an attorney. I informed the press club if anyone was interested in interviewing me, I would willingly oblige them.

After my trial began, I agreed to requests for interviews from the press, including those occasions that conflicted with the unofficial "lectures" being given by the prosecution to the reporters covering my case. Most of the reporters who were sitting in on the proceedings in court did not appear to know very much about the case, and they often approached me for corroboration. They always listened to responses by me and comments by Ishida with open minds and polite respect, and our exchanges served as a deterrent to any one-sided lectures by the prosecution.

The reporters I met this way appeared to view me as an ordinary human being—neither a charismatic business operator nor a businessman with political connections. On a number of occasions, I, always with Ishida, would meet them for a drink in a pub, and we always split the tab equally.

In preparing to write this book, I read through the files of articles clipped from those days. Compared to the fevered coverage by the press before and after my arrest, reporting on my trial was down to a trickle—perhaps 10 percent of what it had been. The more rational level of reporting was likely attributable to the effect of my responding to reasonable interviews; it seemed to deter reporters from going to journalistic excess.

Preparing for the Trial

Prior to the trial, one of my lawyers gave me a copy of the complete record of the court proceedings from the Lockheed case as covered in the press by *Tokyo Shimbun*. It ran to an astonishing sixteen volumes.

"This should give you an idea of what to expect," he said.

I didn't have to read very far into the first volume to see how exasperatingly slow a trial could be. One of the defendants was barraged with an endless series of questions that seemed to have no relevance whatsoever to his case: "What was the seating order at your wedding party?" "Who were asked to make speeches?" "What did they say in their speeches?"

I was also struck by certain revelations that seemed to cast doubt on some of the facts. For example:

- As a result of plea bargaining with the United States, the record of testimony by Lockheed, the bribe-giver in the case, was prepared without the defendants making an appearance in Japanese courts.
- The two defendants accused of giving 500 million yen in bribes, Carl Kotchian and John Clutter, were granted exemption from criminal prosecution.
- Nevertheless, the record of testimony was used as evidence in the Japanese courts, and it was based on that record that Hiroshi Ito, of Marubeni, who served as Lockheed's messenger in delivering the bribe money, received his jail sentence in the lower court.
- Former Prime Minister Kakuei Tanaka had also been sentenced to serve time in jail.

So in the Lockheed trials too, how the media reported events had an impact even on the decisions handed down by the Supreme Court.

My attorney had observed how the amount of media reporting in my case was unprecedented, and he had said I might end up with a jail sentence. I was overcome by the uncertainty of my future.

In November, just as the fall foliage reached its peak of color, I met with my defense team—about a dozen attorneys in all—at the Recruit company resort in Hakone. It was to be a two-day affair, the purpose of which was to analyze the content of the six indictments filed against me.

The indictments were very difficult to understand. The sentences were exasperatingly long, with almost no punctuation. Altogether the six indictments stretched to thirty-eight pages, and it was frustratingly hard to decipher exactly what crimes I was being accused of. Even my lawyers—who should be used to such things—were racking their brains to interpret them.

At first, the team itself was split as to what the indictments were charging me with. Finally, after heated debate that continued for hours, they decided ultimately that in order to make the points of contention in each indictment clear, at the very first court session, they would formally ask the prosecution to clarify the reasons behind each indictment; in other words, what was the basis on which I was being accused of each alleged crime.

Next, my lawyers analyzed each indictment and discussed the content of what they wanted the prosecution to clarify. They hammered out which parts of each indictment were valid and which parts went contrary to the facts, in order to clarify what points should be disputed in court.

After that, they discussed the matter of my statement of opinion to be presented to the court. In typical court cases it suffices for the defendant simply to admit to or not admit to the charges being made against him. In my case, however, I told my defense team I didn't think a simple reply of that sort would do me justice. They saw my point and decided to prepare a statement for me to read at the start of my trial.

Our meetings that first day continued well past the appointed time, and we didn't finish until after one in the morning. Before going to bed, some of us went for a soak in the facility's communal bath, which drew water from the local hot spring.

"I've been on any number of defense teams, and believe me, it's rare to see arguments as heated as what we've seen here today. Ezoe-*san*, I'd say you have yourself a team you can depend on. I'd even bet you'll get off on some of the charges." This was Akinori Sakaeda talking.

Junkichi Kuroda replied, "In my day, I was active in the student movement and was arrested on more than one occasion. That more or less prevented me from getting a job at any private company, so I took the bar exam and became a lawyer."

I was left with the impression he rather liked fighting battles against authority.

The reassuring words of encouragement I received that night from my attorneys, plus the long soak in the bath, enabled me to sleep solidly that night for the first time in a long while.

The next day discussions continued as to how to go about writing up my statement of opinion as well as the corresponding statement to be presented to the court by my defense team.

I left Hakone feeling that much had been accomplished. The ride back to Tokyo through the winding mountain roads from Hakone to Odawara, surrounded by brilliant foliage and within earshot of the gently flowing river below, gave me a welcome sense of calm. Gazing up at the azure sky, I took heart from a burgeoning feeling of confidence that with a defense team like this one, I would surely be found innocent on at least some of the charges against me.

IV

THE TRIAL

My trial, from the opening session to the handing down of a verdict by the lower court, lasted an astounding thirteen years and three months. In total, 322 court sessions were convened and I gave testimony thirty-eight times. When other Recruit trials carried out separately are included, I testified on 128 occasions—a figure unheard of in the history of Japanese criminal trials—over the course of 450 court hearings—a figure unprecedented anywhere.

Court proceedings in real life differ considerably from trials portrayed in TV dramas. In real courts, exchanges between the two sides dwell with dogged tenacity on the smallest details and go on interminably.

Let me relate my experience as a defendant on trial. I will rely on the actual court records as I go along.

Request for Clarification

My trial began on December 15, 1989, roughly seven months after I was served the last of my indictments. The media were so fired up—far beyond normal journalistic fervor—that all the TV stations had their cameras set up in front of my house from the night before.

When the fateful morning arrived, I made my way to the Tokyo District Court by car, accompanied by my lawyers Kyuzaburo Hino and Osamu Ishihara. When we reached Kasumigaseki and the car approached the court building, I couldn't believe my eyes. The entire route from the gate to the entrance of the building was lined with tents set up by the media to serve as a base for their crews. I never imagined that reporting by the media would reach such frenzy.

As we alighted and headed toward the main door, we were beset by the hordes of cameramen eager to capture my every move. I could hear the overlapping voices of the myriad newscasters on hand, all reporting with an excitement bordering on hysteria that I was entering the court building on my way to trial.

I was overcome by a renewed fear. Somehow I recalled hearing how the grander the scale of news, the heavier the sentence.

The trial was to take place in Courtroom 104, the largest of the courtrooms at the Tokyo District Court. I waited nervously in an anteroom while the photographers shot their footage of the inside of the courtroom. Once they were done, I was escorted inside and took my place at the defendant's table.

I composed myself and glanced around. The seven prosecutors assigned to my case—Norio Munakata, Toshiaki Hiwatari, Katsuhiko Kumazaki, Haruo Kasama, Shuzo Yamamoto, Hiromi Nagai, and Hideo Makuta—were already seated at the prosecutors' table to my left.

Sitting with me at the defendants table were Former Chief Cabinet Secretary Takao Fujinami, Katsuya Ikeda of the Komeito, and Toshihiro Ono, my secretary. Our defense team was to our right—in all, more than thirty attorneys, sitting in two rows. On the bench were Tadatsugu Watanabe, the presiding judge, and an associate judge on either side of him.

The visitors' gallery was full, and from what I later read in the evening editions of the newspapers, there was a long line of would-be observers. Another section set aside for reporters was also completely occupied.

Judge Watanabe declared the court in session. The first order of business was the defendants' identifying themselves. That done, our trial was under way.

Munakata, who headed the prosecuting team, then read out the six indictments against us. This was followed by the defense counsel requesting clarification of the charges.

To illustrate, the indictment charging me with having asked Fujinami for favors spoke of "requesting utmost efforts to respond appropriately, within a national administrative organ, in line with the tenor of the gentlemen's agreement on student recruitment." The wording used here was too abstract, and it was unclear just what the issue at hand was. Obviously, if the issue at hand weren't clear, then there could be no knowing what defense one should offer.

Prior to the start of the trial, the defense counsel submitted a request for clarification, encompassing one hundred questions, that ran to sixty pages. In reference to the indictment just cited, for example, clarification was sought on the following matters: What "national administrative organ" is referred to here? What is the content of the "appropriate response" allegedly requested? What constitutes "utmost efforts"? And if, as charged, Fujinami used his influence on an administrative organ, what specifically did he ask for?

By way of reply, the prosecution kept repeating that the points in question would be clarified during its opening statement or when presenting its substantiating evidence, or that no clarification was necessary. In turn, the defense team decided to repeat its request for clarification within the courtroom.

Heated exchanges took place between the defense and the prosecution for a full two days. Here is a sampling:

MASANORI ONO (my defense attorney): In the indictments relating to NTT and the Ministry of Education, references are made to "various favors." Such "favors" are what was allegedly provided in return for the offering of benefits and they thus constitute the core element of the crimes being charged—the *actus reus*. However, the indictments offer no indication as to how the alleged bribes were dispensed. In particular, according to the charges as presented, the "favors" received from Mr. Hasegawa, Mr. Shikiba, Mr. Takaishi, and Mr. Shinto spanned extremely long periods of time— the periods they were in their respective positions—for example, from April 1985 to March 1987, or from January 1986 to June 1988, or from July 1983 to June 1988. With durations of such length, acts of various kinds would naturally have taken place; but from the indictments it's altogether unclear just which of those actions were the alleged "favors." We believe this point should be clarified now—not in your opening statement or presentation of substantiating evidence.

NORIO MUNAKATA (chief prosecutor): We believe in each instance there are no inadequacies with respect to specification of the cause of action, so we will make no further clarifications at this time. Everything will become clear during our opening statement and the proceedings thereafter.

YOSHIAKI ANZAI (Fujinami's defense counsel): We have extracted the main points and submitted a second request for clarification, so I will present the essentials to you concisely. First, earlier, in the matter of who was referred to by "Mr. Ezoe and others," you responded that this was a reference to a plural number of individuals, and you mentioned such names as Toshihiro Ono and Masao Tatsumi, among others. But who is being charged as the perpetrator here? If Mr. Ezoe isn't claimed to be the perpetrator, who is? Second, according to the prosecution's clarification, in response to our request for clarification of the direct recipients of checks and shares, you indicate you will make this clear in your opening statement and during your substantiation of evidence; however, the items whose clarification is being requested are indispensable to the specification of the cause of action and to the exercise of the defendant's right of defense. Once again, we request clarification.

MUNAKATA: Concerning the "plural" raised in your first point, this is a matter relating to the perpetrators and we will clarify this in our opening statement and in the course of substantiating evidence. As to the second point, we believe no clarification is necessary.

ANZAI: The prosecution's second clarification is altogether unacceptable, but as we believe arguing the matter any further would not serve the purposes of these court proceedings, we will not pursue our request for clarification. Let us state, however, we are extremely dissatisfied with the response we have been given.

YOSHIMITSU FUKUSHIMA (Ikeda's defense attorney): In our request for clarification, in reference to the shares of stock involved in this case we asked for clarification of what constitutes the alleged actual bribe. In response the prosecution stated this to be the profit accruable by the bribe recipient as a result of having acquired shares of Recruit Cosmos, which were expected with certainty to rise in value after the company's registration in the over-the-counter market and which are extremely difficult for the average person with no special connections to Mr. Ezoe and others to acquire, at a price clearly lower than expected after market registration. This is an extremely convoluted explanation and one I am unable to understand. Is the bribe the shares of stock themselves, or not?

MUNAKATA: It's precisely as written in our clarification.

TERUHISA MARUYAMA (my defense counsel): In the indictment relating to Mr. Fujinami, in the first reference the passer of the bribe is described in the plural as "partners in crime," whereas elsewhere the bribe-passer is recorded as Mr. Ezoe acting alone. Are we to accept the latter explanation as the correct one? Clearly a distinction needs to be made as to who is being charged with crime here, so please respond.

MUNAKATA: It's just as described in the charge as filed.

MARUYAMA: We're asking for clarification precisely because the meaning of what is written here is unclear.

JUDGE WATANABE: When it says the defendant acted alone, this means he acted alone in the sense only Mr. Ezoe is to be charged here.

MARUYAMA: That doesn't make sense. Since acting as "partners in crime" means the crime was committed with accomplices, treating one of those partners as though he acted alone changes the elements of the crime. It's because this makes no sense we are requesting a clarification.

JUDGE WATANABE: The prosecutor just clarified that point a few moments ago. With that I wish to conclude the proceedings regarding requests for clarification.

In the end, for every question the defense attorneys posed before the court, the prosecution merely answered "it's precisely as written in the indictment" or "the point will be clarified in the opening statement or during the substantiation of evidence." These exchanges proved infuriating in the extreme.

The proceedings relating to our requests for clarification ended around 11:20 A.M. Next, was my long-awaited opening statement. I knew that whatever I did and said in the courtroom would be reported by the media in excruciating detail. Trying to contain my nervousness, I took the witness stand. A hush fell over the entire courtroom. Looking straight ahead, I began by making a public apology:

> The turmoil caused to the public by my actions, the mistrust of the government my actions invited, and the loss of trust in the governing authorities was brought about as a result of my own ignorance. I feel the heavy weight of responsibility for these events, and I wish to apologize sincerely, from the bottom of my heart.

I then proceeded to read my prepared statement. It was fifty pages in length, part of which follows:

> On June 18, 1988, the media reported I sold shares of Recruit Cosmos to Hideki Komatsu, the deputy mayor of Kawasaki City, and he was relieved of his office.
>
> From that time forward, up until the Tokyo District Public Prosecutors Office declared an end to its special investigation on May 29, 1989, over the course of almost a year, on nearly a daily basis the media consistently reported on the Recruit Cosmos stock affair or on my political donations in a critical way, as though what I had done was highly criminal in nature. Even before my indictment, I was portrayed by the media as a man so sinful there was no one who did not already know my name, and as a result many people who acquired the Recruit Cosmos shares suffered damage to their public standing.
>
> In addition, many politicians who received donations from Recruit or its affiliated companies were met with criticism and censure, their social or political standing suffering as a result, with a large number of them resigning from their positions. No words of apology could suffice to atone for the major repercussions the Recruit affair has on society, for the chaos it has engendered, or for the enormous trou-

ble my actions caused those who received the shares of stock or our donations, and I am overcome with shame.

In the course of my interrogations, on numerous occasions statements were drawn up that went counter to the facts or made allegations I adamantly denied. But repeatedly I was told if I didn't sign the statements, the presidents of Recruit and Recruit Cosmos and other parties concerned would be arrested. I agonized greatly, torn between the belief if any more people were arrested the Recruit Group would no longer be able to continue, and the knowledge that if I did sign the untruthful statements it would cause trouble for those individuals who were being accused of having accepted bribes.

Were it not for the untruthful statements I signed, the persons who are seated alongside me at the defendants' table in this court on charges of accepting bribes would surely not be here, in this position, today.

Among the general public, the prevailing view is since indictments have been served after the prosecuting authorities undertook a lengthy and large-scale investigation, adequate evidence must have been produced and substantiation made to warrant the charges. This is only to be expected, for the public places great trust in its national institutions—prosecuting authorities among them. They also place a high level of faith in the media—and the media have reported during the investigation phase as though crimes of a grave nature were committed.

Now that I have signed false statements in the interrogations during my long detention, in court I will be stating facts different from what those statements contain, and I know it will be an imposing task to get the court to understand where the truth rests. People likely cannot imagine the statements taken from me, the other defendants, and those called as witnesses could be false. They surely assume during interrogations we would staunchly refuse to sign any statements that ran counter to the facts.

It is my firm belief, however, the courts are a place where a fair and neutral position is rigidly maintained. I am confident in the trial about to get under way, within the confrontations between the prosecuting authorities and the defendants and defense counsel, it will be brought to light which "facts" of the two sides represent the real truth.

I believe through the trial commencing today, the truth will invariably be made known, and I earnestly hope the court will be circumspect in its proceedings and fair in rendering its judgment.

As I read my remarks, the visitors' gallery was so quiet you could hear
a pin drop. I sensed every eye in the room fixed on me. When at last I
finished reading the statement and returned to my seat, I felt relieved.

The court then recessed for lunch for ninety minutes. The afternoon session
began at 1:30 P.M., starting with the prosecution's opening statement.

In reference to the "favors" I allegedly asked of Fujinami in 1984, the
prosecution stated I requested "utmost efforts to respond appropriately,
within a national administrative organ, in line with the tenor of the gentlemen's agreement on student recruitment," adding on that occasion I
"requested the announcement of results of the exam for high-ranking civil
servants be delayed." Concerning the "favors" I purportedly requested in
1985, the prosecution said I requested "utmost efforts to have the administrative organ make an appropriate response, as in the previous year, in line
with the tenor of the gentlemen's agreement on student recruitment, with
Hisao Tanaka [senior managing director of Recruit] and Masao Tatsumi
again this year getting the personnel directors to prevent the early hiring
of students by government agencies," and Fujinami acquiesced. They also
claimed on that occasion Tanaka and Tatsumi asked Fujinami to bring up
the early recruitment issue before the Ad Hoc Council on Education and to
get this incorporated into the council's recommendations.

As expected, these claims were very vague. For example, although the
issue of what I supposedly asked Fujinami to do in return for my "bribes"
related to his professional authority as chief cabinet secretary and was
therefore an extremely important point, the prosecution's opening statement didn't make this clear in specific terms. Also, the statement claimed
that I requested of Fujinami that he bring up the early recruitment issue
before the Ad Hoc Council on Education and have the matter incorporated into the council's recommendations, but it was unclear whether or
not these were the "favors" I allegedly asked for.

In the second court session, on January 12, 1990, the defense team thus

asked for clarification once again of the specific content of the "favors" I was charged with requesting.

> DAIZO YOKOI (Fujinami's attorney): There are two points we would like clarified. The prosecutor's opening statement states the defendant requested to have the results of the exam for high-ranking civil servants delayed. The first point is whether or not having that announcement delayed is included within the "favors" allegedly requested. Second, in relation to the Ad Hoc Council on Education, the claim has been made a request was made to have Mr. Fujinami take up the early recruitment issue with the council and have the matter incorporated into its recommendations. Is this part of the purported "favors" requested also? Please clarify these two points.
>
> JUDGE WATANABE: Would the prosecutor please clarify these points?
>
> MUNAKATA: With respect to both points, we believe the opening statement is quite clear on these matters, but I will clarify them further. The request to have the announcement of the results of the exam for high-ranking civil servants delayed, and the request to have the early recruitment issue taken up by the Ad Hoc Council on Education and have the matter incorporated into its recommendations, are *not* included in the "favors" recorded in the indictment charges.

At the first court session, in his opening statement Munakata said the favors asked of Fujinami consisted of the request by Tanaka and Tatsumi to have the issue of early student recruitment taken up by the Ad Hoc Council and included in the council's recommendations. But at the second court session the chief prosecutor then stated this request, along with the request to delay the announcement of the exam results, was *not* included in the favors I allegedly asked of Fujinami. Clearly the two contentions contradicted each other.

Munakata's view voiced at the second court session could be construed as saying there was no requests for favors. Later, this served as one basis on which the lower court passed down a not guilty verdict against Fujinami.

At this stage, the prosecution disclosed to the defense only an extremely small portion of the statements it had taken and of the vast amount of evidence seized. In response, Fujinami's defense team filed a formal objection. The resulting exchange in court went something like this:

> JUDGE WATANABE: Mr. Fujinami's defense team has filed a formal objection. Please proceed.
>
> YOKOI: Thank you. In our objection dated January 10, 1990, we pointed out that in its opening statement the prosecution claimed to hold certain evidence. We would like the court to ask for clarification of such evidence now, at this time. Naturally, insofar as evidence to emerge later is concerned, the court can request to examine such evidence at such time; we are not asking to have all evidence examined at this stage. But at least as concerns evidence claimed to be on hand at the outset, we would like to request clarification now.
>
> JUDGE WATANABE: Am I correct in understanding your objection as saying if there is evidence, it should be clarified at this stage and a request to examine it issued, and that not doing so runs counter to the law?
>
> YOKOI: Yes, that's correct.
>
> JUDGE WATANABE: I would like to hear the prosecutor's opinion regarding this objection.
>
> MUNAKATA: We see no reason for such an objection. We would like to see it dismissed.
>
> JUDGE WATANABE: Are you saying you haven't held back on any requests to examine evidence?
>
> MUNAKATA: Yes. In our view, if the defense were to admit all of the large volume of evidence we disclosed, our case would stand, so we have nothing more we will offer.

The defense team was demanding the prosecution disclose all the statements and other evidence taken by the public prosecutors and clarify what the charges were. In response the prosecution's stance was if the defense agreed to admit all evidence it disclosed—mostly statements taken by the prosecutors—it would acquiesce to the defense's demand.

Clearly, if the defense were to agree with the content of the statements submitted by the prosecutors, the possibility of a guilty verdict would be very high, so admitting such evidence was out of the question. The prosecution kept refusing the defense's demand, saying if it would not admit the evidence it offered to disclose, then it would not disclose it. The two sides were thus deadlocked, and the gradual manner in which the prosecution thus proceeded to present its evidence, in dribs and drabs at best, was one reason why the trial dragged on for so long.

The foregoing was excerpts from the proceedings on the first two days in court. The exchanges taking place between the defense and the prosecution were quite intense, and the whole time the judge seemed bewildered as to how he should go about arbitrating between the two sides. Watching all this unfolding before my eyes, I heaved a heavy sigh, pondering the long road ahead. If I thought the interrogations were a lengthy affair, the trial showed every indication of becoming a long haul as well.

Perhaps because the court proceedings were so complicated, the reports in the evening editions of the dailies were more brief than I expected, and they varied widely in focus. While the headline in the *Asahi* concentrated on how the defendants denied any intent of bribery, the *Yomiuri* stated I flatly denied passing any bribes and that Fujinami and Ikeda both demonstrated their strong determination to fight their cases. The *Nikkei* played up the total denial by all the defendants, quoting our contention there was neither any asking for favors nor any making of bribes.

At the end of the day, my defense team and I gathered at a restaurant in Akasaka, where we had a private room to ourselves. Everyone was fuming. They had submitted an enormous quantity of petitions for clarification ahead of the trial and then sought explanations in court, but all their demands were brushed off by the prosecution's self-serving "clarifications."

One member of the team turned to me, trying to conceal the full scope of his vexation. "Usually, the prosecutor in charge of an investigation and the prosecutor who takes charge of the case in court aren't the same," he said. "But here, because they're the same, the opening proceedings were pretty intense. The prosecution must be frustrated at not having procured enough statements during the investigation to ensure a guilty verdict. And we were hot under the collar because our requests for clarification were all sidestepped. The sparks were flying! It wouldn't have happened this way if the prosecutor in court hadn't been involved in the investigation."

Hearing this, I was overcome with discomfort, realizing heated exchanges about the statements taken by the prosecutors were likely to continue, and that the trial would drag on and on.

That night, with the saké flowing freely, everybody vented their anger toward the prosecution's attitude in the courtroom. Once that anger was released and calm restored, we emerged into the blustery winds of midwinter and each of us headed home.

The Political Route

Once the opening procedures, which spread over two court sessions, were completed, the court agenda proceeded to calling witnesses and examining evidence.

The proceedings were to be divided into five phases. The first involved the allegation that I repurchased the shares of Recruit Cosmos stock and then sold them. Next, the court was to focus on each of what it considered to be four "routes" into which I allegedly funneled my bribes. These were, in chronological order, the "political route," the "Ministry of Labor route," the "NTT route," and the "Ministry of Education route."

Allegations of Buying Back, Then Selling the Shares

The prosecution alleged that I had personally repurchased the shares of Recruit Cosmos stock and then sold them to various recipients—which, if true, was a violation of the Securities and Exchange Law. However, the recipients of the shares under investigation all testified before the Diet that the shares were provided not by me but by a company of a friend of mine.

In each instance, the recipient personally concluded a stock purchase agreement with and rendered payment for the shares received to one of the five companies in question. It should have been altogether clear, therefore, that the stock deals were conducted with those five companies—not with me.

The prosecutors insisted, however, that I myself bought back the shares in question and then sold them. This was all a rehash of allegations I responded to during my voluntary interrogations, the prosecutors' grilling no less tenacious now than then.

Following is the testimony given by one of the share recipients, Ippo Hiramoto, president of Kosaido Development Co., Ltd., when he appeared at the seventh court session on March 15, 1990:

TOSHIAKI HIWATARI (prosecutor): The witness purchased shares of Recruit Cosmos, is that correct?

HIRAMOTO: Yes, I did.

HIWATARI: Who approached you about buying the shares?

HIRAMOTO: Mr. Ezoe.

HIWATARI: And did he tell you what shares you would be buying?

HIRAMOTO: I thought the shares had something to do with Mr. Ezoe, but I thought they were shares belonging to somebody else.

MAMORU WADA (defense attorney): I'd like to ask you about the occasion when you were approached by Mr. Ezoe about buying the shares. When you were first approached, did you think the shares were coming from Mr. Ezoe himself?

HIRAMOTO: No, I didn't.

WADA: Why didn't you think they were Mr. Ezoe's own shares?

HIRAMOTO: It is common knowledge the owner of a company doesn't sell his own shares, so in that sense I knew the shares weren't Mr. Ezoe's.

WADA: This loan agreement attached to your report—this is an agreement under which you were borrowing money from First Finance, is it not?

HIRAMOTO: It is.

WADA: Next, this bank transfer application and receipt—this is a document specifying the money you borrowed from First Finance should be transferred into the bank account of Sanki Corporation, is it not?

HIRAMOTO: It is.

WADA: When you were first approached about this by Mr. Ezoe, you didn't know the name of the party whose stock you would be buying, but at the point when you concluded the purchase agreement and prepared the bank transfer application, you knew this information, am I correct?

HIRAMOTO: Yes, that's correct.

As his testimony indicated, Hiramoto was aware the shares were not coming from me.

One provider of shares was Shigeyo Sugawara, a close friend from university days. Two companies he owned, Do-best Incorporated and Big Way, purchased the shares and subsequently, at my request, sold them to third parties.

When he was called as a witness on December 19, 1991, Sugawara gave the following testimony:

MUNAKATA (chief prosecutor): I'd like to ask you how it came about that the companies with which you are affiliated acquired shares of Recruit Cosmos stock. Around April 1985, were you approached by Mr. Ezoe about a third-party allocation of Recruit Cosmos shares?

SUGAWARA: Yes, I was.

MUNAKATA: What did you discuss at that time?

SUGAWARA: I received a phone call from Mr. Ezoe. He said in another two years or so he was planning to have Recruit Cosmos listed, and for that reason they were undertaking third-party allocations of new shares, and he requested shares be held by my companies.

MUNAKATA: Was he asking you to hold 200,000 shares?

SUGAWARA: That's correct.

MUNAKATA: At the time you purchased the shares, did you enter into any agreement to return the shares to Mr. Ezoe in the event he became in need of them at some time in the future?

SUGAWARA: No, there was no such agreement.

MUNAKATA: On the surface, Mr. Ezoe loaned you the money and you had your companies purchase the shares. But since the shares were serving as the loan collateral, you couldn't dispose of them at your discretion, could you?

SUGAWARA: I believed I could.

MUNAKATA: You'd have to provide something else as collateral.

SUGAWARA: Yes, that's right.

MUNAKATA: Didn't you foresee the shares would be returned at some point in the future?

SUGAWARA: There was nothing about returning them to Mr. Ezoe.

MUNAKATA: Didn't you ever consider this was what Mr. Ezoe might have had in mind?

SUGAWARA: No.

MUNAKATA: Didn't you once tell the public prosecutor Mr. Ezoe assumed that, given the circumstances under which Best-do and Big Way came to buy the shares, he could have them returned at any time and dispose of them freely as he wished?

SUGAWARA: No, I never said that. The prosecutor said that, but this is an item on which I disagreed strongly.

MUNAKATA: You're aware a written statement to that effect exists, aren't you?

SUGAWARA: Yes, I remember it. At the time I opposed it, saying such a thing was out of the question.

MUNAKATA: How did you come to give up your shares?

SUGAWARA: I received a call from Mr. Ezoe saying he wanted the officers and others at Recruit Cosmos to hold shares in the company before it was listed. He said since he wasn't in a position to give them any of his own shares, he was requesting my companies render their shares. I acquiesced and sold them.

MUNAKATA: Didn't you feel since they were shares that came your way from Mr. Ezoe, you were willing to return them to him?

SUGAWARA: Forgive me for dwelling on the words "willing to return them," but when I was called in by the public prosecutors, I told them I originally had no mind to return the shares, and we argued on this point. When Mr. Ezoe requested me to, though, I had no objection to selling the shares to the people he wanted to have them.

MUNAKATA: Has your thinking changed between that time and now?

SUGAWARA: No, it hasn't.

The questioning of witnesses who bought and sold Recruit Cosmos shares continued for the next year and a half. Nearly all the witnesses testified in the clearest of terms that I had merely played the role of an intermediary in having the shares trade hands; but some stated they bought the shares directly from, or sold them directly to, me. I had to believe the latter witnesses had signed statements to that effect after being summoned and interrogated on the matter over and over again. I also suspect the prosecutors "reminded" those witnesses, during their "rehearsals" ahead of actually appearing in court, to testify precisely as it was written in their statements.

The charges on which I was indicted were bribery—not violation of the Securities and Exchange Law. I was suspicious as to why the court should dwell on this issue for a whole year and a half. It was later suggested to me that the prosecution was using up time while it was trying to build its bribery case against me.

The Good or Bad of Stock Trading

In April 1990, Tetsuo Mae, who held a middle-management position at Daiwa Securities, appeared as a witness and responded to questions concerning the initial public offering of Recruit Cosmos's shares.

Mae was asked to name who bought the shares; who was in attendance, and what statements were made by whom when the decision was reached to use Daikyo Kanko and Mitsui Fudosan as comparable companies for determining Recruit Cosmos's share price; and approximately what he expected Recruit Cosmos's share price would be at the time of its IPO. Mae testified he thought the initial price would be around 6,000 yen. He testified that Daiwa, the managing underwriter, requested of Seiichi Tateoka, managing director at Recruit Cosmos in charge of financial affairs, that the company prepare a greenshoe option—that is, to have additional shares available for sale in the event the share price rose too substantially from the opening price, thus circumventing an excessive price rise.

On the day of the IPO, several dozen shareholders sold off their holdings under this greenshoe arrangement, and among them were a large number of secretaries of politicians who borrowed funds from First Finance in order to buy the shares. From Mae's testimony, I learned this circumstance was behind subsequent accusations that money was made hand over fist.

Mae was repeatedly questioned by the prosecutors concerning my personal stock transactions, but in court the judge disallowed questioning by the prosecution on this matter. In addition to my defense attorneys' having objected on the grounds this had no direct bearing on my case, there were reporters in the courtroom and the judge may have deemed it better to avoid getting the media worked up about my personal stock transactions.

Neither those sitting on the bench nor the prosecutors had even the most basic knowledge about stock trading and its attendant vocabulary: the greenshoe option was relatively obscure, but even common terms designating monthly and weekly share price movements were beyond their realm of knowledge.

My father, a high school teacher by profession, used to dabble in the stock market. Those were the days when Japan's economy was just beginning to boom, and virtually all stocks rose in value. He passed his stock holdings on to me while he was still alive, and after I finished my education and began working, I sold off those stocks and used the profit to begin my own stock portfolio.

Later, at Recruit I hired Masanori Yamaji away from Nikko Securities and put him in charge of managing our Group pension funds and idle cash. He engaged in arbitrage: he would buy stocks that seemed ripe to rise and short-sell stocks that seemed poised to head downward. Reason would suggest such transactions to generate profits, but Japan's share price movements are linked to those of the New York stock market—the Dow Jones Industrial Average, which incorporates a mere thirty companies belonging to the manufacturing sector. When the Dow moves higher, in Japan gains are typically posted not only by stocks thought to be heading upward but also by those expected to trend downward. But when the Dow moves lower, so too do Japanese stocks. So logic aside, in reality the Japanese investor engaging in arbitrage is by no means assured of always turning a profit. However, if an investor engages in short selling and margin buying of a number of stocks over a prolonged period, in most cases he will make a profit in the long term. In my own case, I used the profits I earned from stock trading to pay for my ski and golf outings and overseas trips with my family, and also to cover losses suffered by Group companies.

Hisashi Ishii of Tachibana Securities, a close acquaintance through golf and Go, related how, in stock market circles, selling was widely viewed as though it were something bad—and this I can vouch for. Earlier, when Singer, then a manufacturer of foot pedal–operated sewing machines, withdrew from the Japanese market, I sold my stock in Riccar, another maker of pedal-operated machines, and bought stock in Juki, which was already producing electric sewing machines. The only thing reported in the press at the time, in the *Asahi*, was my selling of the Riccar stock.

Tomoo Hirooka, former president of *Asahi Shimbun*, once told me about his first assignment after he joined the *Asahi* as a reporter covering the Tokyo stock market. His boss warned him: "Keep your hands out of the market—not just while you're attached to the economic department, no matter what department you get assigned to. If you start playing the stock market, you'll be fired." Apparently, the *Asahi* was of the view that income earned by the sweat of one's brow is income well earned, but income acquired by trading in the stock market is "bad" money made on the quick.

I never thought there was anything bad about providing someone with profit earned from shares that rose in value, but the *Asahi Shimbun* did, and the newspaper's continuing reports of a critical nature were, I believe, one of the characteristic features of the Recruit scandal. I also think the zeal with which I traded stocks, combined with the gap between that zeal and the perceptions embraced by the prosecutors, judges, and the media—all of whom had virtually no connection to stock trading—was a large part of the reason why the Recruit scandal became such a prominent focus of media attention.

My Tax Trial

Another issue surfaced in conjunction with the matter of the shares of Recruit Cosmos that I purportedly bought back and then sold. It was alleged I failed to report the profit I earned from the sale of the shares, and I was told to pay a large sum in tax penalties. Ultimately I fought my case against the national tax authorities in court, challenging their handling of the matter.

Although the court proceedings concerning this tax matter veer from the Recruit trial, some brief comments about this other trial offers a window into this mindset.

On December 22, 1989, I received a call from the Tokyo Regional Taxation Bureau asking me to come in to their offices. Without delay I went to the Shiba Tax Office, accompanied by my attorney, Hino, and by Tadashi Sekine, my accountant. An officer from the division handling individual taxation informed me that I was to be assessed a penalty against earnings I made from the sale of 700,000 shares of Recruit Cosmos stock in September 1986.

In those days the upper limit on untaxed stock trades was fifty transactions per year involving a total of 200,000 shares. The tax authorities contended that because, by their assumption, I repurchased the Recruit Cosmos shares first and then sold them, I exceeded the limit, so the transactions were subject to taxation. They claimed I owed roughly 2.1 billion yen in taxes, including a penalty for underreporting my income, against profit totaling near 3.1 billion yen. I was flabbergasted.

The reason the Taxation Bureau took this step was likely in reaction to a registration statement resubmitted by Seiichi Tateoka the previous July 28. According to that statement, 700,000 shares of the company's stock was sold by me.

The information was untrue, but in court, on October 18, 2001, Tateoka testified that in May 1989 he was summoned by the Ministry of Finance's Securities Bureau and told that the Public Prosecutors Office concluded the shares in question were sold. He said he was then advised to put the company's registration statement in order, and to submit a report stating that the shares were sold by me; otherwise, the officials told him, it was conceivable Recruit Cosmos's over-the-counter registration could be nullified—and also that the company's listing on the Second Section of the Tokyo Stock Exchange (TSE), planned for some point in the future, would not be approved. Under the circumstances, Tateoka testified, he had no alternative but to submit the report as requested.

The Special Investigation Department wields powerful influence over the Ministry of Finance and National Tax Agency. What likely happened was the special investigators had pressed the Finance Ministry, compelling them to view my actions vis-à-vis Recruit Cosmos as a violation of Article 4 of the Securities and Exchange Law. Likely, it was also at the behest of the special investigators that I was levied the taxes on my alleged stock trades.

Recruit Cosmos, which at the time was making preparations toward listing on the Second Section of the TSE, had no other recourse than to follow the Ministry's instructions.

Whatever the motives behind this turn of events, the situation represented a major upheaval for me. If I came up with roughly 2.1 billion yen, including penalties, I would soon be in financial straits—to the extent I might no longer be able to cover the costs of my increasingly lengthy trial.

To deal with this newly arisen situation, I immediately assigned part of my defense team to work on this other problem. In addition to a detailed report explaining the facts of my stock transactions and relevant documents, I submitted a petition to the Tokyo Regional Taxation Bureau.

My actions proved fruitless. On March 12, 1990, I received notice from the head of the Azabu Tax Office that the additional tax and penalties were to stand. I immediately filed an objection with the Taxation Bureau and requested the ruling be nullified, but to make matters worse, while waiting for this appeal to be heard, a further penalty was accrued for being late in making the payment as ruled.

After discussing the matter with my attorneys, I decided as an expedient measure to put up my home and all other real estate holdings as security with the tax authorities and receive legal exemption from being in arrears. What this translated to was a 50 percent reduction in the delinquency tax rate, from 14.6 percent to 7.3 percent; but even so I would still have to pay more than 150 million yen a year for late tax payment.

Subsequently, in October 1992, I petitioned the National Tax Tribunal to reexamine my case. For a long while I heard nothing whatsoever back from them, and so, frustrated at the lack of any progress, in January 1995 I opted to take the matter to court and filed a claim with the Tokyo District Court seeking nullification of the unjust tax and penalty imposition.

Even after those court proceedings began, however, the tax authority representatives showed no sign of submitting their written response to the complaint filed against them. The court even designated a deadline by which they were to respond, but no response was forthcoming. A second deadline was set, and then a third, and still the tax authority failed to comply. Before too long, the original judge was replaced by a second. As the trial continued to drag on without progress, my attorneys vented their frustration. "If we were dealing with the private sector here, we'd be 100 percent sure to win," one said. "The court doesn't want to rule against the state."

I thought it strange that the National Tax Agency should bow to the wishes of the Public Prosecutors Office. I looked into other cases where the state was being sued, and overwhelmingly the state came out on top. In a democratic nation, this did not seem right.

The first verdict in my tax trial was finally handed down in November 2002, more than seven years after I took my claim to court. I lost. The judge stated he found it difficult to regard the actions taken by me, the plaintiff, with respect to trading the Recruit Cosmos stocks as those of an intermediary for the transactions of others; rather, he thought it appropriate to interpret what I did as having myself first purchased the shares of Recruit Cosmos from the five companies and then having sold them to the recipients in the case.

This was shocking. Neither I nor my defense team could accept such a verdict—reached by utterly ignoring the evidence at hand. I reorganized my defense team and filed an appeal.

Heading the team this time was Yukio Nozaki, who had formerly sat as a judge for the Tokyo High Court. He pored over the submitted documents and concluded the verdict was unjust. He offered me his reassurance: "I've never stood in court as a lawyer before, but I'll take up the fight on your behalf."

Nozaki's efforts notwithstanding, in November 2003 my appeal was turned down. This time Nozaki couldn't believe it. "The verdict is totally unacceptable," he fumed. "You don't need to pay me any fees, but let's take this to a higher court."

I followed his advice and appealed to the Supreme Court, only to have the appeal rejected there as well. (I might add that although the court was unwilling to accept my appeal, it was more than willing to charge me 10.7 million yen in appeal costs.) Ultimately, I ended up paying just over 2.15 billion yen in back taxes at the state level, roughly 200 million yen in taxes levied against underreported earnings, and slightly more than 256 million yen in local taxes—a little over about 2.6 billion yen in total.

This entire issue revolved around the simple question of whether I repurchased and sold the shares or served in an intermediary role. Given that objective evidence existed in the form of public and other documents, and testimony was made in support of my claim, it shouldn't have taken very long to establish the facts. Nevertheless, it took *thirteen-and-a-half years* from the time I submitted my first request for a reexamination until the final ruling was handed down—on March 24, 2006.

During each court session, the visitors' gallery had been filled with officials from the National Tax Agency and the Azabu Tax Office, which seemed unusual since it seemed they should have been at work. Some members of my defense team indicated they felt a kind of pressure exerted on them.

Lawsuits filed against the state, except in the most extreme cases, seem to find the court taking sides with the state. Had I not sold shares of Recruit to Daiei during this long interim, the verdict in my tax trial would have left me broke. I came away with the sad realization it was impossible to win against those in authority—I could only suffer in silence.

Questioning about the Ad Hoc Council

Back to the Recruit trial.

During my interrogations at Kosuge, I was asked time and again about the Ad Hoc Council on Education, but ultimately it seemed no specific "problems" were found because at the start of my trial the chief prosecutor clearly stated they would not be charging me on suspicion of having asked for favors from the council. Nonetheless, in September 1990, the prosecution began calling people affiliated with the council as witnesses.

On September 7, 1990 Taijun Saito, who was deputy manager of the council's secretariat, gave testimony, the gist of which is recorded below.

HIWATARI (prosecutor): How did the council come to discuss the issue of student recruitment?

SAITO: At the time, the early recruitment of students—early in the sense the would-be employer doesn't keep to the gentlemen's agreement on when to commence student recruitments—was a social issue. Because the top business corporations were approaching impending graduates of the well-known schools early and offering them jobs, those schools tended to attract many students, which was making for even fiercer competition on the entrance exams. And the tendency of the big companies to offer early hiring only to students from specific universities in itself was a problem.

HIWATARI: So your discussions about early recruitment—and by extension the issue of the gentlemen's agreement—were related to the council's deliberations on how to rectify injustices stemming from a society focused on academic credentials?

SAITO: That's right.

Another witness called in conjunction with the council issue was Susumu Ishikawa, who conducted research into matters of the council's concern. He gave testimony on September 20. The focus of questioning by Prosecutor Nozaki was on the council's discussions relating to lifelong education.

In the testimony of neither Saito, Ishikawa, nor others on the council was anything said to suggest Recruit had attempted to sway the council to take up the matter of early recruitment in its official recommendations to the prime minister. Quite the contrary. What the council members' testimonies revealed was: (a) given that the council was charged with finding solutions to rectify society's focus on academic credentials, the problems surrounding the early recruitment of college graduates were slated for incorporation into its report from the outset; and (b) nearly all members were in agreement with that view.

In its first report, as one measure that would contribute to rectifying society's fixation on academic credentials, the council recommended both the corporate and public sectors cease early hiring in violation of the gentlemen's agreement—a practice that was leading to excessive attention focused on certain renowned schools. It also urged that more aggressive efforts be made to ensure equal opportunity in job hunting by, for example, eliminating the practice of hiring from specified schools.

As said earlier, in its opening statement the prosecution stated unequivocally it was not charging me on anything related to the Ad Hoc Council on Education. Nonetheless, it proceeded to inquire into matters relating to the council in court for almost a full year. During the course of the trial, my chief defense counsel, Tada, went so far as to ask the prosecution whether it was changing the charges against me, to which the answer was "No." I wondered just what the prosecution had up its sleeve in spending so much time on endless questioning totally unrelated to its case against me.

At the end of the final court session of that year, Judge Watanabe, after indicating that the stenographer not transcribe what he was about to say, turned to the prosecution. "I've read over the court records, and I think you've been wasting too much time on exchanges that have no relevance to the case. Please clarify your points of contention as quickly as possible."

The prosecution's fixation on irrelevant questions had irritated the judge, too.

The Issue of the Civil Service Exam

The foremost point of dispute in connection with the "political route" was the question of whether I had asked Fujinami to use his influence to stop the proposal bringing forward the date of the civil service exam.

I had made donations to Fujinami, and if the donations were purely political contributions, there would be no problem; but if in providing him those funds I had asked the lawmaker to do any favors on my behalf, my actions would be considered bribery and I would be guilty of a crime. As such, I was questioned repeatedly as to whether I had sold Recruit Cosmos shares to Fujinami directly, and if not, then who had undertaken the transfer.

Fujinami's secretary, Eiji Tokuda, gave the following testimony concerning this matter on June 25, 1992.

EIJI MATSUNAGA (prosecutor): The transaction involving Recruit Cosmos stock was carried out in your name. Who first contacted you about this, and when?

TOKUDA: As I recall, I think it was Mr. [Toshihiro] Ono.

MATSUNAGA: And did Mr. Ono come to you and ask if Mr. Fujinami would hold the shares in question?

TOKUDA: That's right.

MATSUNAGA: And how did you respond? Did you immediately say yes?

TOKUDA: I told him Mr. Fujinami wouldn't be interested in purchasing the shares.

MATSUNAGA: So you turned him down?

TOKUDA: Yes.

MATSUNAGA: And was that the end of it? Or did something happen after that?

TOKUDA: I believe I said to Mr. Ono something to the effect that, "in that case, how about me?"

MATSUNAGA: After you were approached about the shares by Mr. Ono, did you report anything about the matter to Mr. Fujinami?

TOKUDA: As I recall, I reported the matter to him only after the brouhaha broke out.

MATSUNAGA: So, Mr. Ono first offered the shares to Mr. Fujinami; you turned him down; and then you had in mind to hold them yourself. Didn't you say anything about all this to Mr. Fujinami at the time?

TOKUDA: "I don't believe I did."

On February 3, 1994, Fujinami gave the following account:

YUKUO OMURO (defense attorney): Do you recall having any discussions with anyone from Recruit in 1985 about the Ad Hoc Council on Education?

FUJINAMI: No. I don't believe I discussed the council with Recruit.

OMURO: Earlier I asked you about meeting with Mr. Ezoe in 1984. Do you recall having had occasion to meet with Mr. Ezoe in 1985— your second year as chief cabinet secretary—or 1986?

FUJINAMI: I met with him as one of my supporters, but I don't recall having ever discussed anything with him in particular.

OMURO: Prior to September 1986 had you ever heard Recruit Cosmos, a company with which Mr. Ezoe is affiliated, would be listing its stock?

FUJINAMI: No, I hadn't.

OMURO: Was anything ever said to you about his wanting to sell shares in Recruit Cosmos to you?

FUJINAMI: No.

OMURO: You're aware now shares of Recruit Cosmos were transferred into Eiji Tokuda's ownership?

FUJINAMI: At the time, articles kept appearing in the newspapers about how the shares were sold to various people here and there, so it was likely reported in the press; but I actually learned about it for the first time only when I asked Mr. Tokuda about it.

OMURO: And when you inquired of Mr. Tokuda, did he admit to having purchased the shares?

FUJINAMI: Yes, he did.

OMURO: And at that time, did you reproach him in any way?

FUJINAMI: I've always given myself over entirely to the affairs of state and left matters relating to accounting, business expenses, donations, and the like entirely in the hands of Mr. Tokuda. Having done so, if there is cause for social censure here, then this is my responsibility. I didn't think the responsibility should be foisted off on Mr. Tokuda.

OMURO: Mr. Fujinami, is Mr. Tokuda aware you personally don't engage in any stock trading?

FUJINAMI: I think he knew this.

OMURO: Was there an occasion on which you discussed the matter with him?

FUJINAMI: I was talking about it on an occasion when Mr. Tokuda was present. My father died in 1968, the year after I became a member of the Diet. He had always advised me three things: First, don't lend money to anyone. When they pay you back, you become the bad guy. Second, don't play the stock market. And third, don't smoke: it's bad for your health. I always assumed my father offered this advice based on his own experience. Anyway, it was because of his advice I quit smoking, cold turkey, in 1966 before running for the Lower House. It made him very happy. Mr. Tokuda was present when I reminisced about all this, so I think he knew I don't deal in stocks.

From this testimony it became clear in court that the person I had spoken to about buying the shares was Tokuda, and the person who actually bought the shares was also Tokuda.

During my interrogations I had stated this fact time and again, but when Munakata pressured me to compromise by accepting his "FIN" deal—that is, in return for admitting I had telephoned Fujinami directly and provided financial backing to Katsuya Ikeda, they would not investigate Nakasone—I ultimately signed my name to that statement saying I had initially claimed to have telephoned Tokuda but, after thinking about it carefully, I came to feel the person I had called was Fujinami himself.

In the courtroom, however, I strongly contended the statement in question was taken against my will and the person I had telephoned was not Fujinami but Tokuda. The following is an excerpt of my testimony given on September 9, 1992.

MUNAKATA: Mr. Ezoe, you've told the judge you were coerced to make statements against your will. Is that true?

EZOE: I never made any statements against my will. What I meant to say is that written statements were prepared that were contrary to what I had stated.

MUNAKATA: I'll just ask you about the major point in question here. During the investigation phase, did you on any occasion ever admit to having personally asked Mr. Fujinami for a favor—a favor relating to the gentlemen's agreement on student recruitments?

EZOE: Throughout the investigation I consistently said I had never asked Mr. Fujinami for favors of any kind.

MUNAKATA: Then you're saying you had no direct exchanges or involvement with Mr. Fujinami concerning the Recruit Cosmos stock?

EZOE: I called Mr. Tokuda, and I told the prosecutor any number of times the one I'd called was Mr. Tokuda. At first a statement was prepared to that effect, but in the end I was coerced into signing a statement that said I had dealt with Mr. Fujinami directly.

MUNAKATA: In the "Matsuzaki memo" presented to this court, the date is given as March 15th. Was there something that enabled you to specify the date was March 15th?

EZOE: After I left Mr. Fujinami's office, I returned to Recruit and immediately telephoned Mr. Matsuzaki at Nikkeiren saying I wanted to meet with him. Late that afternoon, a little after four I think it was, he kindly fit me in between other visitors, and I have a distinct memory of having met him. Mr. Matsuzaki has said my visit was on March 15th, which means my visit with Mr. Fujinami had to have been in the morning of the 15th.

MUNAKATA: Are you saying you were able to specify the date from the date written on the Matsuzaki memo?

EZOE: Yes.

MUNAKATA: Did you tell the prosecutor around what time it was when you visited Mr. Fujinami's official residence?

EZOE: Yes. I told him it was in the early morning, around eight o'clock I believe.

MUNAKATA: Altogether, about how long did your meeting last?

EZOE: It was very brief, only five or ten minutes or so.

The following is an excerpt of my testimony given on September 18, 1992:

HIROMI NAGAI (prosecutor): When you went to see the chief cabinet secretary and told him bringing forward the date of the exam ran counter to the will of the private sector, did you think you were acting as a representative of the private sector?

EZOE: No. The reason I went was to inquire, in general terms, what course or form of action could be taken to get the National Personnel Authority to listen to the will of the private sector.

NAGAI: How, specifically, did you discuss this matter with Mr. Fujinami?

EZOE: I told him that what was desirable would be for the date of the civil service exam to coincide with the timing designated under the gentlemen's agreement, and I said what the private sector was hoping for was not that the exam be brought forward but rather scheduled somewhat later. I went to ask Mr. Fujinami how and where to convey this will of the private sector.

NAGAI: So you may have told Mr. Fujinami that the public sector was getting preferential treatment over the private sector, am I correct?

EZOE: Yes. I believe I told him in such a way as to convey the private sector felt it was being treated unfairly.

NAGAI: When you met with Mr. Matsuzaki, didn't you tell him you had gone that same day to see Mr. Fujinami and pleaded your case?

EZOE: I reported to him that I had visited Mr. Fujinami and that he had replied he could do something if an appropriate source broached the subject to the National Personnel Authority.

NAGAI: Mr. Matsuzaki has given testimony before the court. Did you hear his testimony?

EZOE: Yes, I did.

NAGAI: Then you know he said he wrote in the memo what you had told him.

EZOE: Yes.

NAGAI: He said when he wrote in the memo he had heard you met with Mr. Fujinami and appealed for his intervention, he was writing just what you had told him. You discussed the matter with him, didn't you?

EZOE: I told him the content of what I had just discussed with Mr. Fujinami.

NAGAI: Did Mr. Matsuzaki say or do anything suggesting he thought you had petitioned Mr. Fujinami to do something?

EZOE: As Mr. Fujinami had said it was probably a matter for the National Personnel Authority, I merely reported that to Mr. Matsuzaki.

NAGAI: You underwent interrogation by the public prosecutor concerning your visit to Mr. Fujinami's official residence and the specifics of what you talked with him about, didn't you?

EZOE: Yes, I did.

NAGAI: According to your statement dated April 30, you told Mr. Fujinami that the early recruitment of civil servants was one reason why the gentlemen's agreement wasn't being adhered to, and you requested something be done about this early recruitment problem from the public side. Isn't this so?

EZOE: No. I didn't say anything to suggest that I had requested that appropriate steps be taken in the matter.

NAGAI: Setting aside the question of whether you asked for steps to be taken, did you not speak in terms suggestive of the public sector being given preference over the private sector, and also tell the prosecutor about having said the early recruitment of civil servants was a reason why the gentlemen's agreement wasn't being honored?

EZOE: I believe I did speak about the public sector being given preference over the private. But what I said was that such moves by the public sector were a source of dissatisfaction for the private sector. I said nothing about implementing corrective measures.

NAGAI: What was your understanding of Mr. Fujinami's vested authority?

EZOE: The chief cabinet secretary serves as the cabinet spokesman. I believed that since when anything happens he immediately holds a press conference on the same day, he is well-versed in the affairs of the ministries and agencies.

NAGAI: Would you explain for us once more, in simple terms, the reason you went to see Mr. Matsuzaki?

EZOE: Mr. Matsuzaki was head of the Central Employment Measures Council, and as such he was the standard bearer for the private sector with respect to the gentlemen's agreement. As I was a special committee member of Nikkeiren, he and I had long engaged in discussions about problems surrounding the agreement. After having gone to ask Mr. Fujinami's opinion in the matter, I thought there was a need to report this to Mr. Matsuzaki, and that's why I went to see him.

Because the content of my written statement in this matter differed from my testimony in court, my attorneys proceeded to spend quite a lot of time questioning the prosecutors about the circumstances under which I was interrogated.

As indicated earlier, on the day I visited Fujinami, I contacted Matsuzaki and told him what had transpired at that meeting, and Matsuzaki made a memo of what I had said. On November 2, 1990, Kazuo Inoue, Matsuzaki's subordinate for whom the memo was written, submitted the memo to the court as evidence.

Toru Nakamura, who at the time was head of the personnel section of the Prime Minister's Office as well as cabinet counselor under Fujinami, gave the following testimony in this matter on October 4, 1991:

> HIWATARI (prosecutor): On the morning of March 19, did the defendant, Mr. Fujinami, enter his office prior to the opening of the Diet session?
>
> NAKAMURA: Yes, I believe he did.
>
> HIWATARI: And on that same day, did the witness also enter the chief cabinet secretary's office before the Diet session?
>
> NAKAMURA: I believe I did.
>
> HIWATARI: Were you summoned by Mr. Fujinami, or did you go because you had some matter in particular you thought you should report to him?
>
> NAKAMURA: Neither, I believe.
>
> HIWATARI: Then why did you go to his office?
>
> NAKAMURA: I believe I went because there would be questioning in the Diet that day.
>
> HIWATARI: On that occasion did Mr. Fujinami give you any instructions or anything of that sort?
>
> NAKAMURA: Yes, he did.
>
> HIWATARI: What was the content of those instructions or of any questions he posed to you?
>
> NAKAMURA: I believe it was about the question of bringing forward the date for announcing the successful candidates taking the exam to become high-ranking civil servants.

JUDGE WATANABE: What specifically did he ask you?

NAKAMURA: He merely asked me what was happening in the matter. We didn't go into any details.

JUDGE WATANABE: Is that all?

NAKAMURA: As I recall, he didn't ask me anything in detail about the matter.

HIWATARI: What explanation did you offer in response to his question?

NAKAMURA: I believe I told him that bringing the exam date forward was a request that was brought to us in the personnel section for quite some time, and also that this year—this year meaning 1984—the National Personnel Authority was making extreme efforts toward realizing this. I also described the negotiations that took place.

HIWATARI: What was Mr. Fujinami's reaction to your explanation?

NAKAMURA: I don't believe he gave me any particular instructions. As I recall, he merely issued the usual advisement that this was a matter which needed to be monitored closely.

HIWATARI: What response did you make to what he said?

NAKAMURA: I explained we intended to reach agreement on the matter at the next meeting of the personnel section, to the effect we would cooperate with the private sector's gentlemen's agreement.

HIWATARI: Did Mr. Fujinami say anything in response to your explanation?

NAKAMURA: Nothing in particular. As I recall, he indicated his acknowledgment of what I had said.

If I had asked Fujinami to take steps concerning the early hiring of students when I visited him on March 15, one would expect he would have given instructions of some sort regarding the matter before the Diet session of March 19. The fact is, no testimony was given to suggest Fujinami had ever given specific instructions in this matter.

Surprise Evidence

The trial continued in this vein, making no real progress to speak of, the respective arguments of the prosecution and the defense no nearer to a compromise than at the outset.

Then suddenly, on January 22, 1993, Prosecutor Shoji appeared as a witness and broke the deadlock. "I was going through papers in my office before appearing in court, when I came across this." he said, then proceeded to submit the statement he had prepared on May 19, 1989. It constituted a piece of evidence appearing completely out of the blue.

What he submitted was the summarizing statement, as I described in detail earlier, based on Munakata's draft and numerous redrafts—the statement to which I had made certain revisions. Shoji offered the following testimony:

NAGAI (prosecutor): Are we correct in our understanding that you prepared the statement of May 19, 1989, concerning the relationship between Recruit's business and the gentlemen's agreement, and the circumstances behind the approaches made to Mr. Fujinami and Mr. Ikeda?

SHOJI: That's correct.

NAGAI: How did you come to draft this statement?

SHOJI: I believe it was the previous day—around May 18, anyway—I received an explanation from Prosecutor Munakata about the gentlemen's agreement, the circumstances behind the approaches made to politicians, the content of Mr. Ezoe's statements to date, and so on, and I was instructed to prepare a statement summarizing all of that.

NAGAI: How did you go about preparing the draft?

SHOJI: Mr. Ezoe had complained the statements prepared by Prosecutor Munakata were very short. He requested I draw up this statement to make it longer, and he said he would then make corrections to what I'd written.

NAGAI: This document before us now, is this the draft of the statement?

SHOJI: It was in the morning of May 19, I believe. I wrote up the draft and, if memory serves me right, made a xerox of it. Then that evening, I think it was, I handed it to Mr. Ezoe and he made his changes to it.

JUDGE WATANABE: Where did you actually write the draft?

SHOJI: There's a conference room adjacent to the interrogation rooms. Mr. Ezoe was interrogated in Room 15, I believe, and the meeting room was right next to that. I'm pretty sure it was there that I wrote the draft while Mr. Ezoe was meeting with a visitor.

NAGAI: I'd like you to look at the actual document now. Of the additions and corrections made to the original text, was any of that written by you?

SHOJI: You see the part about preventing the early hiring of civil servants and the connection to the Ad Hoc Council on Education? The five lines after that, with the marks through them to indicate they were to be deleted—I did that. The words "the issue of preventing the early hiring of civil servants and the connection to the Ad Hoc Council"—that's my handwriting. The six lines after that—I deleted that part also.

NAGAI: Those things aside, who wrote the remaining parts written in pencil?

SHOJI: That's Mr. Ezoe's handwriting.

NAGAI: When Mr. Ezoe first returned the statement to you, had the text merely been deleted in parts?

SHOJI: No. He also added some parts. And he made some deletions.

NAGAI: When Mr. Ezoe was making his revisions, did you instruct him in any way, ordering him to delete something or to change the text in any specific way?

SHOJI: Concerning the parts deleted, he said he'd already said that yesterday, so I said, "In that case . . . ," and I deleted them and handed the draft to him again. He revised it and then handed it back to me, saying he was finished. I figured nothing more could be done, so I dictated the statement based on the draft as it was.

NAGAI: Your original draft says Mr. Ezoe visited the chief cabinet secretary's official residence and "requested of Chief Cabinet Secretary Fujinami that something be done to prevent the early recruitment of students to become civil servants, and also the date for announcing the successful candidates of the civil service exam be pushed back." Mr. Ezoe revised this to: "I requested measures be taken to prevent the early recruitment of students to become civil servants—specifically, that the date for announcing the successful candidates of the civil service exam be pushed back." But this has been deleted by you, hasn't it?

SHOJI: Yes.

NAGAI: Do you know the process by which Mr. Ezoe went about making his deletions and additions?

SHOJI: He was mulling these things over in his mind. I'm not sure what was behind his specific changes.

NAGAI: So, once again, Mr. Ezoe made changes to the draft, didn't he?

SHOJI: Yes.

NAGAI: And then you dictated the statement to the assistant precisely in line with the additions and deletions he had made?

SHOJI: Yes, I did.

NAGAI: And in the course of dictating the statement, did Mr. Ezoe make any indications regarding anything?

SHOJI: The parts I indicated earlier, in my handwriting—I wrote those while dictating the statement.

NAGAI: So when you were dictating the statement based on the written draft, you wrote in the parts Mr. Ezoe had brought up earlier, about the problem of preventing the early hiring of civil servants and about the connection with the Ad Hoc Council?

SHOJI: That's right.

In the courts, great weight is given to whether written statements have been made voluntarily, and to their overall reliability. The prosecution no doubt submitted this surprise evidence as their way of indicating I had made my statements of my own free will and not under their coercion.

Confounding those intentions, however, the court appeared to glean my perception of the facts from the deletions and "stet" notations remaining in the draft. This cast doubt upon the voluntary nature and reliability of the statement, and was likely one reason why the court ruled I had not asked Fujinami for any favors.

In this way, the prosecution's surprise evidence ended up having the opposite effect from what was intended.

After the court session closed that day, Shoji came up to me.

"You've put on a little weight, I see," he said congenially. "And how are your children?"

Our brief exchange was within earshot of Prosecutor Nagai, who, in contrast to Shoji, had a sour expression on his face. He no doubt thought it was a mistake to have Shoji submit the "surprise evidence."

My Donations to Fujinami

Besides the question of whether or not I asked Fujinami for favors, the timing of my donations to Fujinami was also of great importance in judging whether bribery had been involved. The scenario apparently written by the prosecutors was that after I visited Fujinami in 1984 and asked him for favors, I began making donations to him as a token of gratitude.

But as I described earlier, I actually began making donations to Fujinami before 1984—from the time his support group, Sazanamikai, was inaugurated with me serving as one of its backers, along with Jiro Ushio and Yotaro Kobayashi. This was before Fujinami had become chief cabinet secretary. Documents and accounting receipts corroborating my claim were among the materials seized by the prosecutors, so the special investigators surely were aware of where the truth lay.

A heated exchange took place regarding this matter between my attorneys—Shozaburo Ishida, Teruhisa Maruyama, and Takeshi Tada—and Prosecutor Munakata, who appeared in court as a witness. The major points of this exchange follow, as taken from the court records of May 26, 1993:

> MARUYAMA: The statements you have written are extremely to the point, or I should say they summarize things well and are extremely easy to understand—but I think they are lacking specifics.
> MUNAKATA: That's your opinion. I believe they are abundantly specific.
> MARUYAMA: With the exception, in your statement of April 30, of

where you mention Mr. Ezoe's appointment to go ask Mr. Fujinami for favors, your statements don't present any concrete picture of how Mr. Ezoe came to visit Mr. Fujinami or what they talked about.

MUNAKATA: He said he went to see him, so I wrote up the statement saying he went to see him. I believe it's the discretion of the prosecutor to decide whether to go into detail beyond that.

MARUYAMA: About the defendant's proffering of political contributions allegedly in thanks for favors from Mr. Fujinami, you say he made his offer to Mr. Fujinami, asked for favors, and Mr. Fujinami acquiesced.

MUNAKATA: That's what it says in Mr. Ezoe's statements.

MARUYAMA: Where does it say that?

MUNAKATA: I believe there's something in there about coordinating among the government ministries and agencies. There should be a statement in which it's written clearly that Mr. Ezoe requested Mr. Fujinami do him a favor in that regard.

MARUYAMA: This "coordination among the ministries and agencies"—specifically what does that refer to?

MUNAKATA: I'm not very familiar with the workings of the various ministries and agencies, but there must be various things involved here: having decisions reached to his advantage by the people in charge of personnel at the ministries and agencies, for example, or giving them instructions, being privy to their reports, and so on. I believe it's within the prerogative of the chief cabinet secretary to do a variety of things. This isn't my personal thoughts we're talking about here; what the statement contains is what the defendant had in mind.

MARUYAMA: And this "coordination among the ministries and agencies," what did you think he wanted to have coordinated, and in what way?

MUNAKATA: That would be the things within his prerogative I just mentioned.

MARUYAMA: And you didn't think to press for any further details beyond that?

MUNAKATA: I would say it's sufficiently detailed as it is. In exercising his prerogatives as the chief cabinet secretary, this can take various forms—getting approval or decisions made at cabinet meetings and the like—and one such form would be to pull the different ministries and agencies together. Now I don't know what Mr. Ezoe had in his mind, but I do think the gist of the statement is fully laid out.

MARUYAMA: Now, according to the contention of the prosecutor, you say that Mr. Ezoe offered to give Mr. Fujinami money in the form of a bribe in August of that year, correct?

MUNAKATA: I don't remember offhand whether it was August, but what Mr. Ezoe said was he offered the money before he actually gave it.

MARUYAMA: I could understand if he'd asked for favors, had Mr. Fujinami to agree to his request, and then immediately paid him the money; but are you saying he let five whole months go by and only then told Mr. Fujinami that he would pay him five million yen every six months?

MUNAKATA: That's what Mr. Ezoe said.

MARUYAMA: The question I'm asking isn't what evidence you found. The question I'm asking is why didn't you press Mr. Ezoe to say that the reason he waited five whole months after asking Mr. Fujinami for favors before offering to express his "gratitude" was to confirm that Mr. Fujinami's actions on his behalf were effective?

KASAMA (prosecutor): I object! The defense has asked that question repeatedly and already received its response.

JUDGE WATANABE: The question has been asked before, but the court itself has received no clear response. I think it would be best for the witness to respond on this point once more.

MUNAKATA: Are you asking me whether Mr. Ezoe specifically felt that Mr. Fujinami did something on his behalf?

MARUYAMA: That's correct.

MUNAKATA: Mr. Ezoe stated nothing in that regard.

MARUYAMA: I'd like to ask you about the donations in question. In your previous testimony you stated that quite early on you had obtained information on all the donations made by Recruit to Mr. Fujinami.

MUNAKATA: Well, I'm not sure it was all the donations, but I did know about what's come to the surface as of now.

MARUYAMA: Then you knew about the purchase of tickets to Mr. Fujinami's fundraising party in November 1982?

MUNAKATA: Yes.

MARUYAMA: And so you also knew about the five million yen from November 1983?

MUNAKATA: Yes.

MARUYAMA: Then I'd like to ask you this. According to Mr. Ezoe's statement of May 10—his first statement relating to his donations—there's nothing in the statement about his offer to provide five million yen every six months—ten million yen a year. If your intention was to record the facts surrounding his donations, there should be mention of a contribution in the amount of five million yen made in November 1983 also. Why was that excluded?

MUNAKATA: I was interrogating Mr. Ezoe concerning the flow of money while Mr. Fujinami was in office, and he stated he had promised to provide funds on a regular basis starting in 1984. I'm not sure when he might have stated how much he had given on a specific date, but I believe that's how the statements were prepared.

MARUYAMA: I could understand that if only the donations—presuming they were bribes—made to the chief cabinet secretary while he was in office were being called into question. But if your overriding intention was to take a statement only concerning Mr. Ezoe's donations, then I don't understand why you left out November 1983 or the donations made after 1986.

MUNAKATA: I was looking to get the overall picture from various angles. When I asked him when he'd started giving the money, he said he'd given it on isolated occasions but that on a regular basis, he started after Mr. Fujinami became chief cabinet secretary.

At this point Maruyama passed the baton to Tada, who was in charge of my defense team. Tada indicated that my statements were written according to a scenario fabricated by the prosecution, and he zeroed in on the prosecution's ambiguous understanding of the facts and the course of its investigation.

> TADA: As a defense lawyer, it only makes sense to me that if you knew the facts regarding the donations made in 1983 or 1986 or 1987, you should have taken a statement concerning whether those differed in nature from the ones made in 1984 or 1985. Am I mistaken here?
>
> MUNAKATA: Where they differed was basically in coming before Mr. Fujinami took office as chief cabinet secretary. Maybe that's why I didn't attach much importance to them.
>
> TADA: Judging from the fact the prosecution made no mention whatsoever of the donation of November 1983 either in its opening remarks or in its substantiation of the facts in the court, we suspect it was quite a long time afterward when you came to know about that donation, or at least that you knew nothing about it prior to filing your indictment.
>
> MUNAKATA: But in your documents submitted in conjunction with the change of judges, you wrote as though the prosecution had known this.
>
> TADA: Then would we be correct in saying the prosecution knew about the donation but didn't take a statement?
>
> MUNAKATA: But that's what you yourself contended in your documents, so I find it truly strange that you keep suggesting that I didn't know about it.
>
> TADA: I'm asking from both perspectives because how things transpired seems so strange to us.
>
> MUNAKATA: I understand your feelings, so I'll reply. You're correct: I did know it at the time.
>
> TADA: In the statement of May 10, you wrote clearly that the twenty million yen in question consisted of political contributions. Then later you switch and imply that it was money in the form of a token of appreciation.

MUNAKATA: Isn't that the statement that only addresses the fact money changed hands?

TADA: The statement says "political donations," does it not?

MUNAKATA: I think what it was meant to imply is that the nature of the money would be described later.

TADA: Mr. Ezoe contended the twenty million yen consisted of political donations, didn't he?

MUNAKATA: Let me just say he practically begged me on bended knee that he didn't want to say what the money was intended for. He said doing so would bring an end to Mr. Fujinami's chances of becoming prime minister in the 21st century.

After my trial began, my attorneys sought disclosure of Recruit's accounting records and other documents that were seized by the Public Prosecutors Office. It took the prosecutors' office more than a month but they finally succeeded in locating the records relating to my purchase of tickets to Fujinami's fundraiser in 1982 and to the donation I made to him, in the amount of five million yen, in November 1983.

The battle waged between the prosecution and my defense team went on and on and on. In the end, because it became clear in court I had also made donations to Fujinami before the time when I allegedly asked him for favors, the prosecution lost its definitive "proof" on which to bring a guilty verdict against him.

Ultimately, the testimonies taken in court, the existence of the Matsuzaki memo, and the judgment it would be difficult to certify as bribes only a portion of the donations I had regularly made to him, appear to have contributed to the lower court's ruling in Fujinami's trial.

The Ruling regarding Fujinami

On September 27, 1994, the lower court pronounced Fujinami not guilty of the charge of accepting bribes.

Originally part of my trial, Fujinami's court proceedings had eventually been carried out separately, and on the day his verdict was announced I was with my defense attorneys watching the event on TV in my office.

When the news that he was found innocent broke at just after ten o'clock, we all raised our voices in joy. I immediately received phone calls from a number of friends. Hiroshi Okura of Noevir offered words of encouragement. "This is great!" he said. "Now you're sure to get a suspended sentence." Takeshi Tada also appeared quite pleased. "It took courage to render a verdict like this," he beamed.

I couldn't have been happier at this outcome: first because Fujinami was a man I respected greatly, and second because of what it suggested for me. All along Kyuzaburo Hino, the head of my defense team, was telling me that if even a single not-guilty verdict was handed down in this case, it would mean I'd get a suspended sentence. First, Masao Tatsumi was found innocent by the lower court in 1993 (on this more later), and now with Fujinami's not-guilty verdict I felt the likelihood of my going to jail was receding even further.

My buoyed spirits notwithstanding, the evening editions of the major dailies all reported on Fujinami's verdict in a critical tone.

Among them, the paper devoting the most space to this story was the *Asahi*. Not only was it the top story on the front page—spanning a remarkable eight full columns—there were also related articles on no less than four other pages. The various headlines read: "Hush Falls over Courtroom" and "Sobbing Heard from Visitors' Gallery." But according to Fumihiro Sasaki, head of Recruit's legal department, who was in the courtroom when the ruling was handed down, the moment the not-guilty verdict was announced, Shozaburo Ishida, who was monitoring the proceedings from the gallery on behalf of the defense team, let out a yelp of joy triggering a rush from the room by all the reporters present—and *then* the courtroom fell silent. There was, also according to Sasaki, no sobbing by anyone in the visitors' gallery.

The *Asahi* further claimed that when the not-guilty verdict was announced, employees of Recruit expressed puzzled surprise. This too was tantamount to prevarication. A not-guilty verdict in any trial related to the Recruit affair could be expected to be greeted with joy by Recruit mployees. We snickered that if anyone was surprised by the verdict, it was the *Asahi*'s reporters.

One of the articles in the *Asahi* was a commentary by Jun Okamoto, one of the paper's well-known legal reporters. Fujinami's trial, he wrote, hinged on "whether or not a specific portion of political donations made on a regular basis could be singled out and identified as constituting bribery." The court's decision cast doubt upon the charge that favors were requested—which, had that been the case, would have supported the contention the donations were a bribe—and recognized the checks alleged to be bribes were part of my political donations. Okamoto further stated the court had reached the conclusion it was difficult to prove Fujinami interpreted the transfer of his pre-flotation shares as being nuanced in any particular way.

The *Yomiuri* likewise dedicated almost its entire front page to the not-guilty verdict and its implications. Additional articles appeared on three pages, including one on how the ruling had "shocked" the public prosecutors. The article closed with harsh criticism of the prosecution: "Instead of adding to the number of cases of graft exposed through circumstantial evidence, the Public Prosecutors Office must now address the weighty task of examining the way in which it conducts its investigations."

The *Nikkei* and *Mainichi* also carried articles on the main points of the trial verdict and its implications, and also reported on the shock and disappointment of the prosecution.

Tada, after poring over the press reports, offered the summary, somewhat disgustedly, that the tone of the reporting was overall negative. I, however, took a slightly different view. Given how critical the media was in their reporting on Fujinami all along, I thought they had no choice but to report developments in this way since the not-guilty verdict would reflect poorly on them. Then a friend of mine, a former judge, offered me his insight, which eroded my optimism. The courts, he said, tend to monitor closely how the media report on their rulings, which made me jittery in case the verdict were appealed and the case taken to the High Court.

Once the verdict was out, the media were after me for interviews. I turned them all down. News reporters and photographers for the TV stations were lined up outside the entrance to my office building, though, making it impossible for me to come and go freely. After discussing the matter with my attorneys, I decided I would meet with TV and news reporters at the entrance to the courthouse when I went there two days later, on September 29.

The interview took place in front of the Tokyo District Court building following that day's session. Suppressing any displays of emotion, I matter-of-factly stated I was very happy Fujinami was found not guilty, and I expressed my heartfelt apologies to him for the trouble my actions caused him. The interview was featured on all the TV stations that day.

The prosecution was dissatisfied with the verdict handed down in Fujinami's case and filed an appeal. I assumed I would be called to testify in the second trial because of my obvious involvement in the case, but in the end I was never asked to do so.

On March 24, 1997, based on the very same evidence that was presented in his first trial, the High Court this time found Fujinami guilty. The ruling stated the initial not-guilty verdict—which was based on doubts concerning whether or not favors were requested of the defendant by me and others, and concerning whether or not Fujinami interpreted the money he had accepted to be a bribe—was overturned on the judgment that the evidence was incorrectly evaluated and the facts misconstrued. This time he was given a three-year jail sentence, suspended for four years.

The evening editions again gave this news their top coverage. One prominent headline in the *Asahi* declared that the prosecution had won a "thin-ice victory"—which is to say, highly precarious:

> In the first trial, Mr. Ezoe had already confessed that during his visit on March 15, 1984, he had requested that Mr. Fujinami put back the announcement of successful candidates taking the civil service exam, and the court took that confession as reason for presuming Mr. Ezoe's request was the issue of the exam's scheduling.
>
> As to the subsequent visit to Mr. Fujinami by a Recruit officer on March 24, the purpose of which, according to the prosecution, was to confirm the chief cabinet secretary's response to Mr. Ezoe's request to prevent early student recruitment, the court expressed understanding of the testimony given by persons affiliated with Recruit who contended the visit was to thank Mr. Fujinami for attending a party at Recruit three days earlier.
>
> In the appellate trial, the prosecution sought to undermine that testimony with evidence to the contrary. It extracted testimony from the

former chief cabinet secretary's aides stating that Mr. Fujinami had not attended the party in question, and it contended that (a) if the purpose of the visit had not been to thank Mr. Fujinami for his attendance, then (b) the aim must have been to confirm Mr. Fujinami's response to Mr. Ezoe's request, thus (c) corroborating that Mr. Ezoe had asked him for favors. The prosecution's strategy—to bolster the reliability of the public prosecutors' statements by amassing indirect facts and reenacting what went on "behind closed doors"—proved successful. Even so, as there was no definitive evidence, the victory stood on "thin ice."

Coverage in the *Yomiuri* focused on the prosecution's sense of relief in overturning the lower court's ruling. One article quoted Norio Munakata, who by this time had worked his way up to service in the Supreme Public Prosecutors Office: "As someone who devoted his every waking moment to conducting this investigation for nearly ten months, when I received word of the guilty verdict, I was so moved I started shaking—and that hasn't happened to me in a long time." The article went on to quote an unnamed prosecutor who was involved in the investigation up until the lower court ruling: "Everything turned out the way things were supposed to. Perhaps we were a bit sloppy in making our case in the first trial, insofar as the follow-up visit was concerned as well as the fact that a donation was made the year before the bribes started."

The "follow-up visit" refers to a visit to Fujinami by senior managing director Naotaka Ida and other Recruit members on March 24, 1984. The visit was paid merely to thank the chief cabinet secretary for attending a party held at the Hotel Okura on March 21 in celebration of Recruit's corporate name change—from Japan Recruit Center to Recruit Co., Ltd. The prosecution, however, linked the visit to my alleged asking for favors and contended that Fujinami's schedule on the day in question was too busy to have made it possible for him to attend such a party, and they alleged that since it was inconceivable that Ida and the others visited him to express gratitude for attending the party, their true objective must have been to ascertain whether the "favors" I had requested were carried out.

I greeted Fujinami at the party in question myself. He stayed only a few moments, apologizing that he had another appointment to attend.

Whether or not Fujinami attended the party should have been irrelevant to the case anyway. Also, I acted alone in paying the visit to Fujinami that the prosecution alleged was made to ask favors from him. If a "follow-up visit" were made to check if those favors were carried out, the one paying that second visit would have been me, not Ida. What's more, the judgment passed by the lower court was that no favors were requested. The High Court then handed down a guilty verdict even though the evidence in the case had not changed an iota.

It seemed to me that the verdict of the High Court was reached without taking these facts into account and, as a result of egging on by the media, made a ruling that was virtually a given from the start. "Thin ice," as even the media pointed out, indeed.

What we have here is a vicious circle. Because the courts pander to the media, the media come to wield ever-greater powers—powers that, in turn, have an impact on the rulings handed down in the nation's courtrooms. In the end I was left feeling that if the courts would reach verdicts truly autonomously, the media would then begin to exercise more discretion in their reporting.

Fujinami subsequently appealed the High Court's ruling against him. But while this was a case probing the guilt or innocence of a chief cabinet secretary and was thus a matter that attracted strong public interest, the Supreme Court rejected his appeal. On October 21, 1999, the court upheld the sentence that was handed down on him: three years' imprisonment suspended for four years, and a fine of 42.7 million yen.

I suspect the reason the Supreme Court rejected Fujinami's appeal was to avoid setting a precedent.

Katsuya Ikeda

Katsuya Ikeda, a member of the Diet, was indicted on charges of bribe-taking in conjunction with my provision of Recruit Cosmos stock to his younger brother, Yuzuru Ikeda, and payments made to the building management company, Seiga, run by the younger Ikeda.

I had no acquaintance whatsoever with Yuzuru Ikeda, however, and I had never even heard of his company until the case broke. What's more, my relationship with Katsuya Ikeda didn't extend beyond having once met him at a party. The lawmaker was from the same electoral district as Takashi Kosugi, a Diet member whom, as a friend and classmate in the Faculty of Education at the University of Tokyo, I had long supported, and I would hardly have given political donations and stocks to the rival of a friend.

The younger Ikeda appeared in court five times between May 28 and September 3, 1992, testifying that his brother had had no involvement in the purchase of Recruit Cosmos shares.

NAGAI (prosecutor): This "Seiga" we've just been hearing about—it had a contract on building management and technical guidance consulting with Cosmos Life, didn't it?

YUZURU IKEDA: That's right.

NAGAI: Between December 1985 and May 1988, remittances were made by Cosmos Life to Seiga initially in the amount of two million yen every half-year, then three million yen every half-year, correct?

IKEDA: Correct.

JUDGE WATANABE: At the time you entered into this contract, did you actually intend to provide the technical guidance just spoken of?

IKEDA: No.

JUDGE WATANABE: So you had no such intentions from the start?

IKEDA: That's right.

NAGAI: Are you saying Seiga didn't dispatch any technical guidance consultants to Cosmos Life?

IKEDA: That's correct.

NAGAI: The money was in fact remitted to you, though, was it not?

IKEDA: Yes.

NAGAI: Why did you think Mr. [Toshihiro] Ono was doing this for you?

IKEDA: As an investment in my future. I was thinking of getting into politics myself, and we had talked about it.

NAGAI: So you were aspiring to become a politician, a lawmaker?

IKEDA: Ono was a close friend, and I confided that's what I wanted to do someday.

NAGAI: You are talking about the stocks. You just happened to pay a casual visit to Recruit and met with Mr. Ono?

IKEDA: As I recall, the subject came up when we were talking about something or other.

NAGAI: Did Mr. Ono state clearly the stock was stock in Recruit Cosmos?

IKEDA: He said it was Recruit Cosmos stock, but at the time I knew almost nothing about the company.

NAGAI: Could you please explain a bit more specifically just what Mr. Ono said to you?

IKEDA: I remember him saying I couldn't possibly lose. As to what exchange took place between us after that, I really don't remember. That wasn't what we'd met for.

NAGAI: During all that time, did you discuss any of this with your brother?

IKEDA: No, not at all.

NAGAI: Now about those stocks, did you get the feeling Mr. Ono was approaching you under instruction from his boss, Mr. Ezoe?

IKEDA: Not in the least.

Katsuya Ikeda appeared in court three times—a whole four years later, the first occasion being October 31, 1996. He underwent questioning by both the defense and the prosecution.

HIDENORI AOKI (defense attorney): Have you ever met Mr. Ezoe?

KATSUYA IKEDA: Yes, I have.

AOKI: Approximately how many times?

IKEDA: Twice, I believe.

AOKI: And what was the occasion of those two meetings?

IKEDA: The first was at a party, I believe.

AOKI: Do you recall the nature of the party?

IKEDA: It was a New Year's party for members of the publishing industry held at a large hotel.

AOKI: And that's where you met Mr. Ezoe for the first time?

IKEDA: That's right.

Aoki: And the second time, when was that?

Ikeda: It was when the publishing industry held an exhibition and sale in Ginza at a hall owned by Recruit. I went with industry people to express gratitude to Recruit for allowing us use of their hall.

Aoki: Did Mr. Ezoe ever visit you at one of your offices?

Ikeda: No.

Mamoru Wada (defense attorney): Next, I'd like to confirm some facts concerning the payments from Cosmos Life to Seiga. Did you know a contract of some sort had been concluded between Cosmos Life and Seiga?

Ikeda: No, I didn't.

Wada: Did you have absolutely no knowledge your brother had acquired shares of Recruit Cosmos stock?

Ikeda: Yes, none.

Wada: You'd heard nothing at all about it from him?

Ikeda: He told me about it later on.

Wada: You didn't hear anything from him about it either when he bought the shares or immediately thereafter?

Ikeda: No.

Wada: When did you first learn your brother had acquired the shares?

Ikeda: I believe it was around the end of June in 1988.

Wada: And how did you come to know this?

Ikeda: I was preparing for an appearance on TV when he came in, a newspaper in hand, and said, "Hey, I got these shares too."

Wada: On that occasion, how much did you ask about the circumstances surrounding the shares?

Ikeda: He kept saying it was no big deal, there was no need to worry, and nothing would leak out. I think he also said he'd tried to refuse buying them but ultimately wasn't able to.

Wada: After hearing what your brother said, what was your understanding of the reason he'd acquired those shares?

Ikeda: I thought he'd been offered the shares through his contact with Mr. Ono. Unlike me, my brother's relatively interested in making money, so I thought that was what it was all about.

From the two brothers' testimony it was clear that Katsuya Ikeda had connections with neither Seiga nor the stock purchase. Moreover, Yuzuru Ikeda wasn't his brother's state-funded secretary. I thus assumed the elder Ikeda would be found innocent. But on December 21, 1994, Katsuya Ikeda was handed a guilty verdict, a three-year sentence suspended for four years plus a fine of 18.35 million yen.

A number of reasons were cited for the court's decision. First, it was deemed conceivable that I directly contacted Katsuya Ikeda by phone regarding the stock purchase. Second, it could be presumed Ikeda was aware of and consented to my intention to thank him for his "favors" by having him reap profit from the purchase of five thousand shares of Recruit Cosmos—a stock virtually assured of rising in value and not readily accessible to the general public—at a price of 3,000 yen per share. And third, although Seiga was effectively operated by Yuzuru Ikeda, it was clear he acted under instruction from his elder brother, as illustrated by his quest for instruction from his brother when renewing contracts, etc.

The evening newspaper editions all gave the news of Katsuya Ikeda's conviction their top coverage. The *Nikkei* reported that Judge Mikami had apparently concluded Ikeda had consented to the favors asked of him and had personally accepted my check with the full knowledge it was compensation for the favors he extended. It could be presumed that Cosmos Life's remittances totaling five million yen to Seiga, which was operated by his younger brother (who had previously been his secretary), were requested of Recruit by the younger Ikeda either under the instruction of or with the approval of his elder brother. Further Katsuya Ikeda had to be aware the transfer of shares in Yuzuru's name was payment for the favors he had provided. Thus, the judge found the facts to be in line with the prosecution's contentions: namely, that the check, the funds remitted, and the transferred shares had all been payoffs to the defendant. Finally, the article stated that the judge deemed my statements, admitting to providing both the shares and the check, reliable.

The *Mainichi* reported that the three-year sentence was a harsh verdict for the defendant. Judge Mikami had censured the defendant for acquiring the pre-flotation shares, saying by accepting stock unavailable to the public—and in the process making a sizable profit—Ikeda had eroded people's motivation to work. At the same time, the judge had opted to give the defendant a suspended sentence because Ikeda could be seen as having carelessly gotten caught up in the web shrewdly spun by Recruit, and because the questioning he had initiated in the Diet, aimed at placing Recruit in a positive light, could not be said to have done harm to the nation's interests.

I had had virtually no acquaintance with Katsuya Ikeda, and the only statements I made relating to him were vague at best. I never imagined a verdict of this kind would be handed down based on such flimsy evidence. When I asked one of my attorneys about this, he replied: "Verdicts are decided virtually according to the prosecutors' statements."

But if that was the case, then why on earth were six whole years spent on his trial?

Fujinami's shares had been bought by Eiji Tokuda, and Katsuya Ikeda's shares had actually been bought by Yuzuru Ikeda. Tokuda and Yuzuru Ikeda had profited, but all the same, it was Fujinami and Katsuya Ikeda who were found guilty. How could this be?

One of my attorneys explained that it was because Fujinami and Katsuya Ikeda had played principal roles in the alleged crime while Tokuda and Yuzuru Ikeda had functioned as accessories to the crime.

I found this hard to accept.

The Labor Ministry Route

The foremost point of dispute relating to the "Ministroy of Labor route" was the question of who had approached Labor Vice Minister Takashi Kato concerning the purchase of Recruit Cosmos shares.

All along Kato, who bought the shares, claimed he was approached by Masao Tatsumi. Tatsumi, who was part of the group of founding members and subsequently became president of Cosmos Life, contended he had never gone to see Kato about any stock matter. Meanwhile, Toshihiro Ono, who had performed the paperwork involved, said he had acted under instructions from managing director Shunjiro Mamiya. The testimony given by the two sides thus differed from the outset.

In the course of Tatsumi's interrogation, a statement was taken to the effect that he had approached Kato about buying the shares under instructions from me. But as I described in detail, my relationship with Tatsumi had soured over the matter of his returning his Recruit stocks, and at the time in question, he was hardly anyone I would be sending on a mission concerning the purchase of Recruit Cosmos shares.

As to why he signed his name to a statement that was contrary to the facts, Tatsumi gave the following testimony in court on July 26, 1995:

> YOSHIAKI TORIMOTO (prosecutor): On March 8, 1989, you were arrested on suspicion of passing a bribe to former Labor Vice Minister Takashi Kato, were you not?
>
> TATSUMI: That's correct.
>
> TORIMOTO: And am I correct that you contend not once during the course of your arrest or detention to have given a statement to the prosecutors admitting to the facts as charged?
>
> TATSUMI: Yes. I never gave any statement of that kind.
>
> TORIMOTO: And does the existence of the statement in which you admit to having offered shares of Recruit Cosmos to Mr. Kato under instructions from Mr. Ezoe in September 1986 derive, as you have testified, from a conversation you had with Prosecutor Nagai on March 24, immediately before your written confession was prepared, in which you agreed to speak in hypothetical terms, and that ended up as your written confession?
>
> TATSUMI: That's right.
>
> TORIMOTO: And throughout your interrogation before being taken into custody, did you consistently deny any involvement in the transfer of the Recruit Cosmos shares to Mr. Kato?
>
> TATSUMI: Yes.
>
> TORIMOTO: How would you describe Prosecutor Nagai's attitude during his interrogations?
>
> TATSUMI: When the interrogations began in the fall of 1988, Mr. Nagai was extremely courteous. In January he said he believed what I was saying but that someone above him had a different opinion, putting him in a difficult position. Then, apparently, Mr.

Kato swore repeatedly he'd been approached by me, and the prosecutor's attitude changed completely. He said public servants don't lie and he believed what Mr. Kato was saying not just 100 percent but 120 percent—or even 300 percent.

TORIMOTO: Did he say something to the effect he didn't believe what you told him?

TATSUMI: He did. He called me a liar and said my memory must be failing. About fifteen or maybe twenty days after my arrest in March, I think it was, he became quite hard-edged and threatening. He kicked the table, sending a stack of papers to the floor. He also made me stand facing the wall, shouting at me and ranting and raving.

TORIMOTO: During your interrogations after your arrest, did Prosecutor Nagai ever use physical violence against you—hit you, kick you, twist your arm, anything like that?

TATSUMI: He never attacked me physically, but he did use mental violence. Once, when he made me stand facing the wall for a long time until it caused me great anguish, I asked him if this was the form of torture being used nowadays.

TORIMOTO: Isn't there a statement in which you say you approached Mr. Kato about the Recruit Cosmos shares under Mr. Ezoe's instructions?

TATSUMI: One day Mr. Nagai came in with a statement to that effect and told me to read it. Once I'd read it, he then ordered me to sign it. I told him it didn't coincide with the facts, at which point he said, "These are the facts—admit it!" He said the same thing over and over again, adding if I didn't admit to what it said he'd have me arrested again and thrown in jail—but if I did admit to everything he'd let me out quickly with a suspended sentence. I told him I couldn't do it.

TORIMOTO: Before that, had Prosecutor Nagai ever prepared a written statement for you and ordered you to read it?

TATSUMI: Any number of times, he would first read a statement to me and then make me read it aloud two or three times.

TORIMOTO: So you both read it—which means you of course understood the contents of these statements, right?

TATSUMI: I knew they weren't true but by ordering me to read them over and over again, I thought he was trying to brainwash me.

TORIMOTO: OK, so let's say you read it. What did Prosecutor Nagai say to you after that?

TATSUMI: He would bring in a statement taken from Mr. Ezoe or Mr. Ono, hold it too far away from me to make out what it actually said, and then say things like "Mr. Ezoe has said both you and Ono were at his beck and call" or "Mr. Ezoe says you're responsible for everything." Or he would say a statement was taken from Ono saying he'd gone to see Mr. Kato and work things out because I'd told him to.

TORIMOTO: So then, in the end, you didn't sign the statement?

TATSUMI: I did sign it, either that day or the following day, I believe.

TORIMOTO: Up until then, all along you'd never admitted having anything to do with getting the shares to Mr. Kato, and you'd made no written statements saying you admitted to that. So why do you say you were compelled to sign this particular statement?

TATSUMI: I was exhausted both physically and mentally, and all I wanted was to get out of there as quickly as possible. All along I'd denied the accusation against me, but I began to sense things moving closer and closer to what they had charged me with. I felt like I was being attacked from all sides, with no way to escape, so I decided my best course of action would be to sign straightaway and then tell the truth in court.

TORIMOTO: Did the prosecutor say you might not get out of detention?"

TATSUMI: Yes. Over and over again.

TORIMOTO: And did that affect your thinking?

TATSUMI: Yes. I kept being told if I didn't sign I wouldn't get out, they'd put me in jail.

TORIMOTO: Did you consider on what specific charges you might be placed under arrest again?

TATSUMI: I'd been arrested for something I hadn't done. "So this is what false charges are all about," I thought to myself.

TORIMOTO: At the time you signed the statement, did you think it might be used as evidence in court?

Tatsumi: It was only after the trial started that I came to understand how significant such statements are.

From Tatsumi's testimony, it's clear that in the course of his interrogations he was driven into a corner, mentally, by the prosecutor and put in a situation in which he felt he had no alternative but to sign the statement against his will.

For a person who has been charged with a crime, being threatened with a long detention is a horribly frightening prospect. Tatsumi's experience was, in fact, close to what I experienced in my own interrogations, and I thought he too had suffered a great deal.

Whereas Tatsumi staunchly denied any involvement in the affair, Kato, when summoned before the Diet, testified that he was approached about the stock purchase by Tatsumi. Here is what Kato testified in court on November 8, 1995:

> Torao Tsukuma (prosecutor): How did you come to acquire the shares in Recruit Cosmos?
>
> Kato: Mr. Tatsumi, whom I'd known for quite a long time, told me a Recruit subsidiary was going public, and he was very eager for me to be among those who purchased pre-flotation shares. I acquiesced to his request.
>
> Tsukuma: Around what time did your acquisition of the shares become a problem in the eyes of the media?
>
> Kato: I believe it was on the tenth of October of that year, when the media were suddenly all lined up in front of my house waiting for me. They asked me a variety of things, and I responded.
>
> Tsukuma: Did you say anything to the media in reference to who had approached you about the Recruit Cosmos shares?
>
> Kato: Yes, I believe I told them I'd been asked to buy the shares by someone from Recruit, someone who was an old fishing pal.
>
> Tsukuma: Why didn't you mention Mr. Tatsumi by name?
>
> Kato: Well, I didn't want to cause any trouble by bringing up any names.
>
> Tsukuma: You gave testimony before the House of Representatives' special committee investigating the Recruit affair, didn't you?

Kato: Yes, I did.

Tsukuma: On that occasion you mentioned Mr. Tatsumi by name. You testified you'd been approached by Mr. Tatsumi, am I correct?

Kato: That's right.

Tsukuma: Did the public prosecutor suggest any other names at the time?

Kato: Yes—Mr. Ezoe and Mr. Mamiya.

Tsukuma: And did he bring those names up on the chance that your memory—your memory of Mr. Tatsumi—may have been incorrect on this point?

Kato: I believe so.

Tsukuma: And how did you answer him?

Kato: I told him I'd slept on the matter for a day but that to my recollection I still believed I'd been approached by Mr. Tatsumi.

Tsukuma: Mr. Kato, you also testified as a witness at Mr. Tatsumi's trial, didn't you?

Kato: Yes, I did.

Tsukuma: Mr. Tatsumi testified in this court that he never asked you to purchase shares in Recruit Cosmos. What do you make of that?

Kato: To the best of my recollection, it was Mr. Tatsumi who approached me.

Tsukuma: When you purchased the Recruit Cosmos shares, who came to handle the actual paperwork?

Kato: Mr. Ono.

Tsukuma: And when Mr. Ono came, did you have the impression he was coming on behalf of Mr. Ezoe?

Kato: Not especially.

Tsukuma: In your statement of March 24, I believe you say you thought Mr. Ono had come to do the paperwork relating to the transfer of shares after discussions between him and Mr. Ezoe, correct?

Kato: That's because I kept being told to write that it was Mr. Ezoe, or to convince myself that Mr. Ono was sent by Mr. Ezoe. I don't remember it happening that way, but in the end that's the statement I was coerced to go along with.

When the news first broke that he had bought shares of Recruit Cosmos, Kato, when questioned by reporters as to who broached the idea with him, responded he was approached by Tatsumi. At the time, Tatsumi had already left Recruit and was president of Cosmos Life.

When Tatsumi was later asked why his name was brought up, he conjectured that when Kato was about to face questioning from members of the press about the stock transfer, he had discussed the matter with Shigeru Kano, then in charge of the Public Employment Service Division, and had been advised to say he was approached by Tatsumi, who was no longer with Recruit.

Kato also named Tatsumi when he was summoned to testify before the Diet. Perjury is a serious crime. I speculated it was for this reason that he stuck to his testimony—that he was approached by Tatsumi—after his arrest.

Ono, who performed the paperwork involved in the transfer of shares to Kato, described the circumstances surrounding the transfer and the nature of his own interrogations in court on April 26, 1996. The following is an excerpt:

> TSUKUMA (prosecutor): Were you not asked to handle the transfer of shares to Mr. Kato directly by Mr. Ezoe?
>
> ONO: No, that's not how it was.
>
> TSUKUMA: Didn't Mr. Ezoe instruct you to process the transfer of three thousand shares of stock to Mr. Kato?
>
> ONO: No.
>
> TSUKUMA: When you went to see Mr. Kato about carrying out the transfer, did you first get confirmation from someone that Mr. Kato had agreed to the transfer?
>
> ONO: As I recall, I visited Mr. Kato after being told Mr. Mamiya had already discussed the matter with him.
>
> TSUKUMA: Mr. Ono, we have a statement prepared by Prosecutor [Shuzo] Yamamoto—and signed by you—stating it was Mr. Ezoe who decided to sell the shares to Mr. Kato and that you went to do the paperwork in line with Mr. Ezoe's instructions.
>
> ONO: I believe there was a statement of that kind.

TSUKUMA: Why did you put your signature to such a statement?

ONO: The prosecutor said if I kept to my story, my statement would conflict with what others were saying. And he made the threat that if he was unable to get a statement out of me, he'd get backup support from other prosecutors and have me arrested for a third time, a fourth time, and so on. He worded the statement in various ways, and in the end, having used up every ounce of energy within me, I succumbed and signed.

TSUKUMA: So you're saying you were coerced to sign because what you were saying didn't coincide with the statements made by others?

ONO: That's correct. The prosecutor went on and on about how if I'd sign the statement, it would tally with the others.

TSUKUMA: And what were you told would happen if your story didn't tally?

ONO: I was told I wouldn't be released, my detention would drag on, and I could be arrested for a third time.

TSUKUMA: Did you sign because you'd been told you might be arrested again?

ONO: I was pressured to sign in exchange for promises I'd get released. "If you sign this statement, we'll arrange so you can get out on bail before the end of April." "If you go along with this statement, we'll let you out just after Golden Week." Things like that.

TSUKUMA: What was your interrogation like on that day? Please tell us as far as you can remember.

ONO: My interrogation on the 19th began in the morning. My interrogations before had pretty much provided a general outline, and since I felt the statement didn't reflect what I'd said, I refused to sign it. At that point I was ordered to stand facing the wall, and I had to stay that way for over an hour.

TSUKUMA: What took place while you were forced to stand facing the wall?

ONO: I just kept being told to stand that way, or to move closer to the wall, to get so close that my nose would touch it, and to stay that way.

TSUKUMA: And why did you sign the statement that day?

ONO: Prosecutor Munakata came and told me to say it was Mr. Ezoe, that there was no way Mr. Ezoe wouldn't know about the transfer of shares to Mr. Kato. He said it would also work to my advantage if I said it was Mr. Ezoe. As I'd heard all authority was vested in Mr. Munakata, I thought something dire would happen if I didn't sign. I was scared of the prospect of my detention continuing, so I signed.

TSUKUMA: When Prosecutor Yamamoto appeared in court, he flatly denied having forced you to stand. You weren't really made to stand, now were you?

ONO: The prosecutor's lying.

TSUKUMA: Now, about your reason for signing the statement, what you're ultimately saying then is there's no direct connection between your being forced to stand that day and your signing?"

ONO: I'm not saying that. As I've told you before, to me it was an act of violence. Saying things like my detention would drag on or I wouldn't be allowed out on bail—that's verbal violence.

TSUKUMA: What connection does that have with your signing?

ONO: Through such violence I was coerced to sign.

TSUKUMA: To your mind, March 19 is the day a statement of confession was taken from you, is that right?

ONO: I don't see it that way.

TSUKUMA: You don't?

ONO: What I'm saying is I didn't confess to anything. If I'd made a confession, there would be no need for my asking for it to be amended, would there? The reason I asked for an emendation is because it's not a statement of confession.

TSUKUMA: The statement says by your recollection it was Mr. Ezoe himself who came up with the idea of selling shares of Recruit Cosmos to Mr. Kato and who put his name on the list. Did you say this?

ONO: No.

TSUKUMA: Are you saying the prosecutor made this up?

ONO: Yes.

So, in ways similar to Tatsumi and me, Ono was continuously put through severe interrogations in order to get statements out of him that coincided with the scenario written by the prosecutors.

Ono also said a statement saying he added Kato to the list under my instructions was a fabrication by the prosecutors, but that he signed it after being threatened tenaciously during his interrogation. Here is his testimony in court on May 30, 1996, on this fabrication:

> Osamu Ishihara (defense attorney): During your interrogation of March 31, did Prosecutor Yamamoto say anything to you in reference to Mr. Kato?
>
> Ono: Yes. After asking me about various politicians, he returned to the subject of Mr. Kato. "Why don't you admit what I've been saying about the share transfer?" he pressed me. He then said I must be worried about my family, and he remarked there's no telling when my company might cut me off. Finally, he suggested after my indictment I put in a petition myself.
>
> Ishihara: As far as you can recall, what did you talk about relating to the "political route"?
>
> Ono: Once the topic turned to the political route, just as with Mr. Kato, several times he told me to "forget" things. He'd say, "If you don't wipe that out of your memory, this'll never end, you know."
>
> Ishihara: Was he referring to the political route?
>
> Ono: I kept thinking how I'd been told the same thing when talking about Mr. Kato. Then too, the prosecutor had told me to "lose my memory"; otherwise they wouldn't let me go. I countered by saying the statement was a fabrication made up by the prosecutor. At which point, I remember being yelled at by Prosecutor Yamamoto, blustering if I did anything during the trial to overturn the statement, they'd throw the book at me.

Ono testified he was instructed by Shunjiro Mamiya to go to Kato and undertake the necessary procedures for transferring the shares—but this was steadfastly denied by Mamiya. The following is part of Mamiya's testimony given in court on October 4, 1996:

TSUKUMA (prosecutor): You were partly involved in the various transfers of Recruit Cosmos shares carried out in September 1986,
weren't you?

MAMIYA: Yes, I was.

TSUKUMA: Three thousand shares were transferred to then Vice Minister of Labor Takashi Kato. Were you at all involved in that
transfer?

MAMIYA: No.

TSUKUMA: We have already heard testimony in the court you were
under instructions by Mr. Ezoe and you recommended four people
to him to be included as share recipients. Did you recommend to
Mr. Ezoe that Mr. Kato be included?

MAMIYA: No, I didn't.

TSUKUMA: When did you learn Mr. Kato was selected to receive the
shares?

MAMIYA: I believe it was around the time it was first reported in the
press."

TSUKUMA: And you really knew nothing about it until then?

MAMIYA: Nothing at all.

TSUKUMA: In this very courtroom Mr. Ezoe testified he wasn't the one
who selected Mr. Kato. He stated that at the time there were two
people in a position to decide for themselves who would get the
shares and who were on close terms with Mr. Kato—Tomoyuki
Ikeda and you, Mr. Mamiya—and he said he believed it must have
been one of you who had chosen Mr. Kato. Mr. Mamiya, were you
not, as Mr. Ezoe stated, the one who selected Mr. Kato?

MAMIYA: No, it wasn't me.

TSUKUMA: Mr. Mamiya, did you instruct Mr. Ono regarding the
paperwork for transferring the shares to Mr. Kato?

MAMIYA: No.

TSUKUMA: On this very point, Mr. Ono stated in this courtroom he
was instructed by you to go to Mr. Kato and carry out the necessary procedures; also that you said you had already discussed the
matter with him. What do you say to this?

MAMIYA: No such thing took place.

TSUKUMA: Mr. Mamiya, did you not yourself approach Mr. Kato about purchasing the shares?

MAMIYA: No, I didn't.

TSUKUMA: So you're saying you never gave instructions to Mr. Ono?

MAMIYA: That's right. Never.

TSUKUMA: But you did know Mr. Kato at the time?

MAMIYA: Yes, I did.

TSUKUMA: And you never approached him about buying Recruit Cosmos stock?

MAMIYA: No.

Mamiya was arrested and interrogated on suspicion of violating the Securities and Exchange Law. In the end he wasn't indicted, and it may have been out of a desire never again to return to Kosuge that he testified he had had no connection with the transfer of shares to Mr. Kato.

Mamiya was never charged, while Ono was given a two-year sentence suspended for three years. From Ono's standpoint, he seemed to think he was made to pay for a crime he hadn't committed because of Mamiya's testimony. Once the scandal was over, he left Recruit. As for Mamiya—who had also been the key culprit in the Matsubara case—after discussions with upper management he agreed to step down.

Masao Tatsumi: Not Guilty, Then Guilty

On December 16, 1993, the lower court pronounced Masao Tatsumi not guilty. It seemed that Tatsumi's description to the court of the nature of his interrogations was persuasive enough for the presiding judge, Kiyoshi Kimura, to doubt the reliability of statements Tatsumi signed. The court seemed also to be persuaded by the testimony given by Seiji Shimodaira, Recruit's legal counsel, about the disaffection between Tatsumi and me at the time.

The *Asahi* gave the news top billing in its evening edition, stating that the foremost point of dispute was the reliability of Tatsumi's statement of confession, which Tatsumi had been baited into signing. There seemed to be weaknesses at the core of Kato's statement—that he was approached by

Tatsumi about acquiring the shares—which the court could not overlook either. Other signed statements—including statements with my signature—suggesting Tatsumi's involvement were thought by the judge to be "unnatural and unreliable."

In reference to Tatsumi's confession made during the investigative phase, the *Asahi* reported that the court concluded it lacked credibility for two reasons. First, the content of the confession had undergone several transformations. And second, at the time the shares were sold to Kato, Tatsumi and I were at loggerheads and our relationship was no longer one in which I would have entrusted a confidential matter like the transfer of pre-flotation shares to Tatsumi. In light of these assessments, Judge Kimura, the *Asahi* reported, concluded "although suspicion that Mr. Tatsumi approached then Vice Minister Kato could not be erased, reasonable doubt remained that precluded firm affirmation of his involvement."

The evening edition of the *Yomiuri* focused on the dichotomy between Kato's having been found guilty of bribe-taking and Tatsumi being declared innocent of bribe-giving. It reported that roughly a half-hour after the ruling was handed down, deputy superintending prosecutor Tatsuhiro Ishikawa called a highly unusual emergency press conference at which he fumed at the court's judgment, calling it "completely unanticipated and altogether unacceptable."

Tatsumi was quoted as saying, "It was a long trial, but from the start of my interrogations all along I said I had absolutely no involvement. I'm very happy the court accepted this." As Tatsumi spoke to the press, he showed little emotion, but the report observed that there were moments when he appeared on the verge of tears. When asked to comment on the judge's assessment that the interrogations were "tenacious," Tatsumi quipped that his interrogations were "more than tenacious." "I was never subjected to physical violence," Tatsumi went on to say, "but what I experienced mentally was the same sort of thing—being made to stand facing a wall for hours on end, someone yelling into my ear, being confined to a corner of the room."

The *Mainichi* indicated that the prosecution was very confident of winning its case, but were nonetheless concerned that Tatsumi might go free. "Things don't always go perfectly all of the time," the paper quoted a source at the Public Prosecutors Office.

When I heard the not-guilty verdict handed down in Tatsumi's case, the first related to the Recruit affair, I felt emotions welling up inside me.

Tatsumi was part of the original group of people who founded Recruit, people who had all worked practically round the clock together. He was a very capable young man, and had started up the Osaka branch while he was still a student. When I heard the innocent verdict, I felt sure his fortunes would rise again.

Here, too, was a not-guilty verdict, the first, which as my lawyer Hino earlier suggested, would suggest likelihood of a suspended sentence for me. I took the outcome of Tatsumi's trial as a happy omen.

The prosecution, however, was dissatisfied with the court's ruling and appealed. The High Court, working with the same evidence as presented in the District Court, overturned the original verdict and, on October 8, 1996, found Tatsumi guilty. He was given a one-year sentence, suspended for three years.

The day after this second judgment was passed, the morning edition of the *Asahi* reported the Tokyo High Court supported the findings of the lower court insofar as my having "masterminded" what took place, but undertook a review of the credibility of Kato's statements. The High Court, the article stated, pointed to the lack of any indication to suggest Kato met with Tatsumi in advance of his testimony before the Diet and to the fact that any party named by him would have been placed under suspicion of having passed a bribe. It added that no matter how desperate Kato's situation might be, it was inconceivable that he would have resorted to perjury in naming who had approached him about buying the stock.

The prosecution, having won its case, released a statement to the effect it found the High Court's ruling to be a fair ascertainment of the facts and the sentence handed down to be appropriate.

The *Mainichi* suggested that the District may have relied too heavily on Kato's testimony. It noted how the two sides in the corruption scandal—the bribe-passer and the bribe-taker, which the paper described as "two sides of the same coin"—had originally been handed polar-opposite judgments, but the Tokyo High Court, by honing in on Kato's testimony, had reached a conclusion under which both sides were "uniformly guilty." The

Mainichi stated although neither the prosecution nor the defense called for Kato to give testimony in the High Court, the court, availing itself of its vested authority, cross-examined him. The paper went on to quote a higher-up in the Public Prosecutors Office as acknowledging that during the investigative phase there had been some debate concerning Tatsumi's involvement.

Tatsumi and my estrangement at the time in question was an objective fact that the court chose to ignore, subjectively adopting Kato's testimony on the premise "it was inconceivable [he] would have resorted lightly to perjury." This seemed a highly dubious basis on which to determine another person's guilt. For Tatsumi, on whom the blame was cast, the High Court's verdict was truly unfortunate.

Tatsumi was incensed at having his lower court ruling overturned for what could be seen as a case of *in dubio contra reo*—"when in doubt, blame the accused"—and it was his aim to expose, publishing at his own expense if necessary, all that had really transpired. In my preparations for this book, I offered Tatsumi space if he wanted to write anything in conjunction with the Labor Ministry route. He thought about it, but in the end abandoned the idea because of a lack of material preserved from those days.

The NTT Route

Hisahiko Hasegawa, who was arrested for violating the NTT Law (Law Concerning Nippon Telegraph and Telephone Corporation, Etc.), was indicted on bribe-taking, charged with having acquired shares of Recruit Cosmos in return for providing favors when Recruit purchased the Cray supercomputer. Hasegawa was in charge of NTT's data communications operations at the time. The person I spoke to when buying the computer, however, was Ei Shikiba; Hasegawa had no involvement in the transaction whatsoever.

Hasegawa insisted all along his purchase of the shares and Recruit's buying of the Cray supercomputer were unrelated. He took the witness stand on July 10, 1998, responding to the prosecution's questioning in the following manner:

HISANAO TAKAHATA (prosecutor): Did you ever think Mr. Ezoe offered
you the Recruit Cosmos shares in conjunction with your professional position?

HASEGAWA: That's a point on which the prosecutor and I were in direct
conflict. I repeatedly said offering pre-flotation shares to friends is
something that often occurs in general, but the prosecutor kept
saying it must have had something to do with my job.

TAKAHATA: The data communications division was in charge of supercomputers, is that correct?

HASEGAWA: That's correct.

TAKAHATA: And why didn't you think you might have been offered the
shares in Recruit Cosmos because of your position as head of the
department handling the computers?

HASEGAWA: Because the department dealing with Recruit was different—that department was headed by Mr. Shikiba. Since any requests
Recruit might have had would go through him, Mr. Ezoe never asked
me to do anything on his behalf. I believed he offered me the shares
in Recruit Cosmos because we'd known each other for a long time.

The reason I offered the shares to Hasegawa was because it was confi-
dentially decided he would come to work at Recruit. I wanted him to have
shares in our Group affiliate as someone who would soon be participating
in company management. It had nothing at all to do with the purchase of
the supercomputer.

As described earlier, at the time that I purchased the Cray computer I
was told by NTT's attorneys, through a third party, that NTT wanted me
to refrain from talking about the matter because if it came to light NTT
had merely acted as a middleman in the purchase, it could have an adverse
impact on U.S.-Japanese trade relations. That's why, when I was summoned to give testimony before the Diet, I stated that in purchasing the
computer through NTT I was anticipating its backup support.

In court, however, I decided to state the facts as they were: namely, how
it came about Recruit purchased the supercomputer through NTT at Shikiba's request, and the circumstances behind my having given false testimony
in my questioning before the Diet.

Here is what I stated in court on May 28, 1999:

TAKAHATA (prosecutor): Mr. Ezoe, during the investigation did you
tell the prosecutors Mr. Shikiba had telephoned you with a request
to purchase the supercomputer through NTT?

EZOE: Yes, I believe I did.

TAKAHATA: I'd like to ask you about your meetings with Mr. [Haruo]
Yamaguchi [NTT managing director] and Mr. Isoo Kata [head of
NTT's International Procurement Office]. According to your writ-
ten statement, your meeting with Mr. Shinto was arranged by Mr.
Shikiba. Do you recall anything about that meeting?

EZOE: When I informed Mr. Shikiba we'd decided to purchase the
computer as a way of cooperating with the International Procurement Office, he was extremely pleased and said he wanted to
come over with Mr. Yamaguchi to thank me in person. I told him
there was no need for them to go out of their way, and I said since
Recruit was so close by, I would pay him a visit. Through Mr. Shikiba I was introduced to Mr. Kata, and after that I met with Mr.
Yamaguchi.

TAKAHATA: And when you met Mr. Shinto, did you tell him you would
be purchasing the Cray supercomputer through NTT?

EZOE: I don't recall my exact words, but when I met with Mr. Yamaguchi he said he wanted for me to meet Mr. Shinto also. He said
Mr. Shinto was in a meeting with the managing directors and he
asked me to wait, which I did. When I told Mr. Shinto we'd agreed
to purchase the Cray computer, he thanked me politely. It was
merely an exchange of courtesies.

TAKAHATA: Did you attempt to confirm NTT would provide you its
backup support?

EZOE: I didn't think NTT was in a position to provide backup
support or assistance.

TAKAHATA: After your meeting with Mr. Yamaguchi or Mr. Shinto, did
you feel you'd confirmed the transaction involving the supercomputer would go smoothly?

EZOE: I knew the purchase would go smoothly if we dealt directly with Cray Japan. Cray Japan's president, Mr. Otis, had visited Recruit to promote the company's hardware. I thought going through NTT would only complicate things, but I was able to confirm that cooperating with NTT would help them resolve their prickly problem concerning international procurement.

TAKAHATA: Are you saying you confirmed that NTT was having difficulties with its international procurements, and the problem would be resolved by Recruit's purchasing the supercomputer?

EZOE: That's right. Cray Japan had already delivered more than a dozen units in Japan. Going through NTT would be a special case, and I was able to confirm the transaction would go smoothly.

TAKAHATA: In your Diet testimony you stated Cray's technology was highly advanced. Is that true?

EZOE: Yes.

TAKAHATA: And it's also true NTT approached you with the request not to talk about purchasing the supercomputer through them?

EZOE: Yes. I was told that talking about it would definitely put them in a precarious position.

TAKAHATA: And is that something you yourself were directly told by someone?

EZOE: I heard about it from our legal department, who said they'd been told by NTT's attorneys.

TAKAHATA: Instead of lying, wouldn't it have been better to tell what really happened when you testified before the Diet?

EZOE: I felt that way too, but if I said we'd cooperated with NTT in making international procurements, it would have adversely affected NTT's position. If NTT did anything unfair in terms of Japanese trade protectionism, it would have reignited trade friction between Japan and the United States. NTT sensed it was in a crisis situation since the U.S. Trade Representative, Mr. Yeutter, had said he would take the case to GATT. Recruit and NTT are business partners: Recruit conducts its telecom business using lines leased from NTT. I went along with our partner's request, fully aware I could get charged with perjury.

TAKAHATA: Are you then saying at the time you received the request from NTT, you felt it was a request you couldn't refuse, and that's why you testified so as to cover for the International Procurement Office?

EZOE: That's right.

TAKAHATA: From your point of view, you don't want to commit perjury. But if you say you cooperated with NTT, your Diet testimony would be used in the criminal case against you. So, in order to avoid having it used as evidence in your case, didn't you give testimony just a wee bit off the mark, hoping it would get you off the hook?

EZOE: I admit what I wanted was to get through with some plausible reason and not have to answer to a perjury charge later. But I was told from NTT's standpoint they'd be in a mess if I said my actions were unavoidable, and if I testified I'd cooperated in covering up the international procurement, it could potentially have an adverse influence on U.S.-Japanese trade relations. I testified as I did with full cognizance that in doing so I could be called on a perjury charge.

As I was giving this testimony, I kept reliving my testimony before the Diet, fearful I could be guilty of perjury, and before long I was reduced to tears. The court record makes no mention of this, however.

During Hasegawa's own trial, in spite of my testimony insisting on his innocence, on December 8, 1995, the court had found Hasegawa guilty. He was handed down a two-year sentence with a three-year suspension plus a fine of 22.7 million yen. The court reasoned that Hasegawa had undertaken various actions beneficial to Recruit's operations—concluding the contract on supercomputer installation work and taking steps to enable early development of telecom lines, for example—and these actions were his prerogative as overseer of NTT's Tokyo branch offices and head of the company's data communications division.

Although the court contended the contract on supercomputer installation work constituted actions beneficial to Recruit operations, buying the supercomputer through NTT was—as I cited in my testimony—of no particular benefit to Recruit. It would have been more efficient for Recruit to contract directly with Cray Japan.

The *Asahi*, in its reporting on the court outcome in its evening edition of December 8, alleged that Hiroshi Kobayashi, former president of First Finance, may not have had specific knowledge of the duties performed by Hasegawa but was aware Recruit was putting efforts into new business that would be using NTT lines, and the report claimed he and I tacitly colluded in what it said was a bribery scheme. Once again this was a total distortion of the facts on the part of the *Asahi*, and upon reading the paper's summary of the factors that supposedly led to Hasegawa's sentence I seethed with anger.

The press, including the *Asahi*, gave only low-key coverage to the conclusion of Hasegawa's trial. None of the reports was critical of the court's findings.

In considering Hasegawa's case in *Seigi no wana* (The Justice Trap), Soichiro Tahara found that the data communications operations over which Hasegawa was in charge were actually performed by NTT Data System Service Corporation (now NTT Data Corporation), an altogether private company spun off from NTT in July 1986, thus lying outside the parameters of the NTT Law. Tawara focused on this fact as an indication that the data communication operations in question were not public in nature, and therefore indicting Hasegawa on a charge of violating the NTT Law was in itself unreasonable because crimes involving simple bribery do not exist when the two corporate parties involved both belong to the private sector.

If Hasegawa's defense team informed the court that NTT Data System Service Corporation had become a private firm and drawn up a persuasive press release that would have been reported by the media, the possibility exists that Hasegawa's trial would have been suspended and he would not have been charged with any crime. At least that was what I thought after reading Tawara's book, but my lawyers suggested that given the dearth of any precedents of this kind, the matter would likely have been left to the court's discretion to decide.

Ministry of Education Route

I took the witness stand eight times in conjunction with events relating to my involvement with the Ministry of Education. The bulk of the questioning had to do with my appointment to the ministry's various councils and committees—the Curriculum Council, Japan Scholarship Foundation, the preparatory council for the New National Theatre, and so on—and I was asked to explain precisely how I came to gain those posts. I was also questioned in great detail about dinners and golf outings in the company of ministry officials.

The prosecution's contention, insofar as the so-called Ministry of Education route is concerned, was that I had sold shares of Recruit Cosmos stock to former Vice Minister Kunio Takaishi as a token of gratitude for favor received in the form of my appointment to the ministry's Curriculum Council. The truth of the matter, however—as described earlier—was that I initially turned down the appointment but ultimately, after repeated requests from Takaishi, felt I had no choice but to accept the offer.

Takaishi gave the following testimony regarding the matter on November 8, 2000:

KURIHARA (prosecutor): From what I understand, the Curriculum Council is second in rank only to the Central Council for Education and is the highest-ranking and most important council within the Elementary and Secondary Education Bureau. Is that correct?

TAKAISHI: That's correct.

KURIHARA: In 1985, at the time you headed the Elementary and Secondary Education Bureau, when debate was raging after the Nakasone Cabinet inaugurated the Ad Hoc Council on Education, did you not instruct the various sections under your authority to the effect that you wanted them to select people to serve on the Curriculum Council who would be as eminent as the members of the Ad Hoc Council?

TAKAISHI: Yes, I did.

KURIHARA: And to my understanding, in choosing the members of the Curriculum Council, first you had the various sections of the bureau suggest possible candidates, then the list of candidates was narrowed down by the section chiefs in a joint review, and the final choice was left to you as bureau chief. Am I correct?

TAKAISHI: Yes. That's right.

KURIHARA: And was Mr. Ezoe's name included in the initial list of candidates?

TAKAISHI: I believe it was.

KURIHARA: Did the head of the nominating section provide you with any explanation as to why Mr. Ezoe was offered up as a candidate?

TAKAISHI: As I recall, the explanation I received was it was important to tap the wisdom of someone from the private sector like Mr. Ezoe, whose company puts out publications like *College Management* that are highly trusted for their educational information.

KURIHARA: And did you yourself feel Mr. Ezoe was an appropriate choice as a member of the Curriculum Council?

TAKAISHI: Yes, I did.

KURIHARA: And how did it come about that you yourself directly secured Mr. Ezoe's acceptance of the appointment?

TAKAISHI: We made the request through the head of Recruit's secretariat, but the reply received was Mr. Ezoe was too busy and wished to turn down our offer. I was then asked to go persuade Mr. Ezoe in person.

KURIHARA: How did you make contact with Mr. Ezoe?

TAKAISHI: By telephone, I believe.

KURIHARA: And once you had Mr. Ezoe on the phone, what did you actually say to persuade him to accept the appointment?

TAKAISHI: I explained the Curriculum Council was a highly important body that would be revising the nation's educational curriculum, and we were eager to hear his views on various issues. I said I understood how busy he was, but we were most eager to have him cooperate.

KURIHARA: And what did Mr. Ezoe say in response?

TAKAISHI: He said he was very busy and would be unable to attend every council meeting. I then said when his work commitments made him unavailable, his absence would be unavoidable, but I requested his cooperation as much as it was possible.

KURIHARA: And at that point did Mr. Ezoe accept your offer?

TAKAISHI: He said if we insisted to that extent, then he would acquiesce.

From Takaishi's testimony it was clear my appointment to serve on the Ministry of Education's council was not to be to Recruit's benefit. This testimony proved—I thought—that I had not sold Recruit Cosmos shares to Takaishi out of a desire to thank him for appointing me to the Curriculum Council.

I don't know what the written statements taken from Takaishi and other people at the Ministry of Education contained, but in my own statements all I said was I had sold the shares to Takaishi because he intended to go into politics in the future and I held high hopes for him and wished to deepen our friendship, as well as to maintain a favorable relationship with the ministry. Nowhere did I say I sold him the shares as a way of thanking him for my appointment to the council.

Through a third party I learned Takaishi had an older brother who was a judge, who'd told Takaishi his case didn't qualify as bribe-taking and he would be found innocent. Takaishi himself was convinced of his innocence, and during the course of the trial he ran in the Lower House elections.

But on December 8, 1995, he was handed down a guilty verdict. The *Asahi* reported on its front page that the lower court had found Takaishi guilty of acquiring the pre-flotation shares of Recruit Cosmos, which were "guaranteed to rise in value," as remuneration for appointing me to various councils. It added, however, the prosecution was unable to make its case stand on another bribery charge: that Takaishi had purportedly refrained from investigating or offering official guidance on the issue of high school instructors' providing their student rosters to Recruit in order to assist the company in its distribution of information magazines on furthering one's education and job seeking. A separate article reported the presiding judge had indicated the defendant had readily accepted entertainment from Recruit—in the form of meals and golf outings—even prior to the case at hand, thus demonstrating a lapse in his moral standards.

The *Asahi* also reported on Takaishi's dissatisfaction with the court's ruling. He was quoted as saying while the court did reject the prosecution's allegation concerning the student rosters, which was the main point of contention, its findings pertaining to the selection of ministry council members were altogether contrary to the facts. He said he would appeal.

On January 19, 1998, the High Court declared Takaishi guilty. Again, Takaishi appealed, this time to the Supreme Court, but the verdict was the same.

The High Court gave two reasons for its ruling. First, it said Takaishi had accepted the shares of Recruit Cosmos as recompense for his having selected "officers" at Recruit to serve on ministry councils and committees. And second, the court stated although the issue of Recruit's collection of student rosters from high school teachers for its use in producing information magazines had come to the surface, Takaishi had chosen to make no proactive response out of consideration that such administrative measures would adversely impact Recruit.

Whereas in the lower court only my council and committee appointments were called into question, in the High Court Takaishi's failure to take administrative measures against Recruit—a crime of omission—was used as a basis for finding him guilty. But as I described earlier, Recruit's job information magazines were distributed with the approval of high school supervisors, and the authorities who oversaw those supervisors were the chairs of the boards of education of each prefecture or ward, or those boards themselves; the Ministry of Education was not in charge. For that reason, I found the guilty verdict handed down to Takaishi completely unacceptable. He was convicted for his failure to take administrative action even though he did not possess the legal authority to provide the guidance in question.

With the close of Takaishi's court proceedings, with the exception of my own case, thus ended the trials of all twelve defendants in the Recruit affair. In every case, the final ruling was a guilty verdict with a suspended sentence.

Credibility of Written Statements

A major point of dispute in my trial was the issue of the credibility of my signed statements: whether or not they were made on a voluntary basis. From the outset, the prosecution alleged my confessions were made by my own free will and there was thus no problems as to their credibility, while my defense team contended problems existed in the prosecution's interrogation methods and that because my statements were wrenched from me through intimidation or coercion, they could not stand as credible evidence in court.

Written statements have great weight under Japan's current court system. Given the controversy over the credibility of my statements, questioning regarding how the interrogations were carried out was undertaken on numerous occasions. The following are excerpts from testimony by Prosecutor Kamigaki on June 27, 1996:

> SHOZABURO ISHIDA (defense attorney): Did you ever tell Mr. Ezoe to remain standing for a long period of time?
>
> KAMIGAKI: I did on one occasion say he didn't deserve to sit down.
>
> ISHIDA: Did you say that because Mr. Ezoe was showing an attitude of insincerity?
>
> KAMIGAKI: Yes.
>
> ISHIDA: Didn't you once tell Mr. Ezoe he had lied about Mr. Shinto and demand he apologize?
>
> KAMIGAKI: At one point I believe I did say something akin to that to challenge what he'd said during the interrogation.
>
> ISHIDA: And isn't it true you ordered Mr. Ezoe to get down on his knees and beg for forgiveness?
>
> KAMIGAKI: No, that's not true.
>
> ISHIDA: You never made him get down on his knees and attempted to get him to apologize?
>
> KAMIGAKI: No.
>
> ISHIDA: And when you made him stand for long periods of time, was that one way of rebuking him?
>
> KAMIGAKI: I think it would be fair to see it in that light.
>
> ISHIDA: And was shouting into his ear another way of rebuking him?
>
> KAMIGAKI: I wouldn't deny I have a loud voice.
>
> ISHIDA: You and Mr. Ezoe once discussed Osamu Takita, the defendant who spent more time in detention than the length of incarceration to which he was ultimately sentenced, didn't you?

KAMIGAKI: Yes, we did.

ISHIDA: And it was you who brought the subject up?

KAMIGAKI: I recall wondering why Mr. Ezoe knew about the case.

ISHIDA: Do you know when the verdict was reached in that case?

KAMIGAKI: As I recall, I became aware of it after Mr. Ezoe mentioned it.

ISHIDA: That verdict was handed down on March 3.

KAMIGAKI: Yes?

ISHIDA: Yes, March 3. By then Mr. Ezoe had already been arrested, placed in detention, and was undergoing your interrogation. During that time he was barred from access to the news, so he had no way of knowing it unless you told him.

KAMIGAKI: Yes, and that's why I wondered how he knew it.

ISHIDA: Didn't you tell Mr. Ezoe if he kept denying the charges, or gave statements saying he was being unfairly charged, it would affect his chances of getting out on bail—and that if he didn't believe you, he should go ask his lawyer about it?

KAMIGAKI: I wouldn't deny having exchanges like that in the context of discussing generalities.

ISHIDA: Regarding the statement prepared on the 24th, charging he was being falsely accused, did Mr. Ezoe not seem quite upset and worried the next day?

KAMIGAKI: Isn't there something about that in the statement of the 25th?

ISHIDA: Yes.

KAMIGAKI: If it's written there, that's the way it was.

ISHIDA: Didn't Mr. Ezoe say to you that with the statement drawn up the previous day, he wouldn't get out on bail, so he wanted you to rescind the statement?

KAMIGAKI: I don't recall specifically, but if that's what's in the statement, that's the way it must have been.

On these various points, I was allowed to question the prosecutor myself.

EZOE: You told me I had no right to be sitting.

KAMIGAKI: I think I said something close to that.

EZOE: And after that you ordered me to stand.

KAMIGAKI: I'd say it was more like you said, "I'm going to stand" and you then stood up.

EZOE: You ordered me to stand.

KAMIGAKI: I admit saying something to the effect you didn't deserve to be sitting.

EZOE: And when I was standing, you ordered me to get closer—and then closer again—to the wall. You also ordered me to keep my eyes open, which caused me pain and discomfort.

KAMIGAKI: I said that because you often close your eyes.

EZOE: When I was made to remain standing, you shouted into my ear at the top of your lungs, "You imbecile!" Your voice was so loud I thought my eardrum would break. Do you deny that?

KAMIGAKI: Naturally I conducted harsh interrogations on you, but my intent was never to launch any personal attacks against you.

EZOE: You once kicked the chair I was sitting on, nearly making me fall to the floor.

KAMIGAKI: You must be joking. I absolutely never acted toward you in any way that could be described as physical.

EZOE: Didn't you tell me if I stick to my attitude, the prosecutors would make more arrests?

KAMIGAKI: I admit I responded to the situation as is normally done in such cases.

EZOE: You also told me that although formally it's the court with the right to release someone on bail, no one gets released without the consent of the prosecutors.

KAMIGAKI: I recall telling you the opinion of the prosecutors is important.

EZOE: About my having been down on my knees and begging for forgiveness, are you saying I asked for permission to get down on my knees?

KAMIGAKI: I'm not saying that at all. What I said was that you were down on your knees and said you were sorry for what you'd done.

EZOE: I'm asking you because I don't know the reason why I was made to get down and apologize.

KAMIGAKI: Isn't it because at the time you were evading saying who it was who'd profited from buying the shares?

EZOE: That's because it's not my problem what relationship existed between Mr. Shinto and Mr. Murata.

KAMIGAKI: Weren't you denying having provided profit to Mr. Shinto?

EZOE: No. There's a statement that says I sold the shares to Mr. Murata but had Mr. Shinto in mind.

KAMIGAKI: Well, I'm not too sure on that point.

It appeared before testifying in court, Prosecutor Kamigaki went over the statements he had taken during my interrogations and was prepared to stay in line with what they said. In court he was evasive, repeating that he had no recollection of such-and-such but if it was written that way in the statement, then that's the way it was.

Verdicts are most often decided on the basis of the prosecutors' statements submitted to the court at the end of a trial. That's why in the interrogation room the prosecutors drive the accused into a corner mentally with threats of a long detention and the like, so they can prepare statements to their own advantage.

My own experience, plus the inordinate length of my trial, have convinced me these circumstances contribute significantly to Japan's remarkably high conviction rate—99.9 percent.

Closing Arguments and Sentencing

My trial proceeded at about three sessions per month, each session lasting a full day. Although my lawyers said this was a swift pace for a criminal trial, the proceedings, which included endless questioning on topics unrelated to the charges and argument over the credibility of my written statements, dragged on for more than *thirteen* years—an unprecedented length of time for a trial in the lower court.

Although there were several reasons for the trial's prolongation, the foremost factor was the extreme care exercised by the prosecution in building its case in the wake of Masao Tatsumi's not-guilty verdict in the matter of the Labor Ministry route. This was the first verdict passed down, and coupled with the not-guilty judgment handed down on Takao Fujinami, a central defendant in the entire Recruit scandal, it spurred the prosecution to work the more meticulously on my case.

Ten Character Witnesses, Two Hundred Nineteen Letters of Appeal

During the thirteen years between the opening session and the handing down of the lower court's ruling, there were a number of changes of personnel on both the prosecution and the defense. There were even two changes of presiding judges, from Tadatsugu Watanabe to Hideaki Mikami in 1993, and again to Megumi Yamamuro in 1997.

Judges get transferred every three years or so. In the event of a change in presiding judges, the new judge needs time to read the preceding court records in order to gain an overview of the case at hand, resulting in the court going into recess. When Judge Mikami took over from Judge Watanabe, the recess lasted roughly two months; and when Judge Yamamuro succeeded him, the court recessed for nearly three months. Judge Yamamuro presided for a period of six years. This irregularity may have been allowed in order to avert yet another break in the court proceedings, which would have caused the trial to drag on even longer.

During my thirteen years in court, a variety of changes—some major, others less so—occurred in my personal life outside the courtroom. From the end of 1990 to around May 1992, the Recruit Group slipped into a financial crisis, and in order to avert its entire collapse I took up a position as the Group's special advisor. Ultimately the crisis was settled by my selling my personal holdings in Recruit to Daiei, but the resulting toll on both my time and my state of mind left me physically drained and unable to sleep.

Exhausted, I found myself nodding off in the courtroom, and on not a few occasions I nearly fell out of my chair. Judge Mikami admonished me time and again, and Takeshi Tada, my chief defense counsel, cautioned me that a bad attitude displayed in the courtroom would add weight to my crime. Even so, I was unable to keep myself from nodding off. This went on for more than a year.

Perhaps the most remarkable change that occurred during the course of those thirteen years, though, was the shift in the public's interest in the case. In particular, after the gassing of the Tokyo subway system in March 1995 by the Aum Shinrikyo group—an act of terrorism unequaled in the nation's history—the media promptly turned its attention away from the Recruit scandal.

In autumn 2001, as my trial was entering its final stages, my defense team proposed calling in character witnesses. Their idea was to have people attest to my character and contributions to society, their favorable testimony serving as part of a plea for leniency. Generally, placing a character witness on the stand assumes the defendant is guilty of the crime being charged. All along I had pleaded my innocence, but as Fujinami and all other defendants in the case were found guilty, my defense team saw little possibility that I, as their alleged partner in crime, would get off scot-free. We thus opted to call in character witnesses.

In all, we proposed ten names as potential witnesses. Only one was a blood relation: Chikako Haraguchi, an elder cousin with whom I had spent much of my childhood. The court approved everyone on our list, and three court sessions that year were dedicated to these witnesses' taking the stand. According to my lawyers, both the number of character witnesses and the time allotted them were highly unusual. Among them were Kiyoshi Igarashi, the artistic director for opera at the New National Theatre in Tokyo; Susumu Sugiyama, president of the Professional Ski Instructors Association of Japan; Noboru Nishikawa, advisor to Itochu Corporation and a lifelong friend since middle school; and Takashi Kosugi, a politician.

In addition, in response to a call by Fusako Seki—a one-time grantee of the Ezoe Scholarship Society Foundation and graduate of the Faculty of Law at the University of Tokyo who went on to teach in the graduate school of Hokkaido University—many of my friends and acquaintances wrote letters on my behalf. Nearly everyone who was approached agreed to write a letter, resulting in 219 letters submitted to the court.

A long list of people appealed for the consideration of extenuating circumstances. These included Isao Nakauchi, Minoru Mori, and Kenichi Ohmae; friends such as former president of Haseko Corporation Kohei Goda, SoftBank's Masayoshi Son, Mariko Hayashi, and Rieko Zanma; scholarship recipients, Recruit employees and former employees, people I knew through skiing, friends from my student days, people I knew through my opera connections, etc. Each person was asked to write up to about two pages, but the letter of singer Masashi Sada ran to seven pages. Actress and former Takarazuka star Ran Otori, a friend of thirty years, penned five pages longhand.

Also offering their cooperation were the local officials in Iwate Prefecture where I had developed the ski resort at Appi. In their letters, they described how prior to the resort's development much of the local population had had to leave home after the farming season to go to Tokyo to earn money in the off-season; but now these people were able to work the winters at the resort, thus freeing them from having to leave their families for long periods each year. The officials further noted in fiscal 2000 the resort contributed 25.7 percent of the local government's tax revenues, thereby providing invaluable support to the local economy.

I was deeply moved by and truly grateful for the generosity of so many people who took their precious time to give testimony or write letters on my behalf.

As a rule, the prosecution ascertains whether or not letters of appeal submitted to the court have actually been written by the persons who signed them. Prosecutor Tsukasa Yamashita later told me he had personally confirmed that the local officials at Appi had written their letters, adding it was very unusual for elected officials to write such appeals. He also revealed he checked more than a dozen of the letters and in each case confirmed their authenticity, with the result of the court agreeing to allow all the letters submitted.

The court sessions normally began at ten A.M. and closed at five P.M., with a ninety-minute break for lunch from twelve to one-thirty and a fifteen-minute break around three o'clock. During the afternoon breaks, I would usually pass the time outside the courtroom, in the same corridor as the prosecutors. In the beginning, we never engaged in conversation, but as the trial went into its sixth or seventh year we began exchanging a few words, and by the tenth year or so we chatted frequently.

By the time the trial drew to a close, the prosecutors in charge of the case were more amiable than those at the outset. The passage of time had softened their attitude noticeably.

The Prosecution Asks for Four Years

My court proceedings, a total of 318 sessions in all, finally closed on December 20, 2001, just over twelve years from the opening session on December 15, 1989. The next step was the prosecution's closing argument and call for sentencing, which took place on March 29, 2002. That morning, as rain poured down heavily, I headed to the Tokyo District Court together with my attorneys. I expected the prosecution's course of action that day to be harsh.

The court opened at ten A.M. The prosecution alleged what had occurred was bribery on a major scale, "transfers of pre-flotation shares, guaranteed to appreciate in value, undertaken in the clever guise of an ordinary commercial transaction." They contended that from the outset the share recipients were assured of reaping large economic benefits "hand over fist," so in reality the transfers were tantamount to provisions of enormous amounts of cash.

The prosecution then alleged I had masterminded the various acts of bribe-passing and that, by stepping beyond the boundaries of business ethics and placing foremost priority on the pursuit of the Recruit Group's business profit, I, through the provision of unlawful monetary gains, had corrupted public servants at the national level as well as officials in the telecommunications industry, an industry public in nature, in an attempt to win personal control over government administration and public services. And they concluded for these reasons, I bore heavy responsibility for having significantly impaired the public's trust of the nation's political and administrative systems as well as its public service sector.

As regards the disputed credibility of my written statements, the prosecution contended that not only had I resolutely denied the bulk of the charges against me, I had continuously engaged in irrational and equivocating arguments to vindicate myself, thereby causing the trial to drag on. It further claimed it was "obvious" I had anticipated from the outset I would receive a jail sentence, and had thus purposefully sought to extend the length of my trial so as to postpone incarceration; and it said I had made a mockery of the criminal justice system and not demonstrated even an iota of remorse for what I had done.

The record of the prosecution's closing argument ran to 581 pages. It closed with a statement that my crimes merited a sentence of four years of imprisonment, without suspension.

My defense team was worried the prosecution would ask for the maximum sentence allowed for bribe-passing under law, which was four years and six months, so the actual call for four years was unexpected. "If the prosecution asked for a three-year sentence, you'd be sure to get a suspended sentence," my attorney said, "but with a four-year sentence, you can't be sure." He added there was no precedent for a defendant actually going to prison for bribery on this scale, but cautioned that given the level of media coverage in my case, the judge's decision could go either way.

The defense's closing argument, a response to the prosecution's call for sentencing on March 29, was scheduled for September 18, almost six months later. We set to preparing immediately.

Although the outline of my defense had already been drawn up by the time the court proceedings for the four different "routes" came to a close, writing up the long final argument—not only taking into account the evidence presented and the prosecution's written statements but also necessitating a thorough perusal of all the court records to date as well as the prosecution's final argument—was to be no easy task. My lawyers worked on the text full-time. Then I went through it and changed the wording to make it less stilted. When the draft was ultimately completed, it ran to a hefty 1,611 pages.

Preparing the text was an exhausting process, but one well worth the effort. The final document was clear and persuasive, and I felt confident I would be granted a suspended sentence.

Our Closing Argument

The defense's closing argument began, as scheduled, on September 18 and stretched on into the next day.

As regards the motive behind my providing shares of Recruit Cosmos, we once again denied there had been any intent to bribe. Our argument was I had simply wanted close friends and acquaintances to become shareholders and reap profits; I had not had Recruit's business interests in mind. As to the alleged certainty the shares would appreciate in value, we contended stock investments always entail an element of uncertainty, that there was no guarantee profit would be gained, so as an instrument of bribery, shares were weaker than cash.

Concerning the protracted length of the trial—which the prosecution had made an issue of in its closing statement—we submitted that the cause was the inordinately large scale of the trial coupled with the fact that, in the wake of the not-guilty verdicts passed down first for Masao Tatsumi and Takao Fujinami, the prosecution had become extremely circumspect in building its case against me. We also pointed out how the court itself had urged the prosecution to proceed with greater alacrity. We argued the facts in the case did not coincide with the scenario drawn up by the prosecutors and that ascertaining the true facts had been at issue. "There are just reasons for the arguments carried out by the defendant and his counsel," we countered.

By the time these closing arguments were being presented, only a few reporters were on hand in the courtroom and the visitors' gallery was nearly empty. The media reported that after thirteen years, interest in the trial had waned. But this was by no means the case as far as I was concerned. The trial was constantly on my mind, and I had known no real peace of mind ever since the opening session. Besides my own trial and the preparations it required, I had also appeared in court as a witness at the other related trials conducted separately.

The responses given by a witness tend to vary depending on how a prosecutor asked his questions, and any time a witness makes a statement that varied even slightly from what he might have said in another court, the prosecutors pounce on him. Also, there is always the possibility testimony given in the courtroom might be perceived as false, which could potentially leave a witness facing a perjury charge.

In my own case, although I didn't think I would be convicted on any charge of perjury, I had put a great deal of time and effort into preparing for my appearances as a witness. In order to prevent any discrepancies from creeping into my testimony, I would rehearse by having my attorneys act out the part of the prosecutor and ask me questions from a variety of angles.

By the time my trial wound down to its closing arguments, I was in my mid-sixties. I could feel that my powers of recollection were no longer what they were. "Time and tide wait for no man," the proverb says, and while I had no one to blame but myself for the thirteen years I had spent on trial, the long ordeal had taken its toll.

Still, I was confident I would receive a suspended sentence. Tatsumi and Fujinami had both been found innocent, and the court had, in an atypical gesture, allowed my character witnesses. As I participated in writing up our closing argument, I entertained some hope.

The Court's Ruling

March 4, 2003, the day my fate would be determined, finally arrived.

Unlike the opening session thirteen years earlier when the visitors' gallery had been filled to capacity, on the day of my sentencing the gallery was less than half full.

At precisely ten A.M. Judge Yamamuro declared the court in session. He then called for me to stand as he read the verdict:

"The court sentences the defendant to three years in prison, suspended for a period of five years."

No sooner had the words left his lips than several reporters rushed out of the courtroom. A hush then fell over the room again.

"This is going to take some time," the judge resumed, and he invited me to be seated again while he read the main points behind the court's ruling.

The full text, which was handed over to my lawyers four months later, ran to 1,168 pages. Here are the points covered in the syllabus read by the judge:

The court had found the charges against me largely true and deemed my provision of Recruit Cosmos shares had been a form of bribery. I had been "blinded by the desire to expand my company's earnings and by the pursuit of profits" and my crime was "un-condonable." It stressed the list of recipients I had chosen to acquire the shares spanned a broad spectrum, including members of the government, the bureaucracy, and the financial sector; and it affirmed the gravity of the scandal was reflected in the large number of people involved, the loftiness of their positions, the weight of their official powers, and the high level of integrity demanded of them. The ruling further declared my crime had major impact on society in the form of erosion of the people's trust in their government, which should inherently be clean and fair.

Concerning those who had accepted the bribes, the court stated that although they were each in the wrong, they had all come to grief—being made to sit in the defendant's seat and found guilty—and suffered harsh recriminations from the public, some losing in elections at the national level, others driven to resign from their official posts. It also said a number of my subordinates were implicated as accomplices in my crime, and in this respect too, the court deemed my responsibility to be weighty. It further concluded I caused Recruit and its affiliate companies, Recruit Cosmos included, to suffer great loss of the public's trust, and it was thus inescapable I should suffer the consequences of my rash actions.

Bribery, the court declared, is "a frightful crime that betrays the trust of the people in the fairness of public service and in their public servants and thus shakes the foundations of democracy itself." It added that the case had aroused a mistrust in the public toward collusive relationships between the corporate sector and the government and bureaucracy and that this mistrust would not easily be erased, nor could its role in adding to the public's mistrust of government and administrative processes be overlooked. Furthermore, in view of the string of scandals that broke out after the Recruit affair, scandals that betrayed the public's trust in their public servants' ability to carry out their duties fairly, coupled with the need to eradicate official corruption, it found my actions deserving of strong censure.

As its causes for granting extenuating circumstances, the court first cited the fact the bribes had been offered in the form of pre-flotation shares. "At the time the shares passed hands," the ruling said, "it was uncertain to what extent their value would increase after the stock was registered on the over-the-counter market, thus making the nature of the crime lighter than bribery by cash." It also pointed out that at the time of the crime, entertaining or offering gifts to members of the government or the bureaucracy was not considered a significant deviation from social norms, and in this connection the bribe recipients were not entirely without fault for accepting shares of Recruit Cosmos stock as a matter of course, thinking of the offer in the same way as they did the benefits they received in such forms as wining and dining.

Regarding the Labor Ministry route, the court's assessment was this: The bribery perpetrated in this connection had not resulted in illegal or improper professional actions by the recipients, and in fact neither was the fairness of their professional duties impaired nor was the propriety of the governmental or administrative systems compromised. The continuation of and adherence to the gentlemen's agreement on student recruitment had been strongly demanded by society at large and meshed with the public's interests; therefore, even if taking action to maintain the agreement was aimed at facilitating Recruit's business operations and ultimately served to Recruit's benefit, maintaining the agreement per se did not lead to perpetration of illegal or improper measures nor did it erode the fairness of administrative processes. If anything, keeping the agreement in place was an act according with proper government policy.

Concerning the NTT route, the court maintained that Recruit's purchase of the Cray supercomputer through NTT had in no small part been undertaken to NTT's advantage—advantage in the form of resolving the company's problems vis-à-vis international procurements and U.S.-Japan trade friction.

By way of explaining why it was granting the defendant extenuating circumstances for personal reasons, the court cited the facts that I founded Recruit, that I actively pursued diverse activities to society's benefit, and that I strived to cultivate the capabilities of young people in many areas. It also cited how after the scandal broke I had resigned nearly all my official positions, sold the bulk of my holdings in Recruit in May 1992, and withdrawn from engaging in economic activities. Additionally, the judgment described how, besides matters relating to the crime itself, I had been roundly criticized in the media for private matters having no relation to my case, I had been exposed to severe criticism by society at large, and I had suffered commensurate social sanctions. "For fourteen long years, the defendant sat in the defendant's seat, which took a substantial physical toll on him; yet the length of time required for the trial proceedings did not owe entirely to the circumstances of the defendant." The court further acknowledged that although I had denied all of the charges against me, I had consistently demonstrated remorse and contrition for having caused problems for the parties involved. Finally, the ruling stated many individuals from a broad spectrum of fields had attested to my character and vision, praised my accomplishments highly, and urged the court to show leniency toward me. It concluded that in light of these appeals, combined with the court's impression of me throughout the trial proceedings, it saw in me a human side very different from the condemnations heaped on me as a perpetrator of evil deeds.

In closing, the court said in determining its verdict it had taken the following factors into consideration: one, that all the parties who were prosecuted in conjunction with the Recruit affair and found guilty, including those who had accepted the bribes, had received suspended sentences; and two, that all previous cases of bribe-passing in which the defendant was handed a jail sentence were limited to cases that were pernicious in nature—for example, cases involving extremely large sums of money or cases in which, in exchange for the bribe, an illegal or improper act was performed in the recipient's professional capacity. The ruling ended as follows: "This case cannot be said to demand invariably the imposition of a sentence of imprisonment; rather, the court has found it is fitting for the defendant in this instance to receive a guilty but suspended sentence."

As I sat in the defendant's seat listening to the court's ruling, I felt an escalating sense of relief at the realization that my long, long trial had finally come to an end. Memories of those thirteen years flashed through my mind: the endless interrogations by the prosecutors as well as the exchanges on all sorts of topics with Prosecutor Munakata, Munakata's own difficult position—caught between the demands of his superior and my claims of truthful testimony—and the concern he often displayed toward me.

I wondered what the prosecution was thinking, hearing the court's decision. All of its contentions were accepted and a guilty verdict handed down. But in explaining the court's reason for passing a suspended sentence, it had concluded that although my actions ultimately served to bene-fit Recruit, the provision of shares itself neither induced illegal or improper measures nor compromised the fairness of administrative processes, and if anything, kept the gentlemen's agreement in place aligned with government policy. Further, the court recognized the reasons and the effect of Recruit's purchase of the Cray supercomputer through NTT. These explanations could, depending on one's viewpoint, be tantamount to acknowledgment of my innocence.

Since all my "partners in crime" had received guilty verdicts upheld by the court, I knew I wouldn't get off with a not-guilty ruling. But if the court found me guilty without a suspended sentence, I would surely appeal; and if the prosecution's contentions were rejected, the prosecution would invariably appeal as well. Either way, the trial, which had already dragged on for so long, would continue even longer. Both my defense team and I thus felt that by handing down a sentence of three years with a five-year suspension, the court had skillfully met the circumstances of both sides and done its best to avert an appeal from being filed.

With the close of this final court session, I headed to the exit of the court-house in the company of my attorneys. The security guards went out of their way to enable my car to leave through the rear exit, but there were no TV reporters in pursuit anyway.

The front pages of the evening editions were largely taken up with articles about my verdict, but compared to the time of my arrest, the space devoted to the case was minimal. Also, in reflection of the thirteen years since the case began, for younger readers unfamiliar with the case, the reports were augmented by a separate overview explaining what the Recruit scandal was, plus a table presenting the details of the case chrono-logically.

The *Yomiuri* featured a comment by Prosecutor Munakata under the title "We were right." In response to the court's verdict he was quoted as saying, "With the guilty verdict handed down on the final remaining defen-dant, it shows the special investigators who probed the Recruit case were correct. In that sense, on hearing the verdict I was filled with emotion and felt a strong sense of relief."

The *Yomiuri* also featured a commentary by Takeshi Tsuchimoto, former prosecutor with the Supreme Public Prosecutors Office and Professor Emeritus of the University of Tsukuba, who wrote that the verdict was significant in clearly demonstrating a crime of bribery can stand even in cases when economic benefit is furnished by one party to another for vague purposes seeking vague favors. And he offered that the case would serve as a major warning to those potentially on the receiving end of bribes as well.

The *Nikkei* carried reactions of some of the nation's political leaders. Prime Minister Junichiro Koizumi was quoted as saying, "Thirteen years? That's way too long. Can't a verdict get passed more quickly? This is a problem with our court system that needs to be addressed." Chief Cabinet Secretary Yasuo Fukuda expressed the view that although strict rules were in place regarding members of the government and the bureaucracy, whether or not those rules are obeyed depends on the ethical strength of the nation's politicians and bureaucrats; the Recruit case made him recognize anew the need for the exercise of caution.

That evening's "News Station"—perhaps Japan's most highly regarded late-night news program, on the Asahi TV network—first presented a video review of the Recruit scandal from its initial emergence through to the day's verdict. It then ran film of my post-trial remarks: "I apologize sincerely for the great trouble I caused to so many people and for causing such disruption to the public. These are burdens I will continue to shoulder from now on. For me, these have been a very long and difficult fourteen years."

Hiroshi Kume, the news anchor, then had this to say: "The bribe giver is of course to blame, but the foremost cause here is the existence of a system that allows seeking monetary gain in return for doing favors. It took fourteen years for this trial to be conducted, and the existence of such a system can be said to have ruined the life of one individual." Whereas initially "News Station" had covered the Recruit affair with great zeal, putting together special features on a daily basis, its report on this final day, including its review of the history of the scandal, ran to only about eight minutes.

The Recruit scandal had begun with reporting by the media, and it had garnered widespread public attention as a result of zealous coverage by the media. In the interim, I had passed the days in distress on a level too difficult to express. The altogether nonchalant tone in which the media now reported on the conclusion of the affair was thus astounding, but at the same time I felt peace of mind realizing I would no longer be in the media's spotlight. I would finally be able to live my life in peace and quiet.

That evening I received a phone call from Yoshiaki Tsutsumi of Kokudo Corporation, a good friend and fellow skier. The prosecution might decide to appeal the court's ruling, he said, and he suggested we submit a written appeal to the Prosecutors Office saying we had no intention of appealing the verdict and hoped the prosecution would do likewise. He confessed he was unsure how effective such a move might or might not be.

When I broached the subject to my defense team that evening, a gloomy look appeared on Tada's face. "The judgment handed down is about as close to a not-guilty verdict as there could be," he began, "so the prosecution's probably not pleased in the least. It's possible they'll appeal on grounds the sentence is too light. If they do appeal, you'd have to submit the notebooks you wrote during detention as new evidence, plus you'd have to get yourself an entirely new team of lawyers—younger lawyers. For people new to the case to write up an appeal would in itself take more than a year."

The question of whether to submit my notebooks to the court had actually been discussed as the team brainstormed in preparation for the trial. While the notebooks would certainly be important evidence, everything in them wasn't necessarily to my advantage. There were some things I had written, in the beginning of my detention, that could work against me, but what I most wanted to keep from being exposed was the private personal feelings I had inscribed. I didn't want the media to get ahold of that, which among other things could breach the privacy of my family. This was something I was eager to avoid if at all possible.

Under the circumstances, I had not submitted the notebooks as evidence during my trial. We decided if I received an unsuspended jail sentence, I would then submit the notebooks to the High Court as new evidence and replace my defense team with a new set of attorneys. I was aware that if the prosecution now put in an appeal, not only would I have to submit the notebooks, but that the process could end up taking a total of twenty years before the High Court reached a verdict. Given that the trials of all of my alleged "partners in crime" had come to a close, I felt that, without a major push from the media, the lower court's verdict was unlikely to be overturned and a jail sentence imposed. But when my lawyers indicated that prosecutors are wont to appeal when they don't get a verdict to their liking—and there were instances of prosecutors quitting their job in disgust when their superiors prevented them from going through with an appeal— I grew depressed.

My lawyers also informed me that if the court handed down an unsuspended sentence, in order for me to be released a second time, I would have to provide another one hundred million yen in bail—this in addition to the two hundred million yen already paid. When I asked why I needed to put up even more money than I had already, my lawyers said I was a flight risk. So people who can't come up with bail money end up in custody? What a strange rule, I thought.

The Prosecution Decides Not to Appeal

The time limit for appealing a court ruling is two weeks. I passed the days nervously until March 18, the final day, when it was announced the prosecution had decided not to appeal. My sentence was thus upheld, and after more than thirteen years, my trial was finally over.

That evening my defense team gathered and we drank a toast to their long years of hard work together. Everyone was in good cheer. The following week I accompanied them all to Kyoto, where we passed the weekend reveling in the beauty of the cherry blossoms.

One minor inconvenience of the verdict for me was that my attorneys advised me to refrain entirely from driving while I was on probation. One accident, even a minor one, could be enough for me to be taken into custody. Until that time I had always driven myself on golf outings, but the moment my trial ended and my sentence was finalized, that option was no longer open to me. I was disappointed, but resigned to put up with the inconvenience.

My lawyers also warned me—half-jokingly—not to evade taxes. For better or worse, this was something I no longer needed to be concerned about: I no longer had an income.

Two months later I attended a party celebrating the opening of Roppongi Hills, the stunning mega-complex developed by Minoru Mori in the heart of Tokyo's vibrant Roppongi district. I had been a close friend with Mori for a long time; it was on the top floor of the first building he ever constructed that I had launched Recruit.

"I'm glad the ordeal's all over for you now," he said with a smile. "Let's get together and celebrate soon." He took my hand firmly in his own. "You shouldn't have been so quick to quit as Recruit chairman, you know. It made us wonder if you'd really done something to feel guilty about."

True, if I had remained in my post as chairman and gone on a business trip to "Recruit U.S.A.," or anywhere, I might have avoided being called in to testify and I might not have been arrested. But one thing was sure: people would have assumed I was fleeing from the truth.

We can't relive the past. I accepted how things turned out, and I felt like I was finally able to set down a burden I had carried on my shoulders for a long, long time.

V

LONG POSTSCRIPT

Yusaku Kamekura, who was my mentor, chided me about my infamous donations. "Giving money to politicians won't make this country's political situation any better," he scoffed. His sentiments were shared by Katsufumi Amano—erstwhile director of The University of Tokyo Newspaper and formerly on the faculty at the University of Tsukuba and Nihon University—whom I respect like an elder brother. "I fail to understand why you would go and give so much money to politicians," he said.

One person who did seem to understand why was Keizo Ohga, a longtime ski acquaintance whom I've known ever since joining the Young Presidents' Organization (YPO). As one of my character witnesses in court, he testified that he believed I provided the Recruit Cosmos shares to so many people because I am "the kind of person who always feels a need for the security provided by being surrounded by other people."

I'm not a particularly capable person. In high school my grades were below average, and the only accolade I ever received during those three years was a prize for perfect attendance. When I passed the entrance exam to the University of Tokyo, my adviser expressed total surprise. "I never imagined you, of all people, would get into Todai."

Where I succeeded was in founding Recruit. The business model I conceived—free distribution of a book of advertisements—enabled Recruit to win the public's acceptance. I took pains in hiring, always believing it was imperative that the people poised to take over after us would be better than those who preceded them. And for a fact, Recruit's employees have been outstanding—it was their excellence that propelled Recruit's quick growth.

I once had the opportunity to interview Konosuke Matsushita, the renowned entrepreneur and founder of Matsushita Electric Industrial Co., Ltd. (now Panasonic). The secret for running a business successfully, he said, was in knowing what work to assign to whom—knowing the limits which people are capable of, and then assigning them tasks that bordered those limits. This secret stayed with me. At meetings where targets were set for each division in the next fiscal quarter, Recruit employees would often gripe I was setting goals impossible for them to accomplish. In response I would cite management guru Peter Drucker's injunction that it's in times of crisis that opportunities for growth are found, and I strongly urged them to pursue high goals by methods different from those they had earlier relied on. Having such demands placed on one is a strain; yet it's even more of a strain on the person who must make such demands. Within the company I gained the reputation as the "demon of demands."

I urged my employees to go out after work, to dine and drink and meet new people too, as a way of broadening their outlook. On my part, I made concerted effort to meet people of influence. Among them was Yoshihiro Inayama, then-chairman of Keidanren, and it was he who advised me to make political donations. "It's necessary for running a business," he stressed. Subsequently, I began to attend events in support of specific politicians—opportunities that provided the avenue for my coming to know many of the political leaders to whom I subsequently provided financial support.

It was within this environment that I faced daily pressures on another front. I felt driven by the need to strive ever harder to keep up with the superlative staff I was cultivating. I was obsessed with the need to learn more and more, and the need to grow as a person. This pressure made me tense and increasingly sensitive to my isolation. By mingling with people, many of them in political circles, not only did I learn a great deal, but I also found equilibrium and a sense of fulfillment in their company. In turn, I was pleased to provide these "mentors" with whatever large cash donations they might request of me.

It is only now, in retrospect, that I understand how desperate I was to be something I could never be. I ended up going astray as a result. I regret this folly of my ways very deeply.

In October, 2008, accompanied by my daughter, I attended an event commemorating the completion of the Shanghai World Financial Center, which had been developed by the Mori Building Company. After Minoru Mori, president of the company, said a few words of greeting, he handed the microphone over to former Prime Minister Yasuhiro Nakasone, who proceeded to give an excellent speech—without relying on any notes. So impressed was my daughter with Nakasone's demeanor that she encouraged me to go up and speak to him.

I approached his table and bowed. "I am so sorry for the trouble I caused during the scandal," I said.

The former prime minister stood up. "Let bygones be bygones," he said, grasping my hand. "You are still young. I want you to enjoy every success in what you are going to do."

In this moment, I felt some of the awkward residue of the scandal being cleared away.

The Role of Media Reporting

From the moment it came to light I had offered pre-flotation shares of Recruit Cosmos stock to many people of influence, media reporting on the Recruit scandal began with a vengeance. The weekly magazines put together special features, on a serialized basis, on the scandal and on me. As someone who personally dabbled in journalism, I wondered then, and continue to wonder, if indeed the scandal merited the overheated attention it was given.

I first began attracting the media's notice around ten years after founding Recruit. The media—and especially the publications of Asahi Shimbun Company—took avid interest in, and offered flattering praises of, this graduate of the University of Tokyo who was being hailed as a standard bearer in the new world of venture businesses. I was only too pleased to bask in this attention, for the media exposure steadily enhanced Recruit's name recognition. In the company's early days, any time I would be asked to give a speech at an employee's wedding banquet, I always felt the need to explain what Recruit was; after the write-ups in the media, such explanations were no longer necessary. Later, when I built the Recruit Building in Ginza, the name Recruit was established, making it easier to attract the kind of outstanding staff I was looking for.

I was also asked to appear on television with increasing frequency—especially during the recruiting season for new university graduates—and I was often featured on both the quasi-public NHK and privately owned stations. I now think it was this rising fame—both Recruit's and my own—that led the media to see the company and myself as worthy prey, and I look on our high visibility as a factor contributing to the relentless coverage of the Recruit scandal.

In October 1988, the publishing arm of Asahi issued a book by Hatsuhiko Mizuki, head of the Yokohama bureau, on what is referred to as the "121 days burning with zeal to scoop the Recruit scandal." It was filled with statements such as "according to a Recruit employee" and "according to someone who knows Ezoe well," and although the book as a result does not rely on fact, the way it was written—like a detective novel—aroused the public's interest and kept the reader engrossed in the tale it chose to spin.

In the afterword, Mizuki said this:

> *Asahi's* reporting on Recruit fits into the category of "investigative reporting"—a type of reporting that has increased notably in Japan in recent years. . . . I think this book is also rich in implications in the way a story which initially hit a dead end as a criminal case was dug up and had its fuse lit by news reporters.

I have heard that the *Asahi's* coverage of the story would never have reached the scale it achieved had it not been for three of the newspaper's staff members: Hiroshi Yamamoto, editor at the Yokohama bureau; Shunji Taoka, who today occasionally appears on TV as a commentator on military affairs; and Hiromitsu Ochiai, who joined the *Asahi* after reporting for the *Sankei*. Yamamoto in particular is well known in press circles, having won awards from the Japan Newspaper Publishers & Editors Association on two occasions. The trio later enjoyed the spotlight again for their investigative reporting of *kankan-settai*, the insidious wining and dining of public officials by other public officials at public expense. Thanks to their exposure of this rampant practice, moves were taken to eliminate this scourge.

When the *Asahi* first broke the story of suspicions surrounding my provision of Recruit Cosmos shares to various individuals, I thought it odd the names of the alleged recipients were being reported only bit by bit. I suspected the information was being leaked by the managing underwriter handling those transactions, Daiwa Securities—either its Kawasaki or Yokohama branch—and I went to Daiwa to discuss the matter with Yoshitoki Chino, chairman, and Sadakane Doi, president. I was assured there was nothing to worry about. Still, not entirely convinced, I requested that the company boost its computer security so that this confidential information could not be accessed by other branches. Chino said everything necessary would be done, and then added a comment I at the time found doubly reassuring: "Selling pre-flotation shares is nothing out of the ordinary. Everybody does it."

In *Seigi no wana* (The Justice Trap), Soichiro Tahara touches on this very subject. "When the media started dropping the names of one politician after another, I asked Yoshitoki Chino, then chairman of Daiwa Securities, whether selling pre-flotation shares was a violation of the law. He replied without hesitation it was altogether common for companies about to register on the OTC market or list on the Second Section of the Tokyo Stock Exchange to offer pre-flotation shares to people they did business with and acquaintances who were in the public's trust. 'Its common knowledge in the securities industry,' he stressed. 'Everybody does it. If it were illegal, the securities industry wouldn't survive.'"

In retrospect, I suspect that the *Asahi*'s Hiroshi Yamamoto early on somehow got ahold of a list of the share recipients. Rather than reveal the list all at once, which would get reporters at headquarters involved in the case, he must have thought it would be to his advantage to reveal the names gradually so as to extend his bureau's reporting over a long period of time, put together a criminal case, and enjoy the credit for doing so. In his book *Ja-narizumu to wa nani ka* (What Journalism Is All About), which he published in 2003, Yamamoto wrote this:

It is often said it was the Recruit scandal that brought an end to the LDP's domination of national politics first achieved in 1955, and that without the Recruit scandal there would have been no subsequent political reforms or administrative reorganization. But had it not been for the *reporting on* Recruit by the Yokohama bureau, there would have been no investigation into the affair by the Tokyo District Public Prosecutors Office, and thus no political reforms or administrative reorganization.

Besides the investigative reporters at the *Asahi*, one other factor making the Recruit scandal so sensational was the prosecution. My attorneys said there would have been no case built against me had it not been for the dogged efforts to prosecute me taken by Yusuke Yoshinaga, Norio Munakata, and Seisui Kamigaki. "The years they were in charge—between the Lockheed scandal and the Recruit scandal—were the heyday for special investigators in this country."

Life is a concatenation of coincidences. Like it or not, in my case a variety of circumstances played intermeshing roles that together made the Recruit scandal the life-changing event for me.

"Recruit-gate"

In many ways the events concerning reporting on Recruit and me by the *Asahi*'s various publishing and TV media were reminiscent of the media pressure, launched by reporters of *The Washington Post*, of the Watergate scandal of 1972–74 that brought down U.S. President Richard Nixon. Indeed, Takako Doi, chair of the Japan Socialist Party at the time, coined the phrase "Recruit-gate."

After my arrest, *AERA* magazine, in its edition of February 28, 1989, introduced an analysis by Fred Hiatt, head of *The Washington Post*'s Northeast Asia bureau based in Tokyo, pointing out similarities between the Recruit affair and Watergate. Hiatt had trained under—and had his investigative reporting skills honed by—Bob Woodward, one of the two reporters who exposed the events that subsequently snowballed into the Watergate scandal. According to Hiatt, the similarities between the two cases were:

(1) In both cases, what initially appeared to be a minor incident developed, through tenacious investigative reporting, into a major scandal.

(2) In both cases, those in positions of power whose actions were called into question initially treated the events lightly and contended no laws had been violated; but the general public viewed their actions, whether legal or otherwise, as highly improper.

(3) In both cases, investigative reporting by the press occurred long in advance of any investigation by prosecuting authorities, and the latter's investigations were pushed along by the probing by the press.

(4) In both cases, investigations were conducted by young reporters having no interest in bending to those in positions of power.

The magazine also quotes Hiatt as saying that before the Recruit scandal, Japanese reporters were deemed to be too close to the nation's politicians and bureaucrats to be capable of investigative reporting, but local reporting on the Recruit scandal proved to be fresh and refreshing, the press vigorous in its investigative reporting this time.

Had it not been for the Recruit scandal, Prime Minister Noboru Takeshita would probably have been reelected on the strength of having introduced a sales tax into Japan. Had it not been for Watergate, Richard Nixon, who would not have been eligible to run for another term, was expected to leave office respected for bringing the Vietnam war to an end, restoring diplomatic ties with China, and terminating the Bretton Woods system, that is, canceling the direct convertibility of the dollar to gold and making the greenback a key currency worldwide (measures collectively known as the "Nixon shock"); instead he resigned in shame.

In these various ways, similarities indeed do exist between the Recruit scandal and the Watergate scandal.

Unexpected Musical Connections

About a year after the end of my trial, my younger daughter and I were at a performance of "La Traviata" at Orchard Hall in Shibuya when, by sheer coincidence, there stood Norio Munakata in the lobby. Taken totally by surprise, I froze in my tracks. Noticing my astonishment, Munakata walked over to greet me, a huge smile on his face.

"Why, Mr. Ezoe! How nice to see you."

"Do you often go to the opera?" I asked.

"Why, yes, I do. I've always been a fan of opera and classical music, but it's only since I left my post at the Nagoya High Public Prosecutors Office and became a lawyer that I have the time to attend performances."

I had recently published *Kamome ga tonda hi* [The Day the Seagull Took Flight], which was a memoir of my years before the Recruit scandal, and Munakata was quick to mention he had read it.

"One day I imagine you'll write about the Recruit scandal too," he grinned. "And you'll talk about me."

Before I had time to respond, he continued: "Handling your case was really difficult, you know. It was such a tough case, but I bet if I'd been on the defense side, you might have received a not-guilty verdict."

Surprised at his candor, I decided that this was an opportunity to ask him things which were long on my mind. "Why did the court spend so much time talking about things with no relation to the charges against me—things like the details of how my selling of shares related to the Securities and Exchange Law, and the issue surrounding the Ad Hoc Council on Education?"

Here too, Munakata was surprisingly forthright: "Well, you see, even after your trial was under way, we were mulling how to build a bribery case against you, and we needed more time. We must have dragged the proceedings out that way for two years, maybe longer, while we considered what to do."

I had been plagued with questions as to why my trial had for so long dealt with topics that had no relevance. Now, hearing from none other than the prosecutor himself, at least I had some clarity after the long pall of frustration. I decided to ask him another thing: "Why, in conjunction with the Education Ministry route, did you exclude my appointment to the University Council from the charges against me?"

"As I recall, I think it was because your appointment to the council came way after your selling of shares. So it would have been hard to show you'd been appointed to the council as a thank-you for providing the shares."

Ever since this occasion, I have run into Munakata about once a year at an opera or concert, and he is always very friendly. It is odd how, through our mutual interest in music, the distance between the two of us, former foes, has narrowed so swiftly.

The Recruit trial had taken a toll on both me and my defense team, but I came to see that the prosecution was not immune to hardship as well. It was doing its job, and Munakata, constantly under pressure from his superiors, notably Yoshinaga, to build a case against me had had a difficult time, too.

One other person whom I continue to see through a musical connection is Megumi Yamamuro, the judge who had handed down my verdict.

Yamamuro and I are both avid fans of Masashi Sada, a popular and highly talented folk singer, composer, and lyricist who first made a name for himself in the early 1970s as half of the duo "Grape." He went solo in 1976 and has been an active contributor to Japan's music scene ever since. Yamamuro's fondness for Sada's music garnered national attention in 2002, when in handing down his verdict on two young men who had caused the death, by brutal beating, of a fellow passenger on a train, the judge cited the lyrics of a Sada song titled "Tsugunai" [Atonement]. The incident was widely reported in the press at the time.

I have been a fan of Sada's ever since his Grape days. Sada and I share a fondness for China, and when he gave a series of concerts in Chengdu in 1987, I flew there, which in those days meant an eight-hour flight by propeller plane from Shanghai. Two members of my defense team were also Sada fans: Haruko Shibumura, who, like Sada, hailed from Nagasaki, and Shozaburo Ishida. In 2005 the three of us went together to Sada's commemorative 3,333rd concert held at Tokyo's Budokan Hall. After the show we went backstage to greet Sada, and by coincidence Yamamuro was there also. He had retired from his judgeship and was now teaching at the University of Tokyo School of Law.

"Now here's a rare gathering!" Sada laughed with great amusement.

Yamamuro and I had faced each other in the courtroom through six long years, and during that time I had come to feel a kind of kinship with him.

At one point the conversation turned to the subject of Japan's new lay judge system.

"I know a lawyer who was formerly an associate judge," I said, "He had a case where he handed down a death sentence, and for the next week he had no appetite. He couldn't shake off those feelings, and in the end he quit the judgeship and became a lawyer."

"It's terrible having to hand down a death sentence," Yamamuro nodded. "Just around the time I was beginning to feel maybe I wasn't cut out to be a judge, I handed down a death sentence in the Aum Shinrikyo case. I had no interest in food for a week either. That's one reason why I joined the faculty at the University of Tokyo School of Law."

Like Munakata, Yamamuro, in addition to being a fan of Masashi Sada, had an ear for classical music. His daughter in fact was studying music in Vienna.

My Love of Opera

The first opera I ever attended was Bellini's masterpiece "Norma," in a 1971 performance featuring Elena Souliotis. I still remember the thrill and excitement I experienced on hearing her sing. Up until then I had always listened to Maria Callas in the same role on a set of five 78-rpm records, awash in needle noise. The difference between listening to an opera on a recording and actually seeing and hearing it live in a theater was enormous.

Sadly, opera appears to be on the wane. Norio Ohga, the man who started CBS/Sony Records, once told me in the early years of the record label, classical music accounted for more than 10 percent of total sales, whereas today it contributes less than 2 percent. Of this, opera recordings constitute only 1–2 percent. "Opera DVDs just don't sell," he lamented. Ohga himself was long active as a performer. A graduate of the Berlin State School of Music, he performed professionally as a baritone both before and after joining Sony.

When I sold my stake in Recruit to Daiei in 1992, I was eager to use the earnings for cultural purposes. My dream was to create operas of high quality, record them using high-definition camera equipment, and produce them on DVDs for posterity. In 2001 I founded an opera company named "La Voce," and I went to see Hirotaro Higuchi, first director of the New National Theatre, Tokyo (NNTT), about renting that venue. Through opera I had been close friends with Higuchi for some time, and he proved most supportive. "I'm sure you'll create outstanding works," he encouraged, and he immediately set to checking the theater's availability.

The first opera for which I served as executive producer was Donizetti's "L'Elisir d'Amore," in August 2002. To produce it I hired the remarkably talented Hugo De Ana of Argentina, who came up with an exciting new stage concept based on van Gogh's "Sunflowers." Giuseppe Sabbatini, in the role of Nemorino, and Victoria Loukianetz, as Adina, turned in outstanding vocal and theatrical performances, and the subtitles specially created by the prolifically talented writer Mariko Hayashi were well received. Reiko Ohara, who had personally been invited by Herbert von Karajan to edit his own DVD productions, served as video director. Commentary on the opera was contributed by Tetsuko Kuroyanagi—famed actress, talk-show host, and best-selling author, who herself had spent two years studying opera in New York.

The second opera I brought to the stage at NNTT, in the summer of 2003, was Bellini's "Norma"—fulfilling a long-held dream. "Norma" is brilliant but fiercely difficult to perform, and after its initial run the work remained dormant until Maria Callas sang the leading role and restored the opera to the repertoire forever.

After "Norma," La Voce staged three more operas, all at the same venue: Donizetti's "Lucia di Lammermoor" in 2004, Verdi's "La Traviata" in 2006, and Massenet's "Don Quichotte" in 2007. In all the operas I produced, I always availed myself of the advice of Kiyoshi Igarashi, NNTT's artistic director, and have been aided by my younger daughter, who is involved in theater work in Italy.

As executive producer, my job begins with going to Italy to conduct negotiations with producers and singers. The process of taking an opera, working with the producer and cast, and putting it on the stage, is fraught with an array of challenges; but for that very reason, in my position I can become far more deeply involved in a work than is possible as a spectator in the audience. Experiencing firsthand the enjoyment of producing an opera, the nervous tension of opening night, and the sense of relief after the run closes, has been a great joy, along with the satisfaction of being able to pass on the performance to posterity.

Because La Voce pioneered the recording of opera in high-definition digital format DVD, I have had two thousand copies of each work pressed on the assumption we should be able to sell two hundred a year. I initially contracted with Sony to handle sales, but the contract was canceled after sales totaled only thirty units in the first year. Now sales are handled online by La Voce directly, but sales still lag at only about fifty units a year.

The current state of opera in Japan is as Ohga had assessed. Faced with that dim reality, I decided to donate La Voce's DVDs to high schools around the nation with dedicated or strong music programs, in the hope of arousing interest in opera among young people.

A Free Man Again

On March 18, 2008, the five-year suspension of my sentence came to an end. The following day I invited all the attorneys who were involved in my case out to lunch to express my thanks. I also asked various Recruit employees, particularly from the legal and general affairs departments, to join in. We started to reminisce about the good old days.

My so-called human rights lawyers—people like Shozaburo Ishida, Masanori Ono, Junkichi Kuroda, and Yoichi Okuda—quipped they had fought on the side of human rights thanks to the enthusiasm afforded by youth. "Today, we've become just like every other lawyer in the business," Ishida joked.

Takeshi Tada, who headed my defense, revealed that after Recruit he never took on another criminal case. "In criminal cases, you must have a phenomenal memory," he said. "You have to read the court records over and over again and commit them to memory, to use in your cross-examinations. And my memory today isn't what it used to be."

The next day I attended a gathering of Recruit's former secretaries. Almost two dozen were on hand for the occasion. I had not seen some of them in a very long while.

Shigeru Nakajima, who was secretary to Naotaka Ida, my successor as president, was complimentary of his former boss. "Mr. Ida is a man of steel," he stated with admiration. "During the throes of the scandal, he underwent interrogations practically every day. In the evenings he would cool down at a nearby bar, and nights he'd sleep in a business hotel not far from the office. He went through a lot—but he handled it well."

The secretaries went through a lot in those days too. One recounted how the prosecuting officers conducted a house search at Recruit. "They opened all the drawers and took every document they could find. For a while it was impossible to get any work done." Another complained about the invasion of privacy. "They'd come in and just take away everything," he reported, "even your private appointment book. Without it, I had no idea who I'd made appointments to meet when and where."

In conducting their investigations, the prosecutors appear to have been rather discriminatory. They interrogated the male secretaries—Hitoshi Kashiwaki, Hiroaki Tsuru, Tomohiko Miyajima—rather severely, but lightened up with the female secretaries; they called them in but never questioned them deeply. "They never asked me anything beyond the superficial," one laughed. "One guy actually asked me, 'When are you going to give up this silly job and get yourself a husband?'" Another recalled a similarly chauvinistic attitude: "The prosecutor said to me, 'You couldn't have any information we'd need, so why should I bother asking?'"

Kamekura, my mentor, always used to say I was inscrutable to the people around me. "People who have sudden flashes of inspiration are like you," he once explained. I never realized it myself, but apparently I would often say things out of the blue and cause trouble to those around me. It was at this gathering I learned for the very first time that the secretaries used to have a nickname for me: "Out-of-the-blue Ezoe." Hearing this made me all the more appreciative of the faithful support they always provided.

Recruit Postscript

I resigned as president of Recruit at age fifty-one.

I was succeeded by Naotaka Ida. I had persuaded Ida—with the invaluable help of Takeshi Osawa, one of Recruit's founding members—to join Recruit on the promise he would one day be a candidate to take over as company president. At the time, Ida was at IBM Japan, the manager in charge of hiring.

Ida was a man of few words, but as CEO he was a man of great insight, a man who would listen to the opinions of others. Unfortunately, it wasn't long after he assumed the position of Recruit president that the scandal broke out, pulling him into the maelstrom of the media frenzy. He remained stalwart throughout, however, always exercising strong leadership despite the strain and hardship imposed by his position.

Around the time the media's interest in the Recruit case started to wane, the bubble economy began its unstoppable collapse. As the discount rate notched higher and higher, the real estate market plummeted. Recruit Cosmos's earnings deteriorated significantly, putting Group finances in a highly precarious position. By way of response, I was appointed special advisor to the Group. Then in 1992 I sold my holdings in Recruit—as did various friends—to Isao Nakauchi, founder of Daiei, giving him a 33.4 percent stake in the company. Simultaneously Nakauchi was appointed as company chairman.

Recruit became a company under Daiei's corporate umbrella. Day-to-day operations of the company were left in the hands of Ida and his staff, however, and Recruit continued to function independently. Only rarely did Nakauchi actually visit the company and exercise his powers as chairman. President Ida and I, accompanied by Hitoshi Kashiwaki, who was appointed in charge of the company's financial affairs, went to Recruit's banking partners to request that Recruit's and Daiei's financial accounts be maintained separately, which was another matter to which Nakauchi agreed.

In 1997, Ida was succeeded as president by Eiko Kono, age fifty-one, who had been serving as vice president under him. Ida had long been planning to pass the baton to her, and under her leadership the company focused on improving productivity and pursuing increased profits on reduced sales. In the assessment of some employees, Kono was known as a CEO who "could take a towel that was wrung completely dry and still wring more out of it." In contrast to the days when I and then Ida were in charge, when the ratio of profits to net sales was near 15 percent, under Kono that ratio was elevated to over 30 percent—no mean feat by any account. To reduce the Group's outstanding debt, she sold off Iwate Hotel & Resort, the company operating the Appi ski resort as well as other properties, to an overseas buyer. Upon becoming chairwoman in 2003, in consultation with her successor Hitoshi Kashiwaki, she oversaw the sale of Recruit Cosmos to a corporate revitalization fund. As a result, Recruit became virtually debt-free. Although some employees saw Kono as a severe and highly demanding boss, many regard her as a star among corporate leaders—as do I.

Kashiwaki, one of the first in a group of engineering students hired when Recruit opted to expand into the telecommunications business, became president at the age of only forty-five. The original founders of the company looked upon him as a "crown prince," destined one day to assume the top position. He was, and is, popular among company employees and highly trusted by those outside the company as well. Since he took the helm, Recruit achieved business expansion by entering the Chinese market, undertook a number of mergers and acquisitions that have added hot-spring information services and staffing services to its portfolio, and secured a solid position as the industry leader in human resource services. Most recently, the company forged plans for expanding into the Indian market. Through these and other initiatives, by recasting its business operations and diversifying in step with the times, Recruit achieved an operating structure which stands resilient despite harsh economic times. As a Group, Recruit today is recording sales in excess of one trillion yen.

I am occasionally asked why Recruit has continued to perform so brilliantly even after I resigned as chairman in 1988. I always reply that the company's earnings growth is achieved by taking optimum advantage of the profit center system, which allowed the company to spin off successful operations. The continuous pursuit of ever-higher productivity also spurs growth.

We have had the unwavering support of banks as well. I worried a great deal, once the press began to report on the scandal, whether the Recruit Group could rely on its loans totaling 1.8 trillion yen. But the twenty-one banks that have been Recruit's creditors have been steadfast—not one of them withdrew a loan—and I have been very grateful to them.

Finally, I firmly believe that my departure from Recruit was to the company's benefit.

Post-Postscript

When I was still actively working at Recruit, I interviewed the CEOs of many companies. Afterward, I would listen to taped recordings and looked over the notes I had scribbled on the spot, and then write up an article for publication. On a number of occasions I was later berated by the interviewee.

"That's not what I said!"

"You've quoted me out of context."

"You twisted the meaning of what I was saying."

I was also on the receiving end of many interviews. I recall with slight irony how at times the writer selected only portions of what I said that fit his own priorities.

This book consists largely of my account of what transpired during my voluntary interrogations, the exchanges taking place between myself and my prosecutors in the interrogation room at the detention center, and passages from the court records of my trial. I have modified the original texts in many instances to facilitate reading, but I have done so without altering the original spirit of the text. Much of what I have included may displease the prosecutors who interrogated me. Also, many people may take displeasure at my having named them in the book without their permission. I ask for their understanding of my overriding intent, which was to clarify what truly happened in the Recruit scandal.

While on the one hand I have written things that may be construed as critical of my prosecutors, I bear no ill feelings toward them personally. The severity of their interrogations came from their professions as investigative prosecutors. They carried out their duties, they were not malicious, and they were always straightforward.

Where the problem lies, in my view, is in Japan's existing judicial system—under which interrogations are conducted behind closed doors, interrogations are not recorded on video, and the court gives preferential weight to the statements written up by the prosecuting officers.

This book condenses events spanning fourteen years—from the first news reports hinting at a scandal through my final sentencing—into a comparatively brief narrative. Its contents were gleaned primarily from the notebooks I wrote in while in detention, the briefs prepared by my defense team, newspaper clippings filling twenty-seven scrapbooks, and minutes of the Diet proceedings. Given the enormous bulk of material, a great amount of time was spent just reading through them.

In the twenty-two years since the Recruit scandal began, many changes have occurred:

In 2002, Nikkeiren (Japan Federation of Employers' Associations) was amalgamated into Nippon Keidanren (Japan Business Federation), after which the Central Employment Measures Council was eliminated and the gentlemen's agreement on student recruitment abolished. As a result, college students became able to search for jobs starting in the autumn of their junior year.

In line with the reorganization of central government ministries and agencies in 2001, the Ministry of Labor merged with the Ministry of Health and Welfare to form the Ministry of Health, Labor, and Welfare, while the Ministry of Education united with the Science and Technology Agency, becoming the Ministry of Education, Culture, Sports, Science, and Technology. The national electoral system also changed: the earlier small-scale multiple-member constituency system was abolished and superseded by a system combining the single-seat constituency system with proportional representation. A system of public subsidies was launched in a targeted effort to aid the nation's political parties, and the unraveling of the ingrained existence of political party factions is underway. The tax formerly imposed on securities transactions was also eliminated and the dilapidated Tokyo Detention Center at Kosuge, where I was held for so many months, was demolished and replaced by a gleaming new facility.

Finally, quite a number of the individuals whose names are found in the pages of this book in connection with the Recruit affair have passed on. Although out of respect for the deceased I should refer to them as "the late" so-and-so, I have not done so but rather referred to their position at the time the events took place.

Under Japan's judicial system, weight is accorded to the statements prepared by the prosecution based on interrogations conducted behind closed doors—a practice rarely seen in other developed countries—and only those portions of the statements that contributed to the court arriving at a guilty verdict are open for public scrutiny. As a result, the conviction rate in Japan approximates 99.9 percent. I strongly believe that even now that the lay judge system has been introduced to Japan, fair trials cannot be achieved unless the situation surrounding the prosecutors' statements is changed. I earnestly believe such a change in the current judicial system needs to take place swiftly.

In my trial, more than thirteen years elapsed between my first day in court and the day when a ruling was finally handed down. The number of court sessions, 322, was unprecedented. Neither the defense nor the prosecution appealed the lower court's findings; but if an appeal was filed, my trial would ultimately have gone on for more than twenty years.

HIROMASA EZOE
2010

Acknowledgments

I wish to express my sincere appreciation to Katsufumi Amano for his valuable advice in the preparation of this book. I first met Amano in the days when I was selling ad space for The University of Tokyo Newspaper, and during my years at Recruit I was beneficiary of his insightful advice on numerous occasions. The original Japanese book was published from Chuokoronshinsha, and I would like to thank my editor Takuji Yokote.

I would like to express my gratitude to Masayuki Uchiyama, senior editorial director at Kodansha International, who kindly offered me a chance to publish this English edition. I would like to thank my translator, Robert A. Mintzer. I have also greatly leaned on the kindness and expertise of Junko Kawakami and Elmer Luke. I have been extremely lucky in having them as my editors.

（英文版）リクルート事件・江副浩正の真実
WHERE IS THE JUSTICE?

2010 年 8 月 26 日　第 1 刷発行

著　者　江副浩正

発行者　廣田浩二

発行所　講談社インターナショナル株式会社
　　　　〒112-8652　東京都文京区音羽 1-17-14
　　　　電話　03-3944-6493（編集部）
　　　　　　　03-3944-6492（マーケティング部・業務部）
　　　　ホームページ　www.kodansha-intl.com

印刷・製本所　大日本印刷株式会社